I dedicate this book to my loving parents,
Jim and Toni Barry

MOTHER LEADS BEST

50 WOMEN WHO ARE CHANGING THE WAY ORGANIZATIONS DEFINE LEADERSHIP

MOE GRZELAKOWSKI

Dearborn™
Trade Publishing
A **Kaplan Professional** Company

Vice President and Publisher: Cynthia A. Zigmund
Acquisitions Editor: Jonathan Malysiak
Senior Project Editor: Trey Thoelcke
Interior Design: Lucy Jenkins
Cover Design: Design Solutions
Typesetting: Elizabeth Pitts

© 2005 by Moe Grzelakowski

Published by Dearborn Trade Publishing
A Kaplan Professional Company

Printed in the United States of America

05 06 07 10 9 8 7 6 5 4 3 2 1

Library of Congress Cataloging-in-Publication Data

Grzelakowski, Moe.
    Mother leads best : 50 women who are changing the way organizations define leadership / Moe Grzelakowski.
      p. cm.
    Includes bibliographical references and index.
    ISBN 0-7931-9518-7
    1. Women executives—Psychology. 2. Women chief executive officers—Psychology. 3. Leadership in women. 4. Motherhood. 5. Sex role in the work environment. I. Title.
   HD6054.3.G79 2005
   658.4′092—dc22

                                     2004019869

First and foremost, I want to thank you for caring enough about the evolution of leadership to read this book. I want to express my appreciation to all of you who are working moms and are bringing all the great qualities of motherhood into the workplace. I also want to thank those of you who are not mothers for being sufficiently open-minded to want to learn how motherhood impacts leadership.

None of this would have come to fruition without the moral support and encouragement of my dearest friend and business associate, Paula Serratore. Thank you for helping me cross the chasm between wanting to write a book and actually doing it. Special thanks for connecting me to Melissa Giovagnoli, a local author and networking expert who assisted in the proposal for this book.

I'm also indebted to Bruce Wexler, who shepherded this book from conception to completion. Bruce brought many thoughts to life and gave many ideas elegance with his brilliant wordsmithing. I especially want to thank him for teaching me the valuable lessons of authorship with the gentle demeanor of a mother leader. I appreciate that he both gave me a lot of freedom and reeled me in on the important things, even if I was kicking and screaming.

I am also grateful for the entire Dearborn team, who were quick to recognize the valuable role that moms play in leadership development and provided this book and me with strong support. Jon Malysiak, my editor, has guided this book expertly and helped it become what I hoped it would be.

With all my heart, I want to recognize and thank the real heroines of this book. They are the 50 remarkable executive mothers whose deep human understanding and compassion have shaped the future of business leadership. Every discussion I had with them in search of the explanation for why "mother leads best" left me with nuggets of brilliant wisdom. These wonderfully gifted women, who have a strong, moral commitment to their families, eagerly collaborated on this subject to enrich the world around them. They have graced all of us with their provocative insights and uncanny candor. It has been an honor to get to know each and every one of them.

There would be no book if these executive moms didn't have support, so I am extremely appreciative of those of you who have helped these women live out their dreams, especially their parents, mentors, and devoted husbands. Husbands, you are trailblazers in your own right for joining the struggle of dual, high-impact careers before it became fashionable. Thank you for buoying your wives so that they can be all that they can be.

Resounding thanks, too, goes to the children, who taught maternal leaders life's most powerful lessons. Believe it or not, you helped your mothers become better people and leaders. You opened their hearts and gave them a greater capacity to love. You deepened the purpose of their lives and enabled them to be truly selfless when you and others needed them to be that way. Please know that your mothers are proud of you and their love for you exceeds your wildest dreams. And they asked me to thank you specifically for holding your chin up high on those days you headed off to school late with buttons missing, holes in your socks, lousy costumes, and barely edible birthday treats.

I want to thank members of my personal circle, starting with my incredibly selfless parents who not only love me beyond description but also set the bar on how to create a close family in a dual career situation. You have been a perfect example for me and a wellspring of emotional wisdom over the years. I have a deep sense of gratitude for oh-so-many things, but especially for you, Dad, for inspiring me to write a book and so conscientiously running our joint business while I write, and for you, Mom, for giving up your own career to keep mine going and for caregiving so lovingly for your grandchildren.

I also want to extend my warmest, heartfelt thanks to my brothers and sisters, who, unbeknownst to them, have contributed in innumerable ways to my personal development as a mother and leader. To Joyce, who taught me compassion and who also helped with reading and proofing this book; Guy—humility; Debbie—warmth; Jim—true faith; and Marilyn—staying centered. I also owe a special debt to two young family members. I gratefully acknowledge my niece at Washington University, Talia Bucci, who played an indispensable role in this book and cheerfully provided her hard labor; and my stepdaughter, Blair, part of my new family, who kept me company by writing her own creative masterpieces alongside me.

My greatest debts, without a doubt, go to my sons, Brian and Michael; you are the lights of my life. Thanks for the hugs and the challenges, for the advice and the pranks, for helping me grow as a mother and leader, and for growing yourselves into such fine young men. I stand in awe of you both. You've turned out so beautifully despite all my parental blunders. The world is blessed by your big, loving hearts, and so am I. There is nothing more personally satisfying in my life than your happiness and love.

And my single most important thank-you goes to my husband for sharing the journey. Thanks for your daily encouragement, your ever-growing love, your amazing spirit, your spiritual guidance, and for putting up with me! You fuel my heart, soul, and mind. The way you pursue your life passion personifies the intensity that drives executive moms to accomplish so much and personally makes me hungry for my next leadership adventure.

America is on the cusp of a leadership revolution. Thanks to some trailblazing mothers—50 of whom were interviewed for this book—our culture now accepts and supports women as both mothers and business professionals. More mothers are making it to the top of corporations faster than ever, and they are bringing a new and improved leadership style to big business.

You can benefit from this emerging leadership model in a number of ways.

First, whether you're a woman or a man, a parent or not, you will learn how maternal traits such as compassion, a strong character, confidence, and efficiency can help you become a better leader.

Second, I'll provide specific suggestions and exercises that will help you assess, develop, and strengthen these leadership traits.

Third, I'll tell the stories of 50 incredible maternal leaders, stories that are instructive and inspiring; you'll find a short biography of each in Appendix A. If you're a woman, they are especially relevant, in that they demonstrate how being a mom and being a leader are synergistic roles rather than an either-or choice.

Finally, this book should provide a provocative and enlightening look at why mother leads best. The first three chapters set the stage for this argument, describing the organizational context in which mothers are taking on leadership roles. Specifically, these initial chapters identify what moms can teach businesspeople about leadership, how motherhood can serve as an antidote to the "dragon lady syndrome," and the ramifications of executives deciding to become mothers. The following six chapters correspond to stages in a child's life—from unborn fetus to adolescence—and how these stages impact executive moms and provide leadership skills. The last two chapters place the entire issue of maternal leadership in perspective, offering observations on how motherhood builds leadership character and ways in which you can apply the lessons of the book to a variety of business situations.

With this framework in mind, let's start out with an overview of why mothers are ideally suited for leadership roles in the current corporate environment.

MOMS AT THE HELM
The Capacity to Steer Companies in the Right Direction

It's not that men are bad leaders; it's not that men can't be as effective as women in leadership positions; it's not that dads don't benefit from lessons learned as parents. It's simply that mothers have certain advantages because of nature and nurture that men lack. Hormonally, they are predisposed toward compassion and caring. Biologically, they carry and give birth to the child, and this has a profound effect on their attitudes and actions. Because women generally handle the lion's share of parenting responsibilities (whether or not they work), these responsibilities have a greater impact on them than on dads.

The issue, though, isn't as simple as women being more compassionate than men, thus being better leaders. There are plenty of compassionate male CEOs. To understand how I arrived at my mother-leads-best premise, let's first look at the findings of two well-known research teams who have studied the differences between men's and women's leadership styles. Korabik and Catalyst established that people who occupy parallel positions and perform similar functions do not differ in personality, motivation, effectiveness, or leadership style (Korabik, 29; Galinsky, 4). In other words, women at the top are wired very similarly to men at the top. Leadership DNA is gender neutral; you've either got what it takes to be a leader or you don't.

Though business pundits have applauded the move away from autocratic styles and toward relationship building, CEOs are still mostly admired for their toughness. When you meet high-level executive men or women, you immediately sense that they are inherently more confident, competitive, energetic, and driven than most people. Even if they are first-class nurturers, you are struck by their power rather than their gentleness or emotional intelligence.

Beneath this norm, however, are significant subtleties of leadership style and substance. The best leaders are tough and confident, yet they also add softer qualities into the mix. They come across as hard-nosed and determined, but they also appreciate diversity, communicate well, and aren't afraid of admitting their mistakes. This more balanced approach not only gets results, but it inspires great loyalty and facilitates development.

Contrary to what you might expect, many women who have risen to executive level roles fit the male stereotype. They reached a higher-level corporate job precisely because they were driven, competitive, and assertive. Yet the very qualities that have helped them climb the corporate ladder also keep them a rung or two below the top. Our society does not react positively toward women whose interpersonal style falls into what researchers refer to as the male schema. The prevailing corporate expectation is for women to be less assertive and more nurturing than men. Not only has this situation negatively impacted these women's careers, but it has contributed to a leadership vacuum. We live in a time when we lack leaders with character; too many CEOs have made themselves rich while bankrupting their companies or have been indicted for various legal violations. At the other extreme, we have ethical but ineffectual chief executives. They are traditional, play-it-safe leaders who lack the guts or vision to deliver great results.

Fortunately, maternal leaders are starting to fill this leadership vacuum. Motherhood has helped women executives change from good leaders into great ones. Children transform ultrahigh-achieving women, leavening their highly focused, intensely driven, tough-minded traits with character and compassion. Children provide even the most ambitious, driven women with a selfless patience, helping them understand and support others. Such transformations are profound. They become softer, yet stronger; more confident, yet more humble; more directed, yet more tolerant. All in all, children not only give them a greater capacity to lead, but they stimulate a greater capacity to love. Leadership, coupled with love, is very powerful.

Think about the requirements for leadership today. We need people who can execute, but we also need individuals who can build and maintain relationships. We require savvy strategists who can develop new markets, but we also demand leaders who can develop their own people. We need leaders who are determined and aggressive, but we also need ones with sterling character. In essence, we want a mixture of toughness and softness, of strength and flexibility. Motherhood, far better than any training program, helps bring out this ideal mixture.

FIRSTHAND KNOWLEDGE OF
MATERNAL LEADERSHIP

As you read this argument in favor of maternal leadership, you may think you see an underlying flaw. Skeptics just don't believe that executive moms can do both jobs well. They reason that it's difficult to find the time, energy, and focus to be a great mom and great leader. Some people, though, have an insatiable appetite for challenge and achievement. Doing both well is a rush. It satisfies an inner drive. In my research, I found that most executive mothers had possessed this incredible drive for as long as they could remember. Overdrive is executive moms' natural state, and they apply it to their work and their families.

I know this because I am one of them. I am a former senior executive of Bell Labs, Motorola, and Dell and ran several multibillion-dollar international businesses while I was mothering my two sons, Brian and Mike. I never thought much about these dual roles, though, until I took a break from my hectic routine a few years ago. I started a CEO retreat, called WISDOMQUEST™, which provides CEOs with a one-week break of quiet and reflection. During one of these retreats, I realized that motherhood made an incredible difference in other leaders' styles, not just my own. Although I knew that I was a dramatically different leader after my children were born, I didn't realize that motherhood impacted others in the same way.

I started asking senior-level men and women if they could distinguish between maternal leaders and other leaders. After thinking about it, they all came back with the same surprising conclusion: Mothers were the most skillful leaders on their teams. Many added that they had noticed a significant change in these women since they'd had children. When I probed to discover the specific way they had changed, I received a wide range of responses. They saw a number of different traits emerge that enhanced mothers' leadership abilities. Despite the diversity of responses, each and every one of these traits resonated with me. The more I discussed the issue, the more I realized the multitude of ways in which my children had changed my life, my leadership approach, and my attitude about work. Eventually, it dawned on me how important this realization was.

I also discovered that researchers had overlooked the impact of motherhood on the leadership style of women. Even when their own data proved that mothers were getting promoted faster than their counterparts, researchers ignored it. I understand that some of the researchers were not mothers or parents and perhaps didn't see the data's relevance. In addition, this finding might not have seemed statistically significant because most top leaders today are not mothers. A third deterrent, perhaps, is the potential explosiveness of this finding. Categorizing gender issues has become taboo, so perhaps no one wanted to deal with the repercussions of spotlighting the motherhood/leadership nexus.

Yet, when I came across this connection, it seemed tremendously important, both for individuals and organizations. I've already touched on how this knowledge can help individuals improve their leadership style, but consider one way it might help organizations. If mother does in fact lead best, then companies certainly should make a greater effort to recruit, retain, and develop high-potential moms. Lack of attention to this issue could put them at a disadvantage. Will companies like Southwest Airlines, Xerox, or IBM, who already have quite a few mothers in senior positions, possess a long-term advantage? Will companies who ignore this issue lose ground?

In addition, understanding the impact of motherhood on leadership can also educate young people who have yet to make a choice about motherhood. A significant percentage of women or couples in the past chose to not have a family to focus on their careers. This choice was often gut wrenching and led to regrets. If motherhood actually enhances women's chances of becoming more effective leaders, should the next generation use a different set of assumptions to make decisions?

The concept that mother leads best also causes us to take another look at the glass ceiling. For years, people have speculated on why this ceiling exists and prevents women from advancing to upper corporate levels. While motherhood may not have created the ceiling, it may be one reason the ceiling remains in place years after blatant sexism and misogyny have been dramatically reduced. All this causes me to ask another radical question: Should we establish new CEO selection criteria that makes parenthood one of the job specs?

I raise these questions here not to answer them definitively but to start a long-overdue discussion. I am not a psychologist; I lack the expertise to run an experiment statistically proving that mothers lead best. As a mother and leader myself, however, and as someone who has worked with other maternal leaders, I have seen overwhelming evidence that mothers do indeed possess executive-level skills that others lack. Rather than just share my own experiences and intuition, though, I decided to solicit the opinions of senior level corporate mothers.

My first step was to identify the country's highest-level executives who were also moms. I researched the top two layers of managers for all Fortune 100 companies and the top layer for the remainder of the Fortune 500 (*Fortune,* 60–82). I also reviewed many lists published by magazines, newspapers, and universities, and I networked with America's most powerful male and female leaders. I focused exclusively on corporations rather than on not-for-profits, educational institutions, the government, the military, and so on. I also limited my scope to one mother per company as well as women who were on the CEO track at large, American corporations.

More than half the women I contacted agreed to participate. This was surprising for several reasons. Executive mothers are some of the busiest people in the world. A 50 percent response to any research request is way above the norm, and most of these women didn't know me from Adam (or Eve). These women took the time to talk to me because they resonated strongly with the concept and felt it was important to share their experiences.

Though these women have top corporate titles in common, they also are a diverse group, including individuals who started their careers as engineers, journalists, lawyers, accountants, consultants, and finance specialists, as well as one secretary, one professor, and one teacher. They were or are CFOs, controllers, CMOs, CIOs, CEOs, GMs, sales executives, consultants and executive recruiters, and they also include women who have run start-ups and women who have taken a break in their careers. The interviewees include Caucasians, African-Americans, Hispanics, and Asians; range in age from their mid-30s to mid-60s, and have had between 1 and 5 children.

I also want to emphasize that, based on what I've learned about them, all these women are great moms. I have no doubt that every single one of them puts her kids ahead of herself and her career. As you'll discover, many of these executive moms made significant sacrifices for their children as their careers progressed. These women provide irrefutable evidence that it is possible to be a responsible, loving mom despite the demands made by a top executive position.

In addition, as you read these women's stories, don't expect to witness a 180-degree change. Motherhood did not turn tigers into pussycats or vice versa. While each woman was affected somewhat differently, the most common impact of motherhood was bringing intense, work-obsessed women back to earth. Being a mom added balance to their lives; it enabled them to put their work in perspective; it made them better human beings. They were no less driven after becoming moms, but they were much better able to channel their drive into productive effort.

Perhaps the best way that I can help you understand the impact of motherhood on leadership is by sharing a bit of my story here. Throughout the book, I'll relate my experiences as a top executive. I'll also relate the before-and-after stories of motherhood—how I led and managed before I became a mom and afterwards. For now, let me tell you a little about how tightly wrapped and demanding I was early in my career and what happened when I returned to work as a mom.

REPLACING OBSESSIVENESS WITH BALANCE

While growing up and throughout college, I displayed leadership DNA. I was always focused on achievement, whether in sports, school, or as the rush chair of my sorority. I loved challenges and proving myself, but after getting my first job, as a systems analyst at Amoco, I left within a year. I needed a greater challenge, so I researched the companies that might ask a lot of me and give a lot in return, and I landed at Bell Laboratories. Bell Laboratories requires its researchers to get a Masters degree in engineering within the first two years, and I chose to complete my master's degree at Northwestern while still working full-time. Even this wasn't sufficient for a driven, young businessperson. I asked Bell to send me to MIT to take an advance course in operating systems, so that I could get in line for what I determined to be the most challenging software assignment of all.

When I returned from MIT, I inherited responsibility for the key operating system software of a highly sophisticated computer. When various male colleagues heard that a woman had gotten the plum assignment, they reflexively questioned the decision. Their doubts, though, inspired me to work even harder. Like every woman leader I know, I constantly needed to prove myself.

I got a little fancy with my first simple program, and the senior designer, Chris, ran to Mort, my boss, and convinced him to pull my new code from the software that was being loaded into the system labs. This was an insult. I tried to convince them that my code was fine and that I was just using an advanced feature of the new C programming language. They didn't believe me, which of course was a further insult. So I wrote a test program and reviewed the test with them. It basically printed out one of two messages: If this works, Chris Smith is a big ____hole; if it doesn't, Moe Grzelakowski is an idiot. The test program worked, and I ran it 1,000 times and pasted the resulting messages outside my boss's door.

My next assignment was to speed up the operating system tenfold. The computer's performance wasn't meeting its specifications. I was given six months to do this. Finally, I had a great challenge. I wasn't so sure I was going to figure this out without a few stumbles, but that was fine; the increased degree of difficulty appealed to the competitor in me. Messing with the core software was very tricky business. While the software guys weren't very helpful, the key hardware designer, Murali Narayanan, enthusiastically walked me through the hardware design and gave me some ideas about how the software could take better advantage of some of his hardware features. Within a week, I'd initiated some straightforward changes and achieved more than a tenfold improvement in performance. My project wasn't due for almost six months, so I decided to take on something much more challenging.

The code was like a bowl of spaghetti. It was not neatly organized, what computer scientists refer to as "structured." Every developer dreams of rewriting the code she inherits, and I was no different. I convinced my boss to let me use the remaining time to rewrite the scheduler and memory manager. When the day came for me to submit the new operating system, Jerry, a very sharp Ph.D. in computer science, as well as the other lead engineers, declared that my code would not work, so they didn't put it in the labs. Rather than giving in, I dug in and, in the strongest terms possible, urged them to give it a shot. They put my code in, and the system not only worked but was over 100 times faster.

While I didn't earn any points for being sweet, I did earn the technical respect of some of the most brilliant engineers in the world (Jerry and I are friends to this day), and I received a lot of management attention. Within three years, I was on the management track, an anomaly at Bell Labs where most people on this track were older than me and were men. Nothing could stop me, and I went at my assignments with a single-mindedness and aggressiveness that may have alienated some people. Nonetheless, I was recognized as a rising star and given the plum assignments I craved.

When I became pregnant, I experienced difficulties after about six months and my doctor ordered me to take total bed rest. So I set up an office in my bedroom, complete with computer, fax, and speakerphone. A week later, I was still having trouble, and my doctor told my husband to rip out all the electronics, which he did.

The three months in bed challenged me more than any assignment I ever had at Bell Labs; I honestly didn't believe I was capable of lying in bed and doing nothing. For my entire life, I had been a doer and achiever. I relentlessly pursued objectives and pushed past people who told me I couldn't do this or that. I didn't have the time or inclination to sit back, think, and reflect. Now I had three months to do these things, and it was a long time to be alone with my thoughts. It was a wake-up call in many ways. My friends and family would bring me my meals every day and sit and talk to me. I had so lost touch with everybody in my quest to achieve. I was grateful to reconnect. I felt like I had returned from another planet.

For the first time, I was sacrificing myself for someone else. Carrying another life around motivates you to reassess your priorities and values. When I went on total bed rest, I was 30, the youngest fourth-level manager in Bell Laboratories. I was getting tremendous rewards and positive feedback from my superiors for my team's results. Yet I was not a beloved manager. At a project celebration, my team gave me the Ayatollah Khomeini award. For those of you too young to remember him, he was yesterday's version of Saddam Hussein. Not only was I driven, but I assumed everyone I worked with should be just as driven. I was so consumed by my need for great results that I even endangered my relationship with my first mentor, Bill Schwartz. Right before I had to leave work to stay home in bed, he left me a note that read, "If you can take some of your precious little time away from your very important project for an unimportant person like me, call." It was one of those whacks on the side of the head that I needed. It was only when I was lying in bed pregnant, though, that I was able to grasp fully what he was telling me.

Not only did I reexamine who I was at work, but I worried about who I would be as a mom. While I lay in bed, I started to fear that might be a less-than-ideal mother. I wasn't very patient, and I worried that if I had a timid child, I would intimidate him or her to death. (Fortunately, Brian turned out to be anything but timid.) I read every book I could find on pregnancy, childbirth, and infants. I talked to sisters and friends who had firsthand experience on these subjects and orchestrated the decorating of a nursery from my bed. Nothing, though, could prepare me for the complete life transformation that occurred when Brian was born.

The onslaught of emotions was overwhelming. I experienced joy beyond anything I had ever known before. Brian was a fussy, colicky baby who could never get enough to eat and at times stayed awake for over 24 hours. I didn't care. He was beautiful, alive, and healthy, and I was at his beck and call. I loved holding him, soothing him, nursing him, and helping him learn and grow. The nurturing side of me poured out at home with as much intensity as the workaholic side of me had in the office. In many ways, this child took me out of the driver's seat of my own life. I was headed in a direction I didn't even know existed, and I absolutely loved every minute of this new life.

I had formally taken a six-month leave of absence. At five months, I told my mom I wasn't sure that I wanted to go back to work. She didn't think I should stay home. She called me back the next day and told me she had announced her retirement, having worked as the accounts manager for a family-owned company for over 20 years. I asked her why the sudden retirement, and she explained that she was going to take care of Brian so I could go back to work. I was shocked. Brian was her 13th grandchild. Why quit now, especially when I was not sure I wanted to go back to work? She said, "I didn't send you to all that schooling for you to stay home and have babies. You are going back to work." It wasn't that my mom was telling me what to do. Instead, she knew my leadership DNA better than I did and knew that I would be miserable if I cut myself off from work. Of course, she was right.

I called my executive director, John Becker, and let him know that I was still planning on returning to work on May 14. "But John," I said, "I am going to slow down my pace. I will be at work at 7:00 AM but out by

4:00 PM. I also have a lot of accumulated vacation and plan on taking it going forward." He suggested that I should be put on special assignment and not take on a management position, and I agreed. A week later, though, he called and said that one department was a real mess, screwing up the entire project. It wasn't the typical high-profile job I usually landed, but it was a big department and an area where I had a lot of expertise. He wondered if I could step in and fix it. He'd accept my 40-hour workweek so long as I could hang late for key staff meetings. I was flattered to be able to have a "real job" with the conditions I set forth and accepted his offer.

I successfully turned the organization around, but this time, I wasn't Ayatollah. I was different, very different. I was more Mother Hen than Wild Goose, and it didn't go unnoticed. At first, my coworkers didn't believe my new style would stick, but over time and through a series of crises that tested my new demeanor, they realized I was indeed a very different person.

Some aspects of my leadership persona changed overnight, while others evolved over time. I was still driven, but I wasn't as ambitious. I was still results oriented, but relationships had become more important. I was still decisive, but I became more collaborative. I was still intense, but I became much more compassionate. In essence, I became more human. It wasn't that I was inhuman before my kids were born or even the Ayatollah I was reputed to be. In fact, I probably was more caring than many of my peers. But I wasn't consistent. I had moments of caring followed by impatience or intolerance. As a woman, this impatience and intolerance was especially problematic, because colleagues' expectations were that I—like all women at work—should drip sweetness and radiate light.

After Brian and Mike were born, I began to view my teams as extended family and, like the mother I was, tried to protect them at all costs. This didn't just mean helping them keep their jobs but helping them learn and grow and build their self-esteem. After a while, this maternal instinct became part of my leadership style. It wasn't a conscious decision but rather a natural side effect of motherhood.

Through formal and informal feedback, I learned that people loved working for me. AT&T even asked me to train the other executives on the team how to care! Had I known then what I know now, I would have said to the mom and dad executives, if you put passion into your parenting, the caring part will come naturally. I matured as my children matured, elevating my skills and perspective continuously. The more I cared, the better my teams performed, and the more I was rewarded.

Every single woman I interviewed has a similar story of transformation. Though the specifics of the stories are different, they all changed significantly and in ways that benefited their organizations and careers—all of them became hugely successful. I think we can learn a lot from maternal leaders, and I hope the following pages will provide insightful and entertaining lessons on an emerging style of leadership.

1

THE CASE FOR MOTHERHOOD

What Moms Can Teach Us about Leadership

"The whole concept of unconditional love transforms the underlying basis of your business relationships from emotionless transactions to respect and loyalty . . . . love keeps your group intact and fuels the mission of the enterprise. And nothing teaches you about unconditional love, until you have kids."

Shelly Lazarus, *Chairman and CEO, Ogilvy & Mather Worldwide*

If you look at the people who lead organizations, you'll find that they share similar traits: competitiveness, toughness, ambition, and drive. Whether you're a man or a woman, you don't get to the top without these traits. The problem, however, is that while men are admired for these traits, women are often viewed in a negative light. People refer to demanding and driven women executives as "dragon ladies" and "ice maidens," finding them overbearing and un-feminine.

The irony, of course, is that women who lack these traits rarely rise to the top. Relationship-driven, caring women are seen as too soft to handle the top jobs. From boards of directors to front-line employees, people believe that for a company to be successful, it needs a no-nonsense, take-charge CEO.

Fortunately, motherhood provides women with a developmental process that prepares them for top positions. While it can toughen soft women and soften tough ones, its real benefit is that it helps them achieve a balance between these two qualities. If you're a working mother, you're unlikely to be viewed as a pushover. You've learned when to put your foot down, and you may be even tougher in some ways after having a child than before. At the same time, however, motherhood has also taught you the value of nurture. As a result, you are a skilled situational leader, knowing when to apply toughness and when to soften your stance. To make the case for motherhood, though, we need to define the specific ways it impacts leadership style.

MATERNAL LEADERS ARE NOT JUST SOFT AND FUZZY

June Cleaver, the mother in the '50s sitcom *Leave It to Beaver,* would not have made a good CEO. In any large corporation, June's sweetness and unflagging kindness would have doomed her to a midlevel position at best. Yes, we might all want June to be our mother—or our boss, for that matter—but we probably wouldn't want to work for a company she headed. She would lack the grit to make the difficult decisions and the drive to push herself and others to their performance limits.

In reality, few moms exist like the fictional June. While motherhood does soften the sharp edges of female leaders, it also helps women acquire perspectives and skills that have nothing to do with "softness." In fact, it is fair to describe the high-achieving leaders profiled in these pages as exhibiting a feminine type of toughness. I'll address the specific traits of maternal leaders shortly, but first I want to be clear that I'm not equating bottomless empathy with motherhood. Much has been written recently about the need for leaders to be more empathetic and communicative, and these are certainly good traits for top leaders to possess, but they don't completely define a maternal leader. Highly successful female executives, like their male counterparts, are successful because they possess what I refer to as "leadership DNA."

In other words, they're energetic, intelligent, competitive, passionately driven, tough-minded risk-takers. They are also dominating, decisive, and focused. There is nothing stereotypically feminine about them as they move upwards in an organization.

When they have children, their leadership DNA doesn't disappear; they don't undergo 180-degree personality changes. But they do change. When a woman becomes a mother, her transition is physical, emotional, and spiritual. Not only do women become warmer leaders, but they also experience other, more subtle and not so obviously gender-related changes. For instance, maternal leaders often develop superior negotiating skills, the result of all the bargaining they must do with their children. They are not so quick to become entrenched in a position, instead seeing the benefit of using tradeoffs to achieve a goal.

Similarly, women who are mothers tend to work better with men. Moms need to learn to work well with dads to bring up kids, especially when the children are little. Compromises and tradeoffs must be made, and many women learn to appreciate their husbands in ways they never did before. Yes, there may be arguments before that appreciation is achieved, but generally, mothers tend to forge stronger bonds with their partners and learn to function more effectively as part of a family unit. The ability to create stronger relationships carries over into the workplace and results in an enormously effective, maternalistic leadership style.

Shelly Lazarus, the chairman and CEO of Ogilvy & Mather Worldwide, observed that motherhood radically improved business relationships. She said:

> In business, the leaders who can establish very strong relationships at work gain loyalty. The whole concept of unconditional love transforms the underlying basis of your business relationships from emotionless transactions to ones based on respect and loyalty. When your teams trust that there's love underlying the relationship despite the conflict, that love keeps your group intact and fuels the mission of the enterprise. And nothing teaches you about unconditional love until you have kids.

ELEMENTS OF STYLE
How Moms Lead

Obviously, leadership style has a lot to do with an individual's personality, and I'm not suggesting that all mothers lead alike. Not all moms parent alike, after all; one mom may be stricter or more controlling than another. All mothers, though, go through the same set of powerful experiences relative to a child's development, and these experiences shape their leadership style. To give you a sense of this style, let's look at the stages of a mother's life and the qualities that emerge from each stage.

- *Pregnancy.* Many of the women I interviewed remarked that this was the first time in their lives that they put someone else ahead of themselves. The impending responsibility for another life made them reflect on their assumptions about what was important. As one woman said, "When I was pregnant, my whole perspective at work changed. I found myself listening more and talking less." Pregnancy brought out warmth in these women and also caused them to be incredibly concerned for their unborn child, avoiding behaviors that might put that child at risk. These protective and risk-aware tendencies translated into work behaviors such as standing up for (protecting) their people as well as taking smart risks—their heightened understanding of what real risk was (as opposed to groundless fear) made them more willing to take a chance when potential rewards were high and risks could be managed.
- *Infancy.* Taking care of a baby teaches moms the value of patience and the need for nurturing. During this first year, moms also must set priorities, delegate, compromise, and learn to operate in other ways that may have been alien to them before having a baby. From a work perspective, moms exhibit much more patience with people and projects than they did before. Perhaps surprisingly, they also sharpen basic managerial skills and get things done faster and more effectively.
- *Toddlers.* Crisis management, multitasking, and spontaneity are all things that moms get good at fast when their kids start walking and talking. The ability to drop everything and do something on the spur of the moment, for instance, is a challenge that many women executives have trouble meeting. They resist changes to their schedule, even when an event demands their immediate attention. Once they are responsible for toddlers, however, they loosen up and recognize the benefits of responding to the immediate situation rather than the formal schedule.
- *Elementary school.* Moms become skilled networkers and teachers, taking on these roles to help their children learn and grow. Mothers also master the art of play and become good at saying no. From

a leadership standpoint, women executives become skilled at forging alliances and communicating more clearly with their people. They also make work more fun for themselves and others, and they are more skilled at rejecting ideas or turning down projects without making other people feel demeaned or degraded.

- *Tweens.* Today's preteens are prematurely faced with many adult choices—alcohol, drugs, and sex to name three—and mothers become skilled at staying connected and tuned in to their children. They learn to listen attentively, read between the lines, bite their tongue, and be open to their children's ideas, concerns, and criticisms. As a result, they are likely to pick up signals both at home and at work that they might have missed in the past.
- *Teens.* These are the times that try parents' souls, and mothers emerge from these trials with a variety of new skills and traits: receptivity, boundary-setting, open-mindedness, negotiation, and influencing through others. Being the mother of a teenager is a maturing process, both personally and professionally. Leadership maturity is in short supply at many organizations that need their top people to be calm, thoughtful, wise, and insightful. Moms acquire hard-won wisdom during their child's teenage years, and it helps them to lead wisely.

The net effect of these traits is a balance and perspective that leaders often lack. The best leaders are not the toughest kids on the block, nor are they the most empathetic. Instead, they can be tough when toughness is called for and supportive when encouragement is the best approach. Maternal leaders sense which approach is best in which situation; they don't lead with one, inflexible way of doing things. As a result, they are great situational leaders, an increasingly valuable commodity when leaders are confronted with so many new and unfamiliar situations.

What we're really talking about here is leadership instinct, which is not much different from maternal instinct. Moms can sense when their children are coming down with something even in the infant stage or when their kids are struggling with an emotional issue in the adolescent stage. They intuitively know when to discipline and when to encourage, and this knowing is not always based on a logical evaluation of the facts.

More than ever, leaders need to rely on more than the facts when making a decision. In a world of information overload, where rapid change renders today's truths invalid tomorrow, leaders must trust their gut. Motherhood provides the experiences that help women gain a sense of what to do in situations without clear answers. A mom's decisions often involve paradox, ambiguity, and unpredictability. She must learn to read between the lines to hear what her child is really trying to tell her or determine if her baby's cry is normal or signaling distress.

The maternal instinct is especially useful in organizations when tough people decisions must be made. Many executives—both men and women—have trouble reading their direct reports. They don't really know if someone is ready for a big assignment or if something is troubling them and affecting their performance. As a result, leaders often make mistakes in matching people and projects, or they promote individuals who simply aren't ready to take on more work or responsibilities. Moms, on the other hand, are much better at reading their people. They pay attention to their direct reports' behaviors—they hear the change in tone when a direct report is excited about a project or notice the awkward body language when an assignment makes them uncomfortable. Many times they absorb these signs and signals unconsciously, similar to the way they absorb various communications from their child. The cumulative weight of what they see and hear feeds their instinct, helping them make good decisions.

YOU DON'T HAVE TO BE A MOM TO BE A MATERNAL LEADER

I'm not suggesting that the only people who can manifest these traits are mothers. While being a woman and having a baby is the most "natural" way to acquire these traits, you can also integrate them into your leadership style if you don't have children or if you are a man. You just need to be conscious of these targeted traits and make an effort to practice them regularly. Because you don't have the benefit of practicing them daily as a mom and haven't undergone the physical changes and emotional impact of motherhood, you must go out of your way to incorporate them into your daily work routine. The information and exercises in this book will facilitate this process.

Even if you are a mother, however, there's no guarantee that you will immediately become a maternal leader. Plenty of women resist what they learn as mothers, and they tend not to be as successful or as effective as other executive moms. Sometimes these women consciously reject what they learn as moms, adhering to a leadership mode that is overly hard or soft. Sometimes they don't spend much time or invest much of themselves in raising their children; they go back to work a few weeks after having a child, assign the majority of child raising responsibilities to their husband and/or caregiver, and don't interact with their child in a way that helps them learn the lessons of motherhood.

The key for a woman with children, therefore, is to be a conscious and involved mother. Figuratively speaking, this is also the key if you are not a mom. Many business executives are not particularly aware of how they lead. They lack the time or inclination to reflect on the elements of their leadership style and how it should be modified. People who pay attention to the 360-degree feedback they receive and take it seriously are much more likely to be motivated to change and to know how to change.

In particular, some of the women who succeed in organizations are hard-nosed, amazingly focused individuals. Like successful male leaders, they don't spend much time looking inward or talking with coaches about flaws in their style. They develop thick skins and feedback bounces right off of them; they may protect themselves from undeserved attacks, but they also filter out constructive criticism.

Many male executives are parents. But for some reason or another, they do not experience the same level of transformation that mothers do. I surveyed the 50 mothers about their thoughts on this. All but one of the women I interviewed were married and had supportive husbands who helped a great deal. Their husbands, though, did not undergo the radical leadership changes that they underwent. In most cases, they did not take ownership of the responsibilities of raising a child in the same way that the moms did. Most of them entered marriage in the '70s or '80s with expectations of stay-at-home wives and an often-unconscious belief that women would take on the lion's share of childrearing responsibilities. Even if they wanted to help out and do their share, they often reverted to secondary roles.

When I asked the women why they were this way, they all said something along the lines of "Because they are guys, they don't know how, and they don't want to know how!" There are many studies that show, despite women's role in the workplace, women and men see this unequal division of labor at home as fair. Studies also show that men do not help out more as women earn more (Valien, 40–41). As a result, men don't make as many changes because they aren't forced to juggle, adapt, and carry the burden of responsibility.

One of the executive mothers said, "My peers who are dads didn't necessarily learn how to let go of things (habits and routines) when their children were born, the way the moms do. Letting go is the fundamental basis for change. And, while they can't fully escape some change brought on by their children, executive fathers don't typically make the profound change that we do."

So for all nonmothers, including most dads, you can start your own process of transformation by paying more attention to how your behaviors and attitudes impact others and your group's productivity. If you discover a negative impact, consider incorporating the traits of maternal leadership that emerge during a child's development, using the information and tools in the following chapters.

DISPELLING THE MYTHS OF LEADERSHIP

It can be difficult to let go of long-held beliefs about leadership and understand how a maternal model has helped top women executives succeed. If you believe the myths, the successes of women CEOs may seem like flukes or exceptions to the rule. Let's clear up two major misconceptions right now.

1. Women are better than men at the "soft" skills, but men are better at "hard" skills such as finances and strategy.
2. Employees want to be led by someone who is a people person—compassionate, humanistic, open, and broad-minded.

These misconceptions fly in the face of the facts, and they can discourage women from embracing and strengthening a maternal style. According to the research, my interviews, and my experience, women lead better than men, but both men and women prefer a man's leadership style. Martha Barletta, author of *Marketing to Women,* notes, "Women get better business results because women are better managers. . . . There are seven different studies available that unequivocally prove women are better managers. And that's according to their bosses, their subordinates, and their peers." (Barletta, 3)

Surprisingly, women aren't just better at the soft skills, but they are better at just about everything. Shari Caudron, author of an article titled "See Jane Lead" in *Controller* magazine (now *Business Finance*), wrote, "Conventional wisdom has long held that women are good at the touchy-feely side of management: interpersonal communication, team building, and staff support. But when it comes to the sweaty details of problem solving, planning, and controlling, it's generally been assumed that men are better managers. To put it bluntly, conventional wisdom is all wet. A study of more than 900 managers conducted last fall by the Foundation for Future Leadership reveals that corporate women outperform their male counterparts in 28 of 31 categories, including 'hard stuff' like recognizing trends, evaluating and acting on new ideas, controlling performance, and maintaining high productivity." (Caudron, 1)

Before we become too carried away with female leadership superiority, we need to be aware of the other side of the coin. According to Gary Powell, who edited the *Handbook of Gender and Work,* employees still accept and prefer the masculine leadership style. (Powell, part 3) My experience at Fortune 100 companies confirms this statement. Employees generally prefer tough, competitive, risk-taking leaders, especially in senior-level positions. They want to be led by people they consider winners. This does not mean they are jerks or lack compassion, but it does mean they project tremendous confidence and authority. Jack Welch (despite his post-GE fall from grace) was the type of leader who convinced everyone he was a winner. He personified the hard-driving, results-focused, masculine leader.

To help you understand why employees generally prefer this type as opposed to the seemingly more effective feminine type, let us look at two examples.

I was at Motorola when Chris Galvin was at the helm, and he was much more participative and communicative than Motorola senior executives had been in the past. Prior to his taking charge, however, the culture had thrived with dominating, authoritative leaders at the top. When Chris became the head of the company, he replaced veteran, dominating leaders with more humanistic, people-oriented executives. Middle managers were used to looking up for vision and decisions and did not know how to embrace empowerment. As compassionate as

Chris was, and despite his intelligence and integrity, a significant percentage of employees had doubts about his approach.

This surprised me, in that I thought Chris's humanity was exactly what the company needed. For instance, he would send a monthly e-mail to employees telling them what he was doing, who he was seeing, and decisions he was making. Though these and other actions certainly improved management-employee communication, for some, it had a downside. One of my vice presidents—a woman—told me, "I am so tired of him (Chris) sounding like my dear, sweet dad. We don't need a father type or a priest running this company. We need somebody to stand up and lead." Believe it or not, she thought he was too nice! She was used to someone pounding the tables and not caring about keeping employees informed.

Michael Dell of Texas-based Dell Computer, on the other hand, favored a command-and-control leadership style, and it helped him run the company with great efficiency. When I was there, Dell spent very little effort, time, or money on the soft issues. The company gained margins in a low-margin business by squeezing suppliers, having world-class processes, and running a no-frills company. They motivated their people by targeting and beating competitors and raising employee's wealth through stock options. Because Dell invented very little and spent less than 1 percent of their revenue on R&D, they did not depend on in-house technical experts, making retention less of a concern than at other companies. Employee benefits were minimal, and a "just the facts" focus didn't allow for much creativity or intuitive thinking. Despite all this, the majority of employees embraced the way things were run, because the stock was soaring and they were reaping the dividends.

Michael Dell favored renting large sports stadiums for annual employee meetings. I attended one that was held at the dinner hour, and the company provided employees with one soft drink and one cookie, a miserly allotment in even a cash-starved company. Nonetheless, the 6,000 or so employees greeted Michael's entrance (he literally rode in on a horse—this was Texas, remember) with thunderous applause. His speech was not the typical, balanced, thoughtful, CEO-type annual talk you might expect. Instead, it was all about crushing Dell's competitors. He poked fun at them and bragged about taking market share. There wasn't one sign of compassion in his speech for the companies he was driving out of business. It was ruthless, macho stuff, and employees loved it.

So why can't a woman simply adopt Michael Dell's leadership style? After all, many of the top women at companies are already hard-driving types like Dell. What is wrong with this style? First, this "damn-the-torpedoes, full steam ahead" approach only works in companies like Dell. Perhaps, even more narrowly, it only works in companies like Dell as long as their stock is soaring. In most companies today, people want the top people to balance this overly pragmatic approach with behaviors that demonstrate employees are valued—in essence a Galvin/Dell hybrid. They expect their top people to exhibit appreciation and compassion, values that maternal leaders embrace.

The second reason, though, is even more instructive. As I noted earlier, the masculine style is only respected if you are a man. Research indicates that women who use the masculine style are disliked and distrusted. *Psychology Today* reported that, although women make better leaders, "Women who use a tough 'command and control' style meet with resistance and suspicion from employees." (Carlin, 1) In addition, Korabik's and Ayman's report, "Should Women Managers Have to Act Like Men?" concludes:

> Women whose style is masculine frequently are disliked by their subordinates and called names such as dragon lady and bitch because they do not display the feminine qualities that we expect women in our society to have. If women choose instead to embrace the traditional feminine role, however, while they may be viewed as likable people, they may also be perceived as poor managers or leaders, because they lack the task-oriented traits we associate with competence. (Korabik, 29)

What we can learn from this is that women need to forge their own style. Though emulating classic male leaders is no doubt tempting, that strategy is flawed. What women really need to do is learn from the maternal leadership role models profiled here. As tough as these women are, they also exhibit attitudes and behaviors that come straight out of family situations. Therefore, don't believe for a second that you have to stick to the soft stuff or else lead like a man. Maternal leaders provide you with a third option.

THE DIFFERENCES BETWEEN YOUR IDEAL BOSS AND YOUR IDEAL CEO

The following exercise may help you understand the value of maternal leaders. First, circle the traits in both columns that you would like your boss to possess.

Authoritative	Participative
Realistic	Imaginative
Methodical	Spontaneous
Tough	Tender
Critical	Accepting
Competitive	Collaborative
Conventional	Unconventional
Forceful	Considerate
Outspoken	Good Listener
Daring	Thoughtful
Excitable	Calm
Determined	Content
Dignified	Down to Earth
Demanding	Helpful
Driven	Clever
Strong	Tactful

Now, use another color of ink and circle the traits that you want your CEO to possess; you can circle a trait that you've already circled, if you feel it is appropriate.

Contrast your two lists. The odds are that you circled more traits from the second column in your boss list, and more traits from the first column in your CEO list. The second column consists of traits that motherhood confers, and it is natural to want a boss who exhibits these qualities. Not many people want a critical, excitable, demanding boss, yet these and the other qualities in the first column are exactly what we want in our CEOs.

Now, using a third color of ink, circle the traits that you exhibit most often at work. Remember, these qualities comprise your most common behaviors (as opposed to how you act at home or how you perceive yourself). If you're like many successful women in organizations, you've circled more traits in the left column than the right. You have probably learned to downplay your tender, calm, and helpful characteristics, assuming that you must be tougher than any man if you want to get ahead. Many women have played a tough, hard-nosed role for so long that they don't realize its downside. If, on the other hand, you circled many of the maternal column traits and not many from the other side of the ledger, you probably are stuck in a midlevel or lower-level position.

Just about every woman interviewed for this book had an almost uncanny knack for balancing these two columns of traits, and this balance helped them achieve their senior leadership positions and do well in them.

DEALING WITH MIXED ORGANIZATIONAL MESSAGES

At certain points in their careers, women managers are told that they are too nice . . . and that they are not nice enough. When I started at Bell Laboratories, most of the women managers were sent to assertiveness training. In these classes, we were told to stop saying *I think,* because it made us appear weak. The trainers wanted us to become more sure of ourselves, more definitive. So I took the *I thinks* out of my vocabulary. Shortly after doing so, my bosses told me I was too sure of myself. They advised me to soften what I said, perhaps prefacing it with *I think.* Feeling that I had no choice but to accommodate their circular reasoning, I again added the dreaded *I think* back into my vocabulary.

In her excellent book, *Why So Slow? The Advancement of Women,* Virginia Valian said:

> Women must appear neither too feminine nor too masculine. At either extreme, they make others uncomfortable. A woman who is very feminine (e.g., nurturing, expressive, communal, and concerned about others) runs the risk of seeming less competent . . . On the other hand, a woman with masculine traits (agentic, assertive, instrumental, and task oriented) runs the risk of appearing unnatural and deviant . . . Women who do not have a soft, genteel way about them may be told—despite their manifest competence—that they should wear more makeup and go to charm school.

Professor Alice Eagly of Northwestern University is at the forefront of research on women and leadership. Her perspective on these issues is instructive:

There is a lot of evidence that women in management are held to a higher standard than men. This is of course unfair. I advocate trying to change this aspect of organizations rather than asking women to accommodate to a system of double standards. Women and organizations struggle with the fairness issue, and there is progress toward greater equality of opportunity. With respect to advice for women who aspire to be leaders, research does not yield any simple prescriptions. However, many studies show that women receive more favorable reactions from others if they convey warmth and concern. It is possible for leaders to behave in this way, because these roles entail much discretion in the sense that leaders can behave in somewhat different ways and still be effective. Conveying warmth and concern allows women to project conventional femininity but, of course, has to be joined with task effectiveness and authority.

Because this double standard is so entrenched in corporations, in their own, muddled way, they are sending women the message that they need to be both tough and warm. Many times, women make serious efforts and companies spend serious money attempting to find this balance. Training programs, coaching, and "off-campus" activities are all designed to help them change their work behaviors, but they often don't meet with much success. The training lacks an emotional component that is critical to change, or the programs lack focus or fail to provide the motivation to change.

Though behavioral change of any type is always a challenge, the maternal model provides a clear, accessible set of behaviors that can inspire change. The women I've interviewed all have different personalities and backgrounds, yet motherhood helped them develop a uniform set of traits and skills. If you are a woman who is also a mother—or soon will be—you can use this book to embrace rather than suppress the leadership qualities that come to you naturally. If you are a man or a woman without children, however, you can still rely on this book as a behavioral guide. It provides a road map for being both strong and compassionate, assertive yet accommodating. In other words, you'll receive more direction than keeping or eliminating the *I thinks* from your speech.

It will also help keep you from turning into a "dragon lady," a scary and increasingly common fate for women executives today.

2

THE DRAGON LADY SYNDROME

"I really started to see that being a workaholic was not healthy. Diversifying my life made me a lot more impactful at work. It's interesting to think I would have become a one-dimensional workaholic if I didn't have children. I wouldn't know any different and I would probably view myself as successful."

Marla Gottschalk, *President and COO, The Pampered Chef*

No one sets out to be called a dragon lady, ice mistress, or any of the other pejorative terms used to describe some women bosses. Nonetheless, we all have encountered dragon ladies in different areas of our lives. They may have been our bosses, teachers, lawyers, doctors, or clients, and when we saw how they acted, we responded negatively. It was not necessarily one or two specific characteristics that caused this negative reaction but a range of behaviors. Our reaction may also have been caused by our perception of these behaviors, a perception colored by specific situations or biases. A woman—especially a powerful woman—is labeled a witch, or worse, if she's abrupt or harsh, arrogant or indifferent, demanding, crabby, rigid, contentious, ambitious, or dismissive. Luckily, because women are so thoroughly vetted during the organizational hiring and promotion processes, the most extreme examples of dragon ladies rarely make it past first-line supervisor.

In a recent *Harvard Business Review* article titled "Coaching the Alpha Male," executive coaches Kate Ludeman and Eddie Erlandson wrote, "Like alpha males, some female leaders do have problems with anger and bullying, and they can be defensive and resistant to criticism. However, the corporate environment—and society as a whole—is much less tolerant of these characteristics in women than in men. So, far fewer women with these tendencies ever reach executive positions." (Ludeman, 3)

In fact, dragon ladies that ascend to top management levels usually don't fit the stereotype. They lack the classic dragon lady traits of sharp tongues and manipulative, amoral attitudes, even though some people in the office may perceive them that way. One remark may create the impression in an individual's mind—especially if they were on the receiving end of the remark—that this woman is as caustic as battery acid. In reality, most dragon ladies are relatively friendly and professional, but they do have an edge that turns people off. At the start of their careers, these women simply work extraordinarily hard at something about which they are passionate. They put in many hours and bring great diligence and high standards to their jobs. If they commit any sin, it is putting too much of themselves into their careers and taking work too seriously. If you are a woman who works harder and longer than your peers, doesn't have much going on in your personal life, and achieves great success, you may well create the perception that you are a dragon lady.

Catherine West, president of Capital One Bank and U.S. Card, admitted that she possessed some sharp edges before she had her son, Will. She said:

> My prior style was very hard charging. I was a perfectionist—very detailed oriented and results oriented. I did a lot of work myself and underutilized the people around me. I told people what to do instead of listening. I worked 24/7. I commuted to my job and returned to my husband on weekends, where I still worked day and night. In a nutshell, I overperformed and overdelivered. I always had the answers, which was difficult on others.

Does this sound like you? If so, you're well aware that you have achieved a certain level of success as a woman in a corporation by acting a certain way. To veer away from the style you've established feels unnatural, and it takes a significant amount of concentration and effort to change, even if you have received negative feedback about being too rigid, ambitious, or unapproachable.

Motherhood, fortunately, provides a method and a model for change. It naturally helps women let go of the little things and take themselves a lot less seriously. More than that, it helps women executives transition into more mature leadership roles. As we'll see, maternal leaders possess a wider range of skills than many male or female executives who have never had kids.

All this is not to suggest that motherhood weakens or diminishes women in any way. I have never seen anyone transformed from a warrior into a wimp. Instead, the change is less dramatic but no less positive. Employees call Mindy Meads, the president and CEO of Lands End, the "velvet hammer." As a CEO, she needs to be tough, but she apparently has found a way to execute effectively without leaving a trail of wounded associates in her wake. Before examining how motherhood promotes the velvet hammer rather than the dragon lady leadership style, let us start by examining the hidden costs of being overly workcentric.

FROM WORKCENTRIC TO WORK BALANCED
Get a Life

In one sense, it is perfectly natural for both men and women to become workaholics when they love what they do. Think about nonwork activities that excite you—volunteering, coaching, exercising, golf, tennis, crafts, or any hobby. If you are passionate about it, you probably are consumed by it. When people have a passion, they talk and think constantly about the subject of their fervent interest.

People who are rising in corporations can easily become consumed by their work. Success is intoxicating, and the more successful leaders are, the more intoxicated they become. Consequently, they dedicate more of their time to business. In the beginning, it consumes what previously was downtime during office hours. When their downtime runs out, they start squeezing hours out of their personal lives. To protect precious time with their families, many corporate executives learn to live on less sleep. They also learn how to work while eating, exercising, driving a car, watching TV, and even while taking a shower.

Jack Scanlon, one of my favorite bosses at both AT&T and Motorola, was the epitome of 24/7. He'd frequently e-mail or call people in the middle of the night. During off hours, he'd usually be calling from an airplane or from his exercise bike, huffing and puffing in the latter instance. Because we were in the wireless telecom business, we worked very hard to ensure that, wherever Jack traveled, our mobile service performed well; we knew we would hear from Jack if there were transmission problems. One morning Jack called John, one of my managers, before dawn. John heard a great deal of hissing and static-like sounds, and he assumed that Jack was phoning to complain about the transmission quality. In fact, Jack was calling about a different matter, but he was making the call from his shower. While calling someone from the shower might not sound so eccentric today, a decade ago, Jack was considered borderline crazy.

Being workcentric isn't a bad thing, but it can become a bad thing when you take Jack's workcentric tendencies to an extreme. Not surprisingly, some workaholics lack a well-rounded life; they aren't involved in family, community, or church. If you've ever worked for someone overly centered on work, you probably don't remember the experience fondly. It isn't fun. Work-obsessed bosses take work and their role way too seriously. They sweat the little things and often they expect everyone around them to invest the same amount of time and energy as they do.

In his book *Beyond Ambition,* Robert Kaplan, a prominent CEO coach, wrote, "Performance problems found among executives are often due to a condition of imbalance. The drive to mastery is overdeveloped even for their specialized roles as institutional leaders. Their anxiety about their worth gets into the high ranges, and they become prone to taking extreme and often self-oriented measures to allay the anxiety—to demonstrate their worth." (Kaplan, 226)

In the high-stress, volatile world in which we live, more people than ever are falling into this workcentric mode. While women with leadership DNA are particularly susceptible to it, other women managers are becoming increasingly vulnerable. For instance, Gloria had become a successful accountant in a major corporation, due in no small part to her quantitative skills and thoroughness. A genuinely nice woman who took work seriously but who also wanted to get married, have children, and stay at home, Gloria fell in love when she was in her 20s and was certain she had found the right guy. He unfortunately grew bored with her, as did the next three or four men in her life.

Gloria eventually grew bitter about her bad luck with relationships and fell into the "work is my whole life" trap. She worked obsessively, driven by her need for recognition as well as financial security and by the company's need for financial accuracy. Gloria became a perfectionist and took her job so seriously, she fostered the impression that her accounting role was the center of the universe. Her obsession with perfection became annoying to those who worked with Gloria and detracted from her considerable talents. Her workcentric approach made her less effective than she was earlier in her career.

A few months ago, I was participating in a women's leadership event hosted by Sidley and Austin. I was on a panel with their most senior female partner, Virginia Aronson. She attributed some of her success to the fact that she had interests that went beyond law and advised the participating women to be multidimensional and not just centered on work. While she didn't have children, she and her husband had become well-known magicians. She talked about how her hobby intrigued her co-workers and clients and how it created opportunities for her to connect to people at work on a personal level. People treated her differently when they knew she was more than just a good lawyer; being a magician humanized her in their eyes.

Marion McGovern, president of M Squared, which brokers senior-level consultants to key client projects, said, "We always ask the question, 'Would they pass the beer test?' You ask yourself this question: 'Would I want to go out with this person after work and have a beer?'" She said they do this because employees enjoy their jobs more and are more productive if they work with interesting people. Executives who are totally workcentric would not pass the beer test.

Conducting an informal survey of senior leaders, I asked them to list characteristics of workcentric executives. Here are the traits that recurred on their lists:

- Are perfectionists.
- Expect everyone else's lives to revolve around work.
- Don't appear to have a life outside the office.
- Wear their ambitions on their sleeve.
- Take work and themselves too seriously.
- Are out to prove something.
- Sweat the small stuff.

I asked these senior leaders if they knew more women or more men like this. Women came to mind more often, even though, on average, fewer women were in leadership positions at their workplaces. None of the women they were thinking of were mothers, and most possessed un-flattering nicknames such as ice queen, nitpicker, and "the nun."

Interestingly and tellingly, not all hard-working executives harbor these negative traits. Jack Scanlon worked harder than any of us, but he was down-to-earth, approachable, and fun. While he was very ambi-tious, he did not appear to be selfish. His ambition was for our team and our company. While he was a workaholic, he had a life outside of work. He was passionate about his large Irish family, golf, car racing, and traveling.

The moral of this story is especially relevant for women. Rightly or wrongly, they are more likely to be viewed as workcentric than men. If they don't clearly come across as balanced people, they may be pigeon-holed as dragon ladies. This is especially true if you are a childless woman who works long hours and drives people hard. If you are child-less and unmarried, the stereotype is even more tempting for others to apply. You may think of yourself as a balanced person with interests out-side of work, but you still come across as workcentric, and people as-sume that work is all you have in your life. As a result, this image is an obstacle on your career path.

When Pat Russo was appointed to the CEO position at Lucent, two staff reporters at *The Wall Street Journal* wrote the following in their ar-ticle: "'There are no plans for any changes,' says the 49-year-old Ms. Russo, who maintained perfect posture during a 40-minute interview Monday." (Berman, 1) The reference to Pat's posture struck me as sug-gestive of the dragon lady stereotype, of someone rigid and militaristic. Pat doesn't strike me as being this way at all. Would the reporters have used the same posture reference if a man had been appointed to this position?

If sharp reporters from the *Journal* can inadvertently fall into this stereotyping trap, anyone can. Time and again, I've seen executive women unfairly portrayed as dragon ladies. While some women cer-tainly deserve this label, many do not. In fact, I've seen the label applied to women at all levels of an organization, including women who were generally humanistic and supportive but had moments in which they snapped at someone or refused to compromise on a position.

To maximize your effectiveness and career success, you need to find a way to moderate this image, even if it is undeserved. If you spend in-ordinate amounts of time at work, make an effort to chill out and talk about subjects other than deadlines and processes. More importantly, find a passion outside of work. I'm not talking about taking up just any hobby or adopting a pet, but rather finding something that fully engages you intellectually and emotionally—that engages you as much as work does. In this way, you can make yourself more well-rounded and less obsessed about doing everything perfectly when you are in the office.

The 50 women I interviewed all agree that having children achieves this goal. Without exception, they found that motherhood helped them become more balanced and interesting individuals and less rigid than they were before having children. Marla Gottschalk, the president and COO of The Pampered Chef, observed, "I really started to see that being a workaholic was not healthy. Diversifying my life made me a lot more impactful at work. It's interesting to think I would have become a one-dimensional workaholic if I didn't have children. I wouldn't know any different and I would probably view myself as successful."

I'm not suggesting that these executives achieved an ideal balance—top women executives need to be driven and dedicated to their jobs in ways that may seem unbalanced to an outside observer—but they moved more toward the center of the continuum after becoming mothers. Let us take a look at the different ways in which they became more balanced and less likely to be perceived as dragons.

LETTING GO OF PERFECTIONISM

With the exception of one individual, who felt her job mandated perfectionism, all the executive moms I interviewed agreed that motherhood helped them learn how to "let go." There was so much demand for their time and energy at home, these women could no longer afford to be perfectionists or sweat the little things. They could no longer obsess about unimportant work issues. They had to let others do things they would normally do themselves. They lacked the time to stand over a direct report's shoulder or insist to a supplier how something must be done. They had to let go and roll with the punches if tasks didn't get done right or on time.

When you give birth, you spend the next year or so making adjustments. Even if you take time off from work or only work part-time during that first year, your days (and nights) change. You are up at strange hours and sleeping when you used to be awake. More is going on in your personal life, too, so you learn to change your sleep patterns, work patterns, and other routines in order to adjust.

When moms return to the office, they work just as hard but also make small but significant changes in their work style. They send fewer and shorter e-mails, call fewer meetings, and delegate more often. These women often become early adopters for any new process, tool, or technology that improves their efficiency. They also learn to rely on their administrative assistants.

Once I learned to let go and delegate, I actually became good at this task. My assistant took control of my calendar, filtered and prioritized my office mail and e-mail, coordinated my budget, handled administrative disputes, routed phone calls to my management team, blocked nuisances, prevented interruptions, and so on. After becoming a mother, one of the first things I would do upon joining a new organization was to hire an assistant for my assistant. Two administrative assistants were usually taboo, but I wouldn't accept a job without two, and neither would many of my mother peers. Because even working in tandem, our administrative assistants worked longer hours than any of their coworkers.

While maternal leaders learn to let go of certain work tasks, they don't let go in a sloppy manner. Instead, they work smarter, prioritize much better, and finish important projects on time. They give up the luxury of detailed advance planning, but they also organize the next day or week much more efficiently than before.

Carrie, for instance, was a micromanager prior to having her first child. A senior vice president with a financial services company, Carrie was as smart as they come and brilliant at achieving or exceeding goals. Carrie believed that her success was due in no small part to the fact that she never screwed up. Throughout her career, Carrie had avoided the types of snafus and mistakes that she viewed as black marks on a record. She would routinely check and double-check any significant projects or programs completed under her watch to make sure that nothing would come back to haunt her.

Carrie took six weeks off when she had her first child, and when she returned, everyone agreed she was much easier to work with. It wasn't that she stopped being tough, demanding, and vigilant for mistakes. It was simply that she had learned to let the small stuff slide. As effective as Carrie was and as well as her teams did, people had mixed emotions about being on her team before she became a mother. No one likes a boss who looks over her shoulder, and Carrie was a classic over-the-shoulder looker. Over the years, Carrie had lost a number of highly talented people to other groups within the company as well as to other organizations. Though Carrie always rationalized these losses (she felt the deserters lacked her ambition and drive), the organization viewed them as a real black mark. After having a child, though, Carrie was a much easier boss to deal with. Though she still came down hard on anyone who made a major error, she had a much greater tolerance for minor mistakes. As a result, fewer talented people left Carrie's group.

HAVING MORE UNDERSTANDING OF OTHER PEOPLE'S TIME

Dragon ladies often are intolerant of other people's schedules, problems, and idiosyncrasies. They don't accept excuses, no matter how valid, and they certainly don't feel the need to make allowances for another person's schedule. Jocelyn Carter-Miller, a past chief marketing officer of Office Depot, remembered how her peers who did not have children insisted on 7:00 AM meetings. Joceyln had the early parenting shift at home, so that she could work as long as she needed to at night. She complained loudly about 7:00 AM meetings but didn't receive support, until a coworker's wife went out of town. Because he suddenly had to get his kids up and out the door in the morning, he became very sensitive to 7:00 AM meetings and supported her the next time she asked to have the meetings moved to 8:00 AM.

As a mom, Jocelyn recognized the importance of being flexible; she discovered that what may seem like a reasonable time to one person might not be reasonable to another. Her male colleague learned this lesson because he was in charge of his child's care for a brief period (many men still don't take charge of a child's care for even one full week), but women without kids don't have this opportunity. Jocelyn has made every effort to avoid putting other people in the position where her colleagues had placed her.

While maternal leaders are sensitive to other people's situations, they don't allow the work to suffer. Many child-rearing executives have learned how to use their sensitivity and adaptability to increase productivity. Marion McGovern established a culture that thrives on flexibility, and she feels it has resulted in tremendous employee loyalty. She shared: "A couple of years ago, one of my friends had lung cancer. I would take off on Fridays to take her to chemotherapy. Someone told me, 'Gee, you're lucky that you're the president and can do that.' I let the employees know that they have that privilege, too."

This doesn't mean that executive mothers accept every excuse and accommodate every schedule. Instead, they learn to be reasonable when reason is called for. When someone offers an excuse for why they can't go to a conference or meet a deadline, they don't immediately dig in their heels and adopt rigid positions. Maternal leaders are willing to listen and consider before they make a judgment. It stands to reason that they are especially sensitive to the schedules of mothers who work for them, but they don't grant them any undeserved favors. Melinda Brown, the controller of PepsiCo Beverages and Foods, said, "I view balance (between work and family) as a personal choice, and I fully support personal choices. However, if you choose an assignment that cannot accommodate flexibility and balance, then I expect you to honor your commitment and do what it takes to get the job done."

Excuses come with the leadership territory, and all leaders hate to hear them. Maternal leaders, though, listen to the reasons why something can't be done or why someone is late and try and come up with solutions. Similar to a mom whose child tells her why they can't do an assignment on time, she works at finding an alternative way of getting the task completed.

Amal Johnson, partner at COM Ventures and past executive at IBM, talked about how her experience helped her find better solutions and encourage women in the midst of crisis:

> One of the people working for me at the time was a single mom with a toddler—when her child was sick, she would call in and indicate she needed to line up some emergency care and would be a little late. Initially, I would say fine, no problem. And she'd show up as promised, but I could see that her heart wasn't at work. After a while, I suggested that she work from home

when her child was sick. She was so relieved and grateful; I sensed she worked twice as hard. Once you've been there and done that, you know the situation is temporary.

Similarly, Marilyn Seaman, president and CEO of M One, observed that the tellers in her bank would start trying to track down their kids to make sure they got home from school around 3:00 PM. A dragon lady boss might have been furious at how much time was wasted as the clerks were on the phones trying to track down their kids. As a mother herself, Marilyn recognized that a small accommodation to the tellers' schedules and concerns was reasonable. More than that, Marilyn saw it as an opportunity to provide her people with a win-win benefit. Marilyn instituted a hotline for these employees. All the kids coming home from school had to call into the hotline by a certain time, or the employee would be notified. This policy eliminated a lot of distractions in the afternoon, lowered the tellers' stress level, and enabled them to work harder.

TAKING THE EDGE OFF

From both a career and an effectiveness standpoint, few things hurt dragon ladies more than their edges. Taking work and themselves too seriously makes them come across as edgy, and it causes others to be uncomfortable, not to mention annoyed. Because they are frequently on edge, agonizing over the details, they have difficulty inspiring the loyalty and forming the relationships that companies require from senior leaders. At the same time, of course, this edginess has helped them advance through the ranks. They depend on their seriousness and detail orientation to get things done. As a result, they are reluctant to soften their apparent strengths.

This edge is naturally blunted when you have children, in large part because they provide you with a life outside of work. The excitement your child shows when you walk in the door takes the edge off even the worst days. Gnawing problems are pushed aside and replaced with hugs, smiles, and the presence of someone who needs you more than anyone else in the world. Nursing your baby in a rocking chair in the middle of the night is about as far removed from sitting in your office chair during the day as anything can be. This beautiful infant clinging to you for food and love changes your perspective on everything. As your kids become older, their pictures, school plays, or sporting events all take your mind off work.

Before having children, many women executives have a hard time letting go of negative experiences at work. They obsessively worry about a mistake or an argument, rather than just moving on like the guys seem to do. They often are unable to shake their negative feelings for days. After having children, though, their kids distract them from their negative emotions and replace them with joyfulness. These moms get over things faster and are able to shake off the anxiety that comes from the unavoidable conflicts and snafus at work. The residual good feeling carries them through the day and stops them from being overly critical or short with their people, at least more often than not.

No matter how successful these women were before they had children, they saw improvements in their leadership skills after they became moms. These changes weren't just internal—a new way of looking at things, for instance—but external. Ellen Kullman, a group vice president at DuPont, said, "Normally, people have a hard time convincing others that they have changed and evolved. This doesn't seem to be the case with mothers. Our changes are readily apparent. As my style has evolved over time, I think I surprised even my boss. The adjustments I had to make to my changing family dynamic (like more empathy and flexibility) carried over directly into my business dynamics."

HOW TO BE LESS OBVIOUSLY AMBITIOUS

Though you can't get to the top without ambition, women need to make a distinction between healthy and unhealthy ambition. Dragon ladies often appear to be overly ambitious, and this perception hurts their careers. I remember when a *Fortune* 50 company, one that had long supported women executives, hired a young, talented female CFO. At the time, it was a significant win for women executives, but this CFO frequently noted in media interviews that she planned to become the company's next CEO. Such naked ambition was unbecoming; it made her appear egotistic and selfish. Corporations are reluctant to reward people with top positions who seem excessively self-centered. In fact, this woman's desire for the top job quickly earned the ire of colleagues, and she self-destructed before long.

Admittedly, this woman was an extreme example, but many successful women suffer because they appear to have an ambitious agenda. While they may not make statements to the media that they want to be CEO, their singular focus on their work leaves the impression that advancement is all they care about. Because they are viewed as too pushy or overly focused on their own success, they end up inadvertently thwarting their own ambitions.

Being perceived as overly ambitious is the kiss of death for any executive. Because women are expected to be more nurturing and held to a higher leadership standard than men, edgy behaviors are often judged harshly. Consequently, powerful women have to go out of their way to avoid being labeled ambitious. Interestingly, when powerful women at work announce their pregnancy or start wearing maternity clothes, they often are immediately viewed in a more favorable light. Their pregnancy raises questions in people's minds, such as, "If all she cared about was getting ahead, why would she have kids? Could this mean that work isn't her only goal in life? Does she possibly have a giving side that I've missed?"

Many executives who become moms say that they remain ambitious, but this ambition is no longer the most important driver in their lives. As one senior executive said:

> Before I had my son, all I could think about was that I wanted the chance to run one of our company's businesses. Just about everything I did at work was done with this goal in mind. Afterwards, it was still a goal, but it didn't consume me. I didn't make decisions with this goal in mind. I didn't complain to confidantes at work how the company rarely made women business heads. I had thought this was what I wanted most, and I learned that there are more important things in life. Ironically, when I gave up trying so hard, I was given a line of business.

When you no longer want to achieve your goals at all costs, your behavior naturally moderates. You don't walk around in a tizzy when someone else receives a plum role. You are less likely to overreact to small, routine examples of corporate bias or unfair practices. Perhaps not surprisingly, the less executive women feel the need to get ahead, the faster they get ahead. When they ratchet their ambition down a notch, they appear to be much more qualified candidates.

AVOIDING THE HIGH HORSE SYNDROME

Some VPs start thinking they really are VIPs. Increased responsibility, larger offices, huge raises and bonuses, publicity, use of the company jet, and other perks can produce a superior attitude. Men adopt this attitude as easily as women, but with men it often comes off as self-confidence, while with women it appears as haughtiness.

Carly Fiorina, perhaps the most powerful businesswoman in America, was immediately criticized for this alleged sin after being appointed to run Hewlett Packard. Carly was featured in HP commercials and had recently purchased a controversial $30 million corporate jet. In his March 28, 2001, column, Matthew Harper wrote, "After she arrived in July 1999, her predecessor, Lewis Platt, told *Forbes* that her celebrity style seemed strange to him." (Harper, 2) Would Platt or anyone else have been comfortable drawing attention to a male CEO as having a "strange, celebrity style" if he had acted as Fiorina did?

When women executives actually exhibit high horse traits, caring for a child, especially an infant, can quickly knock them off this horse. When you get little sleep, change an endless number of diapers, and deal with crying and spewing babies, you are quickly brought down to earth. Executive dads may escape these responsibilities—or at least not have to deal with them regularly—but just about every executive mom interviewed has spent much of their time engaged in these activities, even if they had childcare help. There is nothing like putting on a nice outfit to go to work and having your baby take the opportunity to spit something gross on your clothes. It is very difficult to maintain a high and mighty pose in these circumstances.

In fact, when you can no longer primp and prepare yourself like a queen, you are less likely to act like one. On average, the high-powered women I interviewed take less than five minutes to put on makeup in the morning and rarely check up on it or refresh it during the day. When women were pressed for time, grooming was one of the first activities to be cut.

Acting superior is indeed an act, and women are less likely to sustain this performance with nursery rhymes and baby talk running through their heads. I was so used to rocking a baby back and forth, that I often embarrassed myself by rocking while giving a presentation. Women see themselves differently after they have a child, and the image is warmer and more down-to-earth. They trade in their sports cars for SUVs and minivans and are seen leaving in jeans on their way to soccer games. They also are knocked down a peg or two by their teenager's perceptive criticism of their mannerisms, clothes, or hairstyles. One of the most consistent lessons of being a mom is not taking yourself so seriously. Women who come down to earth are still confident in their abilities, but they don't feel the need to display this confidence in every word and gesture. As a result, they are less pushy and more likable.

THE PROOF IS IN THE PUDDING
Being More Real

Because women leaders have the added curse of bias throughout their careers, they face an even greater inner battle than their male peers. This is why so many women feel they need to prove they are better than anyone else. While I was not conscious of this impulse at the time, I see in retrospect how it manifested itself. For instance, I never missed a schedule, even if it involved a trivial task that no one ever completed on time.

The drive to prove yourself in even the smallest of ways is big-time irritating. I know my peers were upset with my behaviors in this regard, either because they were unable to keep up with my pace or because they preferred ignoring relatively minor duties to concentrate on more important matters. If you go around with a chip on your shoulder, you will turn off people. If you constantly have to demonstrate that you are a better strategist, decision maker, innovator, deadline maker, and the like, you will end up proving only that you are obsessed with showing your competency.

Proving yourself becomes less important once you have a child. To understand why, recall Kaplan's view that an executive's anxiety about her self-worth triggers performance problems, like the need to prove yourself. He goes on to say:

Executives can grow and improve by redressing imbalances. The dominant parts of the self, in which so much is invested and in which the person so strongly believes, lose some of their power and preeminence. The submerged parts of the self, in which so little has been invested and which have gone undervalued, gain favor and are given increased expression. All the mastery-oriented "shoulds," which have virtually tyrannized the executive and, in many cases, led him or her to tyrannize others, are relaxed somewhat. (Kaplan, 227)

Children bring out the submerged parts of driven women. Caring for them overwhelms many work anxieties. Though being a mother doesn't eliminate the impulse to prove yourself, it does push this impulse off to the side. Some women focus instead on being the best mom they can be, while others find that they receive so much more love at home that the opinions of bosses, colleagues, and direct reports matter less. In either case, they let go of the need to prove how smart or sharp they are and spend more time being smart and sharp.

All this letting go, chilling out, taking oneself less seriously, and becoming more down to earth helps women act in ways that come across as authentic. This genuine quality resonates with colleagues, who see these executive moms as "more real."

TAMPING DOWN THE DRAGON'S FIRE

If you are a maternal leader who has become less obsessed with work and is leading a fuller life, you know the benefits of making this transition. The worst dragon ladies are loathed, and you have learned it is much more effective—and much more pleasant—to be someone who passes the beer test.

Some of you, though, may still be stuck in dragon lady mode, either because you've resisted the lessons of motherhood or because you have never had children. You need to bring out your submerged, undervalued traits, and there are many ways to achieve this goal. Certainly, being aware of what these traits are—and the downside of being a dragon lady—is a good start.

If you're not a mother, you can moderate your dragon lady posture in a variety of ways, including following earlier suggestions such as volunteering, finding an interest you are passionate about, meditating, traveling, becoming more involved in your religion, and so on. Broadening yourself will dilute the dragon lady's fire. When work is not your entire life, you are not as consumed by it, and you are not as likely to consume others.

Be conscious of your dragon lady tendencies. Some of these tendencies are obvious, including a perfectionist mentality, inflexibility, and taking work too seriously. There are a number of less obvious signs, though, and the following exercise will help you to identify them.

On a scale of 1 to 10 (1 meaning never, 10 meaning always), respond to the following 20 statements. Score yourself, then ask coworkers to score you. Use the scoring guide for a calibration.

1. I walk past people in the hallway without seeing them or saying hello.
2. I daydream.
3. I am the first one in the office.
4. I get numerous personal calls at work.
5. I am the last one to leave the office.
6. I use small talk to start meetings.
7. I have a clean car and park straight in the same spot every day.
8. I go 24 straight hours on a weekend without reading e-mail.
9. I respond to all my e-mails each day.
10. I celebrate my direct reports' birthdays, weddings, and children's births.
11. I fill a briefcase with work every night.
12. I book my lunches first on most days.
13. I have a clean desk.
14. I know everyone in my work area on a first-name basis.
15. I have a clean house.
16. I mentor a lot of people regularly.
17. I read certain business newspapers or magazines religiously.
18. I volunteer my time outside of work at least once a week.
19. I change my purses frequently to match my outfits.
20. I eat ice cream at least once a week.

Scoring guide: Add up your answers to the odd-numbered questions, then add up the answers to the even-numbered questions. Subtract the even from the odd. Divide by 20.

–4.5–0	Dragon-free
0–2	Some dragon tendencies
2–4	Baby dragonette
4–4.5	Dragon lady

3

THE MOTHERHOOD DECISION

"Motherhood absolutely impacts your leadership style. It rounds you out. Overall, it makes you a more complete person. By virtue of raising children, you become a much more complete leader."

Linda Wolf, *Chairman and CEO, Leo Burnett Worldwide*

To be or not to be a mother is a question that many executive women wrestle with, and most decide in favor of having children. Whether you made this decision long ago or are just starting to grapple with it, you probably have not given much thought to how it will increase your leadership effectiveness. Typically, women focus on more practical matters, such as how the time away— whether it is a relatively short maternity leave, a longer sabbatical from work, or a decrease in hours—will negatively impact their careers.

The executive mothers in this book did not experience a serious negative impact. And, while there's no magic formula about when to have kids or how many to have, Appendix B summarizes the choices these women made. If you have not had children yet, thinking about this decision from an informed leadership perspective can be eye opening. If you have had children, you can learn a lot about how the decision may have shaped the leader you've become; it can also provide you with new ways to take advantage of this choice, even if you made it years ago.

As you saw in the last chapter, the dragon lady syndrome is not a permanent condition. Motherhood and an understanding of its impact can have a tremendously beneficial effect. Similarly, the very decision to become a mother not only changes your life but, as we will see, changes your leadership style for surprising reasons.

THERE'S MORE TO LIFE THAN WORK

Perhaps it seems counterintuitive, but people who eat, sleep, and dream about work do not make the best leaders. Yes, they devote all their time and energy to business issues, but this devotion makes them less rather than more effective. In many instances, career success is intoxicating, and these individuals often don't see clearly how they operate as bosses and managers. Only when they step back and put their life into perspective do they discover that work isn't enough and that a work-centric approach has negative consequences. Their self-indulgent drive for career success at all costs inhibits leadership growth.

Like politicians or Hollywood stars, business executives have become so driven by their own agendas and goals, they have lost sight of larger organizational needs. A significant number of *Fortune* 500 CEOs have exhibited self-indulgent, greedy behavior recently, and they have not just been men. Martha Stewart is not an isolated case. Just about every organization has a number of dragon ladies who are difficult to work with and have high horse attitudes. While some of these women are mothers—who have resisted the positive qualities that motherhood instills—many are childless and have concentrated on their own issues to the exclusion of other people or social concerns.

Despite all of their success, the women in this book are not egotistical. As Elizabeth Buse, the executive vice president of product development and management at Visa explained, they have healthy egos because "you don't have the space to be narcissistic if you are going to be an involved parent. When you have kids, you suddenly have something that is more important than you are. Most everything you do, including work, is secondary."

In my mid-30s, I was pursuing my career and raising my two sons, and though I was doing well, I wasn't doing much for the less fortunate people in the world. My husband thought I was doing plenty, because I had just finished running a huge benefit for the Chicago's Infant Welfare Society, and he wanted me to reduce my volunteer work. Instead, I asked AT&T to let me take off a year to work on urban education reform. Instead of giving me a leave, they "loaned" me to the city of Chicago and paid me a full salary. Besides starting some good programs in the city, I ended up spending more time with my family than I had in a while and returned to work refreshed and guilt-free.

I don't mean to make myself sound like Mother Theresa—as my previously mentioned Allatolah Khomeni moniker suggests, I have my flaws. I relate this story, though, to identify a common struggle that successful business people experience. At certain points, you realize that there's more to life than your company and your career. You have the urge to escape it in one form or another. Sometimes this escape is travel. Many times, though, the impulse is to do something more socially or culturally valuable than furthering corporate goals. You want to do something for people who really need the knowledge or services that you can provide.

You should seize the opportunity to involve yourself in a giving way over a sustained period of time. Serving those in need rather than your organization creates an effect similar to that of becoming a mother. In both cases, your perspective shifts. As a leader, you become better able to place events in perspective and avoid the overreactions and permanent-crisis mentality that often comes with top jobs in big companies. For men or women who don't want to have children, this altruistic decision is just as important as the motherhood decision.

The drive to do something more, the need to make a real difference, is found in even the most outwardly successful and business-focused executives. Responding to this drive can make a difference, not only for people in need but for leaders themselves. Kevin Dunn, a former president of McDonald's, was asked in a recent interview at DePaul University for his thoughts on this. He said:

> Be sure that you're giving to life as much as you're taking from life. Be awake and aware of the signals that it's time to give back to the world that has given you so much. There are many ways that this self-actualization or awakening can occur—for me, it was the birth of my first child—and if we're awake we see them and grab them. It helps us develop into a complete human being. We each have the responsibility to be contributing members of our community, serving others and giving back to a world that's given us so much.

Unfortunately, not all of us can respond to our save-the-world impulses because of our situations. We lack organizational permission or the financial wherewithal to take a sabbatical from work. Deciding to be-

come a parent is generally a more common road and provides significant leadership benefits. Though women tend to receive more benefits
than men for reasons I've already enumerated, both male and female executives who are parents tend to be more mature leaders than those who
are not. It is no coincidence that most CEOs are parents. Peter Senge discussed this in *The Fifth Discipline* when he quoted a reference as follows:
"The more I understand the real skills of leadership in a learning organization, the more I become convinced that these are the skills of effective parenting." (Senge, 310) Similarly, in a 2003 study by the Families
and Work Institute, Catalyst, and the Boston College Center for Work
and Family, called "Leaders in a Global Economy," Ellen Galinsky, president of the Families and Work Institute, reports, "Executives who are
dualcentric—who give equal weight to work and personal life—feel more
successful at work, are less stressed, and have an easier time managing
the demands of their work and personal/family lives." She continues,
"Women who are dualcentric (as opposed to women who are only focused on work) have advanced to higher reporting levels and feel more
successful in their home lives." (Galinsky, 4)

In fact, all the executive mothers contributing to this book agreed
with Leo Burnett's worldwide chairman and CEO Linda Wolf's statement, "Motherhood made me a more complete person." Wolf went on
to add that "motherhood absolutely impacts your leadership style. It
rounds you out. Overall, it makes you a more complete person. By virtue
of raising children, you become a much more complete leader."

Achieving this completeness is especially tricky for women, who
may view the decision to have children as a subtraction from, rather
than an addition to, their leadership persona. Logically, women must
subtract time and energy from work when they have children, especially
early on. Over time, however, this decision helps women add a sense of
perspective and other valuable traits to the leadership mix.

Thinking about why women have children reveals how this choice
broadens and deepens leaders in ways that many other experiences cannot. In a very real way, the decision helps women fit work into the larger
purpose of their lives. As a result, they lead with a sense of purpose
rather than just being propelled by a need to achieve.

DECIDE IN THE CONTEXT OF YOUR LIFE VISION

Let us start with two exercises. First, imagine your own deathbed scene. You know you only have another day to live, and you want to gather the most important people in your life. You can invite only 15 people. Create a list of the 15 (or fewer) who would be on it. They can include anyone you currently know as well as people you might imagine coming into your life at a future time.

Second, picture attending your birthday party. You're about to blow out the candle on your cake and make a wish. In this instance, however, it is no idle wish. Fantasize that whatever you wish for will be granted. The only condition is that the wish must be specific and significant. It cannot be a general wish for happiness or an insignificant wish for a sports car.

Now compare the results of these two exercises. Consider whether a number of the people you invited to your deathbed were people you know through work. Consider also if your wish had to do with work or career goals. Conversely, imagine how it would feel if the attendees and the wish both involved family or contributions to other people or society.

I've asked you to do these exercises here, because the decision to have children has a direct impact on your responses. Women who have chosen to be moms tend to populate the deathbed scene with children and grandchildren, and they usually wish that the two generations that follow them achieve their goals and have good values. Women who have decided not to have kids—or who have kids but resist the changes motherhood catalyzes—tend to surround themselves with work-related individuals and wish to achieve a capstone job or some other career goal.

The decision to have children is transformational. It doesn't make work less important but instead shifts a woman's perspective on it. It is almost as if the decision removes the blinders from a woman's eyes, allowing her to see work for what it really is rather than for what it can never be. This realistic, balanced perspective helps women become realistic, balanced leaders. They are no longer as likely to overreact to problems or to overanalyze situations and suffer from analysis paralysis. Deciding to have children liberates women from their work myopia, and over time, their broader vision helps them view work issues in a more objective light. While the decision doesn't catalyze an instant transformation, it is crucial to starting the process.

I had already made the decision to have children when I did a version of the first exercise. At the time, I was working at Bell Laboratories, a place that was incredibly supportive of women and minorities, thanks to the efforts of a few great men such as Jack Scanlon and Dan Stanzione. When I was promoted to supervisor at Bell's Naperville headquarters, they had several hundred managers, and I was the 13th woman to be promoted to this rank. At the time, this was the only level of management that included women, and only one of these leaders was a mother. Because of the supportive environment, a decade later women had penetrated three more levels of management, and more mothers were in the management chain than nonmothers. By the early '90s, women had started penetrating the executive ranks of this traditionally male-dominated, research industry.

At this point in time, Bell Laboratories had hired ARC and Associates to provide leadership training to their supervisors, managers, and executives. The executive course was a one-week program called Vision-Quest. The goal of this course was to help us understand our life—as opposed to our work—vision. The organizational theory was that, if we were more authentic and in touch with our life goals, we would make better decisions at work. Leaders who are centered around a vision, whether a corporate vision or a personal vision, are stronger, more trustworthy, and stable. A couple of dozen women executives across the country were intrigued by this concept, and we enrolled in the course as a group.

When we arrived at our hotel, the facilitators sent us to our room to engage in private meditation on the deathbed question. This was the first time most of us had given more than a fleeting thought to this issue. In fact, it was probably the first time any of us had sat quietly in a room by ourselves for three hours! Remember, women don't usually work out their problems in caves. We like dialogue.

After much fidgeting, I finally slowed down enough to concentrate on the assignment. I pictured myself as a very old woman. I also pictured that my family was at my bedside—kids, grandkids, and great grandkids. I assumed that my kids were in their 70s and grandkids in their 40s, so I worried the most about my great grandkids. I struggled for a while but then zeroed on what I wanted most: for the people at my bedside to love themselves and feel inspired. I didn't want them slobbering over me or talking about what I had accomplished. Whatever their own personal gifts were, I just wanted to leave them inspired to be all that they could be.

These feelings were in stark contrast to the pictures painted by the other women in my group. When we returned to the room, we were asked to share our thoughts with each other. Remember, I adored the women I was with; they were my support system, my mentors, and my friends. Their responses, though, surprised and saddened me. As they talked, they communicated that their accomplishments at AT&T were an integral part of their deathbed scenarios. Even more shockingly, they assumed that the other women in the executive group would be at their bedsides. Only the moms mentioned young people being there in the final moments. For many of the others, the deathbed scene resembled a Bell Labs conference room meeting. Assuming that we would die in our 90s meant that they expected us all to be best friends for the next 50 years. As we talked, I realized that for many of them, their role at work would be their major life accomplishment.

The next step was that we each committed to our search for a life vision and to support each other through the process. During the course, we all had epiphanies of one sort of another, but the reactions of several nonmothers in the group are particularly relevant. These women either had been postponing motherhood or thought they didn't want children, but within a year or so after this event, they changed their minds and started families. In addition, two or three other women who weren't married either became more committed to finding a life partner or adopted children. These women were able to look at the motherhood decision in a fresh light. Instead of seeing it as just an obstacle to their career goals, they saw motherhood within the larger context of their life goals. They realized that, though being a mother might present fresh challenges to their business careers, it could also help them become more purposeful, insightful leaders.

I am not saying that every woman—or every female business executive—should become a mother. What I am suggesting is that taking the time to reflect on this decision can be an important growth experience. It can help you make the right decision for who you are and the leader you wish to become. Too many women consider the motherhood decision within narrow parameters. They don't explore how this choice might impact their development as leaders or their ability to fulfill larger life goals. It can be a remarkable turning point in both your career and your life, and at the end of this chapter, we'll discuss how you can maximize what you learn from this choice, whether you're a mom-to-be or have many years of motherhood behind you. Susan Hogan, a principal at Deloitte Consulting LLP, referred to the decision as a turning point:

> I was scared to have kids . . . I didn't think I had maternal instincts. And now, I cannot imagine life without kids. They have completely changed my life. They have made me a better leader and a better person. My life didn't have true value or substance or meaning until I had kids.

Catherine West didn't want children at first, either, but realized after having them how important they were to her life and leadership. She said, "I wouldn't have been as good a person. My son brought out a sensitivity and selflessness I didn't know I had. And because I am a different person and I am changed, I am much more successful."

I'm encouraged that an increasing number of powerful, executive women are considering the motherhood decision within a larger context. Even some of the most ambitious, younger female executives I've talked to don't cavalierly dismiss motherhood. They recognize that there is more to life than work and are trying to make a wise decision about being moms in terms of their life goals.

I think that Ann Fudge, a mother and CEO of Young and Rubicam, summed it up well in *Business Week*. (Brady, 1) She said, "I do think about what I want my obituary to say. I don't want it to say, 'She did this job, and she did that job.' I want it to say, 'She made a difference in how people view themselves individually and how they view themselves collectively.' Over and out."

Ann's emphasis on her life's mission is not unique. Recently, I attended a women's senior executive roundtable in Chicago sponsored by Lee Hecht Harrison. Twelve of us met each other for the first time, and for an icebreaker, our facilitator unexpectedly asked us to go around the table and share our life vision. Normally, everyone in the room would start squirming at this point. Surprisingly, though, this group was quite introspective. Every senior executive had her life purpose at the tip of her tongue. No one viewed her life as being all about a business role or title. In fact, all of them were concerned about giving to others. Not all the women in this group were mothers, but all of them had consciously made the decision to leave the world a better place and help other people prosper and grow.

Having a clear sense of purpose is the type of decision that creates leadership authenticity, whether it involves a choice to have kids, nurture others, or support those in need. Making this choice based on your vision of creating a better world starts you on the road to being a more mature individual and leader. It keeps you focused on others as well as on yourself, and this dual perspective is the mark of a strong leader.

DECIDING TO BE MATERNAL WITHOUT BEING A MOTHER

One of the themes you'll find running through these pages is that motherhood is not just a physical state but a state of mind. You can choose to give birth to children or choose to give to others. In either case, this decision shakes you out of a completely self-involved mind-set and enables you to mature as a leader. While becoming a mom was a no-brainer choice for me, deciding not to become a mom is a no-brainer choice for others. It may be that you have not found a partner with whom you want to have children or you believe that you're simply not the type of person who would make a good mother. Whatever the reason, if you are convinced that this would be a bad choice for you, don't let me, or society, convince you otherwise. Not everyone should be a parent, and if you have strong instincts against this, listen to your instincts.

If you choose not to become a mother or life's circumstances prevent you from having children, find other means to attain the leadership lessons of motherhood. Oprah Winfrey, for instance, is incredibly nurturing and empathetic as well as a very powerful CEO, yet she has no biological children. In a recent interview, Oprah says that she is focusing a portion of her $1 billion net worth on helping "the world's children." She is devoting her private time to help build 12 schools for girls in Africa. "I went to Africa to create the best Christmas possible for kids who'd never had one, kids who didn't even understand the concept of a present, and the joy in that room was so thick you physically feel it. And in that moment, it hit me. Now I see why I am not married. Now I see why I never had children. I am supposed to work with these children." (Limbacher, 1)

Another childless executive, Sue Palmer, the managing director of London-based accounting firm Grant Thornton, is quoted in Susan Hewlett's book, *Creating a Life: Professional Women and the Quest for Children*, as follows:

> Round the time I realized I would most probably not get married and not have kids, I met this industrial psychologist . . . He told me that to remain strong and vital, I needed to find something in life that could be as important to me as children. If I could do this—find some interest that had deep, personal meaning—it would force me to balance my life. Otherwise, there was a danger my soul would shrivel—I still remember his exact words—and I could become some kind of one-dimensional workaholic. This conversation had such a profound impact. I mean, I just knew he was right. (Hewlett, 70–71)

Sue went on to discuss the things she got involved with and summarized her involvement by saying, "These are now my babies, and I know they are food for my soul." Many childless, giving women, like Sue and Oprah, channel their generous spirits into good causes. Not only do they receive food for the soul, but they become balanced and complete, much like mothers, and ultimately become more complete leaders.

While some women are absolutely certain that they do or do not want to have children, many are on the cusp. One day they worry that if they don't have kids, they will regret it, and the next they are so enmeshed in work issues that having children seems completely unrealistic.

Be aware, also, that a couple of the maternal leaders I've interviewed were dead set against having children at one stage in their careers but changed their minds later on. Priscilla Lu, who was an executive at AT&T and went on to become the chairman and CEO of InterWAVE, a high-tech company in Silicon Valley, said that she was adamant about not wanting kids and shared this sentiment with her colleagues. When she got married, though, she changed her mind and decided to have children. She recalled:

My first pregnancy was pretty traumatic. When I found out, I was shocked. I was worried how I was going to handle being a mom. It was very overwhelming. I knew my life was going to be very, very different. I wasn't 100 percent sure of my decision. I went into a sort of denial—like, "Nah, this isn't happening." But when Douglas was born, my fears went away. Everything did change, but it was wonderful. I guess it's Mother Nature. I don't know where my nurturing side came from, but I immediately felt passionate love for my son and went on to have two more children.

Moms such as Priscilla make extraordinary leaders, but some women never experience the joy of motherhood or the rewards of maternal leadership, because common myths discourage them. Unlike women who make the motherhood decision with their eyes open and their minds clear, women who say no to motherhood often do so because they subscribe to false fears about how being a mom will impact their job effectiveness and their careers. Exploring and exploding these myths can help everyone in organizations by both preventing women who have already had kids from feeling guilty about or hamstrung by their choices and assisting women on the cusp to make the right choice for themselves.

THE MYTHS ABOUT MOTHERHOOD FOR FAST-TRACK WOMEN EXECS

Myth #1: Motherhood will make it more difficult to get to the top. Corollaries of this myth include, "Moms can't devote the time or energy necessary to qualify for these positions" and "Organizations are reluctant to select mothers for top jobs because of the fear that they will give in to the demands of their family over the demands of their jobs." While some organizations may subscribe to this myth, most companies are more enlightened. The authors of "Leaders in a Global Economy Report" determined, "Women at reporting levels closer to the CEO are *more likely* to have children and less likely to have decided not to have children than women executives at lower levels." (Galinsky, 3)

Shelly Lazarus, the CEO of Ogilvy & Mather, said, "It is certainly possible to be both a mother and a CEO. You learn how to set priorities, and you learn how to enjoy the ride." Shelly noted that this belief isn't necessarily shared by all women, as evidenced by a commencement speech she recently heard: "I was startled because the speaker gave a speech that you cannot have both. These were young, impressionable women, and she was telling them not to believe it. It really bothered me. There's enough evidence that you can do both."

No doubt, some women in certain fields and in specific companies will face roadblocks because they are moms. Balancing career and family certainly can be a challenge, but in the majority of situations, it is not an impediment to securing top corporate positions. In fact, the "Leaders in a Global Economy Report" suggests that motherhood is viewed as a positive rather than a negative quality when selecting candidates for executive positions. The tide is indeed turning. No doubt, organizations are recognizing that the qualities of maternal leadership—perspective, balance, nurturing, and so on—are exactly the skills needed to manage a diverse workforce in turbulent times.

Therefore, when you think about your motherhood decision, don't beat yourself up because you chose to have kids and believe that you haven't achieved your career goals because of that decision. Unless you work for a truly backward organization, this isn't the case. Similarly, if you're a younger woman trying to decide about becoming a mother, don't let this myth stop you from starting a family if that is what you really want to do.

Myth #2: Mothers are opting out at alarming rates. The opt-out myth places pressure on working moms to quit their jobs and join the trend to stay at home with their kids. It also discourages women from having children, because it creates the fear that becoming pregnant signals the beginning of the end of their careers. Though it is impossible to find reliable statistics about how many professional women opt out after having children, everything I've learned from my interviewing and research suggests that the number has been inflated.

The media has had a field day with this trend, and articles in *USA Today, The New York Times Magazine, Business Week,* and *Time* have all declared that more women than ever are leaving the workforce to stay at home with their children. I would caution everyone to take what they read in the media with a grain of salt, as the following example illustrates.

A *New York Times Magazine* and *Business Week* article declared that only 38 percent of the female graduates from Harvard Business School's 1981, 1985, and 1991 graduating classes were working full-time. (Conlin, 1) In a follow-up article, Bonnie Erbe noted that she called the Harvard B-School media office and received the results of the Harvard survey cited in the *New York Times* article. Erbe wrote: "It was made clear this was not a statistical reliable sampling. I was told each of those classes of 900 graduates (in 1981, 1985, and 1991) she cited were roughly 30 percent female. That means, to get a statistically accurate sampling, the professor would have had to receive approximately 810 responses (or 30 percent of 2,700 responses). She received a grand total, I was told, of 150 responses. And who would have more time to respond to such a survey than women home full-time versus women crunching hours and putting in face time at high-velocity jobs?" (Erbe, 1–2)

Opting out is also a nebulous term. Some mothers quit executive positions for the same reason nonmothers do: They are dissatisfied with some aspect of their organizations, their jobs, or their lifestyle. The time-out that women take for maternity leave gives them an opportunity to assess their career and life. One of my bosses used to tell me, "As soon as your team completes a huge project or solves a crisis, put them on another one right away. You don't want to give them too much time to think about how hard they've been working." Maternity leave provides women with time to think.

Perhaps most significantly, my interviews suggest that fast-track women executives with kids are less likely to opt out than women who have lower-level jobs. It stands to reason that most women with highly successful careers have more to lose by opting out than other women, that the financial rewards and satisfaction they derive from their jobs are greater than if they had been less successful. Therefore, while a woman in a dead-end job who has a child might find it easy to stop working, a woman in an exciting, fulfilling executive role will find such a prospect less enticing.

Opting out is also less of a possibility if you work in a mother-friendly environment. Many of the women I interviewed noted that they were eager and able to return to work after having children, because their organizations valued maternal leaders. Mindy Meads of Lands'

End said, "I am fortunate to work for a company that is so family oriented. I have been able to go to many of my son's soccer games. There are lots of moms working with me, and kids are respected as an essential element of our lives. In fact, some of our senior executives occasionally bring their children along on European business trips."

Myth #3: To become a CEO, you must carefully plan your career and life around your goal. While you need to get the right mix of academic and job experiences to be even considered for a CEO position, you cannot plan every aspect of your life to the point that you significantly increase the odds of becoming a CEO. When I hear women complain that they would have been considered for a CEO job if they had never had kids, I know they are under the influence of this myth. When they decided to have children, they did not automatically destroy their chances of being a chief executive. Though being a mom might not have fit into a formal CEO career plan, it also didn't throw them off the fast track.

When my son was young, he wanted to be a professional athlete. While he was very talented, the probabilities were still a million to one. Now that he's a scholarship athlete on a Division I football team, his probabilities are more like a hundred to one. His odds of making it, while better, are still pretty low. He knows he's at the mercy of certain factors beyond his control, such as injuries and luck. As a result, he is not planning everything in his life around playing professional football, even though he still would like to achieve this goal.

Similarly, women who decide not to have children because it doesn't fit with their CEO plan are forgetting that factors beyond their control will impact whether they ultimately become a CEO. Only so many top jobs are available, and if you sacrifice a family for this long shot, you are making a bad bet.

Myth #4: Women who have to leave work because of family problems become bitter and resentful. In other words, you feel that the decision to have children will eventually come back to haunt you. You fear having kids because you feel they will need you, you'll have to quit a job you love, and this second decision will make you miserable. Or you have already had children, and you're just waiting for the other shoe to drop—for the moment when the family/work balance becomes impossible to maintain and you have to quit.

In reality, when high-achieving mothers stop working, they usually do so because they have decided they prefer to be at home rather than at work. No one puts a gun to their heads. Contrary to the myth, they don't look at motherhood as a sentence to life in prison. I interviewed a number of very talented, ambitious executive moms with senior corporate executive aspirations, but they had gladly stopped working or changed career paths to spend more time at home. Some felt they could not be good at both, some didn't like the incredibly hectic pace, and others had children in distress. Not one regretted her decision to become a mother. In fact, they all said their children were the best part of their lives. Though some had struggled with the decision to leave the corporate world, all of them eventually came to terms with their departures.

In fact, a trait of many maternal leaders is an ability to derive meaning from more than work. Though they may miss aspects of the business world, they don't miss it in the same way that many men do. Too often, powerful male leaders derive the bulk of their identity from their work, and fatherhood is seen as a secondary role. Powerful executive mothers, on the other hand, have a more balanced viewpoint. This balance is why senior women leaders are not as likely to be consumed by the quest to be CEO as men are. Warren Farrell, the author of *The Myth of Male Power,* finds the following:

> When a woman gets near the top, she starts asking herself the most intelligent questions. The fact that few women make it to the very top is a measure of women's power, not powerlessness. Women haven't learned to get their love by being president of a company. They've learned they can get respect and love in a variety of different ways—from being a good parent, from being a top executive, or by a combination of both. But here again, women are opting off the CEO track because they believe they found something better, namely, love. (Farrell, 1)

Myth #5: If I do take a break, I cannot get back on the fast track. The "High-Achieving Women 2001 Report" stated, "Fully two-thirds of women who left their careers would like to go back to work." (National Parenting Association, 2) While many high achievers want to return, some fear that they've lost too much ground to get back on track. It is a myth, however, that getting off the fast track means that you cannot get back on it. When you decide to become a mother, you do not condemn yourself to mid-level or below positions when you return to work.

Again, the media's fascination with this topic has helped foster the illusion that, once you leave work for family, it will be difficult to pick up where you left off. Article after article warns of the difficulty of making up for lost time or convincing bosses that you are sufficiently "serious" about work to be considered for an important role.

In reality, you must battle to stay on the fast track no matter what your situation might be. More significantly, organizations don't view "time off" with the same suspicion as they did years ago. CEOs often take breaks in their corporate climbs without penalty. Jamie Dimon was fired as president of Citigroup and took 16 months off before being appointed CEO of Bank One. Ed Zander became CEO of Motorola a year-and-a-half after leaving his COO role at Sun Microsystems. Ann Fudge was appointed CEO two years after voluntarily leaving Kraft. And Brenda Barnes, who left a top position at PepsiCo in 1997 to spend more time with her children, returned as the COO of Sara Lee after a seven-year break.

I heard many wonderful stories about corporations who went out of their way to support their talented senior women executives during and upon return from breaks. In addition to taking maternity leave, many of these executives have taken a break for family and balance purposes at one time or another. In my case, AT&T paid me a full salary to perform public service. It is not the only company to do something like this. One of the strongest women leaders I've known was at Sun Microsystems when she took a sabbatical to spend more time with her teenage daughter who was struggling with depression. "Scott McNealy was so supportive," she said. "He wouldn't even put me on a leave of absence. He paid my full salary while I took the time I needed with my daughter. Scott has three kids. He understood how important it was for me to be there for her."

HOW THE DECISION TRANSLATES INTO LEADERSHIP MATURITY

Deciding to become a mother or to devote a period of your life to helping others doesn't instantly transform you from an immature to a mature leader. It does, however, provide you with the opportunity to mature. Once you choose to devote at least part of your life to others, you are changing what you value and how you see the world.

The following two checklists describe immature and mature leaders. Not surprisingly, maternal leaders tend to have some or most of the mature traits, while others often have a significant number of immature traits. Look at both lists and determine which traits apply to your leadership style.

Immature	Mature
__ Makes fast, impulsive decisions	__ Reflects before deciding
__ Takes a position and digs in	__ Is willing to rethink positions
__ Thinks short term	__ Thinks long term and short term
__ Becomes impatient when things don't go according to plan	__ Can adapt when things go off course
__ Resolves conflict unilaterally	__ Resolves conflict with wisdom after listening to all sides
__ Looks for easy solutions	__ Tests alternative solutions
__ Works poorly with people outside their inner circle	__ Creates good relationships with a diverse group of people
__ Is unwilling to compromise	__ Knows when to compromise and when not to

The decision to be a mother or to help others doesn't instantly make you a mature leader; it merely points you in the right direction and increases the odds that you will gain the traits of leadership maturity. Of course, you may never have had children but still possess many mature leadership traits. Your particular life experiences may have helped you mature in ways similar to those of moms.

It is also possible that you are a mother but made a number of checks next to the immature traits. If so, recognize that motherhood is a lifelong process. There's always an opportunity for growth. Earlier in your life, you made the choice to be responsible for someone else, to make sacrifices, to view the world through someone else's eyes. Sometimes we don't let our home-based skills translate into our professional life. The odds are that you're a responsible, wise, and balanced person as a mother. Your goal should be to apply these same qualities to how you lead and manage others at work.

To help all of you apply the qualities of motherhood to your leadership role, let us start by examining what we can learn from bringing up babies.

4

PREGNANCY

Transitioning to a Softer, More Accountable, More Value-Conscious Style

"People didn't think I ever wanted kids. When I announced I was pregnant, people were shocked. It changed their perspective of me. Knowing there was something else in my life made a big difference to them."

Dawn Lepore, *Vice Chairman, Charles Schwab*

Contrary to what some people might think, executive women love being moms. The notion that these women view motherhood as secondary to their work—that they are too ambitious and busy to appreciate the joys of motherhood—is probably a mixture of Hollywood stereotypes and societal attitudes. From CEOs to senior vice presidents, these women emphasize that there is no greater reward in life than being a mother, and they have also stressed that their children have helped them to become better leaders and people in a variety of ways. In fact, many of them mentioned pregnancy as a life-changing, leader-making experience.

This shared sentiment makes sense when you realize that, up until this point, these women have been wrapped up in fast-paced, high-altitude careers. Pregnancy is a radical, new experience for women in leadership positions who are accustomed to immediate results and being in control. Waiting nine months for results and having to go with the flow runs counter to a leader's nature.

It is impossible to prepare for this experience. As much as some women may have thought about what it would be like to be pregnant, the actual fact of pregnancy affects not only how they think but how they feel. Specifically, most women feel joy and trepidation. In varying ways, they all talk about how they are uplifted, ecstatic, and magical. Paradoxically, they are also anxious and worried. The huge new responsibility combined with the prolonged uncertainty of pregnancy shakes even the most confident of women executives. The women I've interviewed expressed concerns about balancing work and family and about being responsible for the well being of another human. More than that, they acknowledged their accountability. They recognized that they were not only responsible for the life of their children, but that they were accountable to these children. For strong, independent women, this accountability was humbling.

The paradox of being pregnant presents wonderful opportunities for learning and growth. It creates a true "teachable moment." Just as the decision to become a mother starts this process, pregnancy provides a transition period in which women can assimilate the joy and trepidation that are part of motherhood and learn the lessons that are necessary to be a good mother—and a good leader.

Let's look at the following pregnancy traits and how they relate to leadership:

- Accountability
- Rational risk taking
- Balanced perspective
- Clarified values
- Emerging softness

ACCOUNTABILITY

Accountability comes in many shapes and forms. For corporate leaders, it's all about choices and decisions. Corporate leaders are often risk seekers, but the best leaders learn how to manage their risk-taking impulses. Pregnancy helps women acquire the wisdom of country singer Kenny Rogers's gambler, who knew "when to hold 'em and when to fold 'em." The vulnerability of carrying around an unborn child for nine months gives even the most risk-embracing women pause. Certainly, they no longer feel invulnerable. Pregnancy doesn't stop women from making decisions, but their deeper sense of accountability helps them to make smarter ones. They are less likely to say "What the heck" whenever an opportunity comes along. Instead, they only say "What the heck" after they've assessed the downside of a venture. Rita Kahle, an executive vice president at Ace Hardware says, "My pregnancies were ten years apart. Both times I became more measured."

Managing accountability is an increasingly important leadership skill in an age when otherwise brilliant and accomplished CEOs have sold out right before it becomes obvious that they have destroyed or weakened their companies. Often, they fail due to being overly optimistic and not adequately weighing risks. Psychologically, a high propensity to take risks goes hand in hand with being extroverted, assertive, analytical, and capable of doing ten things at once. In addition, risk-taking cultures tend to reinforce this behavior by rewarding leaders for taking these risks.

Risktaking.co.uk—a Web site that provides an introduction to the psychology of risk taking—suggests that "a large number of studies have shown that people who engage in a range of high risk behaviors tend to be high Sensation Seekers. . . . Studies involving identical twins that are reared apart suggest that a large proportion of Sensation Seeking is genetically determined." The Web site goes on to say that people who take extraordinary risks do so because they are confident they can manage the risks.

Unfortunately, this confidence is sometimes unfounded. Both men and women who have achieved great success in organizations are often extremely confident that their risks will pay off, but just one bad gamble can get them into serious trouble. Though both men and women tend to be given a certain length of rope with which to hang themselves, a woman's rope tends to be shorter and flimsier. Men are often given second chances after they blow an opportunity or lose a lot of money, while women are deemed "in over their heads" and moved out of their leadership posts. One has to wonder, if former Kraft CEO Betsy Holden were a man, would she have been given more time to prove herself?

Don't delude yourself into thinking that women aren't as Sensation Seeking as men because they are less likely to gravitate toward macho adventuring; the news media seems to focus on wealthy male businesspeople who climb mountains or sail around the world in boats or hot air balloons. In fact, I know or have read about many women executives who have engaged in similar types of adventurous activities. Gail Evans, retired executive vice president at CNN Newsgroup and author of several women's leadership books, bought herself a purebred Arabian mare for her 50th birthday. She said, "I'd have to pay full attention to what I was doing. If I wondered about work while I was riding her, I would surely fall off. But that invigorating ride and pure removal from work would bring me back totally refreshed." When Leo Burnett landed the U.S. Army account, Linda Wolf agreed to jump out of an airplane and parachute with the Golden Knights. No wonder her nickname is "Indestructible Girl."

In fact, until women executives become pregnant, they often feel indestructible and have the propensity to engage in behavior that is physically and organizationally on the edge. I can recall a number of experiences in my own life that, with hindsight, epitomize my fearlessness (though you could also argue that they also epitomize my foolishness). Once, an employee from another country, who had just been fired along with a number of others, was upset because he had to leave the United States. I didn't know him, but he somehow decided that I might intervene on his behalf. Margaret, my assistant, indicated that he wouldn't take no for an answer, so she put him on my calendar. In the meeting, he pulled out a weapon and threatened me. He told me that Allah had sent him to stop me from going through with the downsizing.

I should have been frightened, but I remained calm. Executives at Bell Laboratories had silent panic alarms under their desks, and I pressed mine while I kept up a conversation with him. Margaret quickly figured out what was taking place, called security, and explained to them that a disgruntled employee was confronting me. In a few minutes, a plainclothes guard knocked on my door and quickly opened it. He acted as though he was oblivious to what was happening and insisted he needed my signature right away, positioning himself between the employee and me. The distraction allowed another guard to position himself behind the guy, and the situation was diffused.

Any "normal" person would have been terrified. I suspect, however, that most executives with a healthy amount of leadership DNA would have reacted in a similar fashion. This fearlessness is essential for making tough decisions or taking chances on projects that can make or break you. It only becomes counterproductive when you act before evaluating the consequences. Whether it is an employee, boss, customer, or shareholder, someone will hold you accountable for excessive risks.

Gail Evans talked about how, when you become pregnant and start thinking about your child, you become more attuned to feelings of fear and when they should be heeded. She said, "Your children teach you what real fear is. Screwing up a contract is not scary. Something life threatening with a child helps you realize that fear is relevant."

You can see clearly how women become less reckless when they are pregnant. It starts with simple things like wearing a seat belt, driving more carefully, and taking care of their bodies as if they belonged to someone else. They cut out all alcohol, caffeine, and medication, substituting food that is good for you even if it doesn't taste very good and even worse-tasting, nausea-generating vitamins. From checkups every month to Lamaze classes to researching everything there is to know about raising happy, healthy children, women move toward a safer, saner stance.

At work, everything from their habitual behaviors to their decision-making process evolves. Pregnant women are much more likely to weigh alternatives than make impulsive choices that they may regret later. Mothers instinctively consider their accountabilities before charging ahead. If all this sounds like a deepening of the leadership maturity, which I referred to in the previous chapter, it is exactly that.

Again, these changes don't happen overnight. While some women learn to adopt less reckless behaviors at the start of their first pregnancy, others require more time . . . or more pregnancies. Though being pregnant helped moderate my hard-charging, damn-the-torpedoes approach, the lessons sunk in gradually, and I experienced some recidivism along the way. For instance, I was pregnant with my second child in the winter of '87, and I was scheduled to fly to Washington, D.C., for a visit with the National Security Agency. A snowstorm socked in D.C., however, and my plane was the last one to be allowed into the city before they shut the airport. After an hour of circling, instead of landing at Dulles where my limo was, I was diverted to National. I was one of the first off the plane and raced toward the taxi stand. All I was thinking about was that I was going to be late for this important meeting.

I really needed to stop at a restroom. Pregnancy gives a whole new meaning to "having to go." The restroom was crowded, though, so I decided to check out the taxi stand. There were only three taxis and the first driver said it would only take 45 minutes to get me to the NSA. I saw the crowd lining up behind me and decided I could wait to go to the bathroom. Seven hours later we had only gone three miles. I didn't have to hold it any longer. I had become totally dehydrated. We were stuck on the highway with no way out. Trucks ahead of us had not made it up an incline; they rolled back, slamming into the cars behind them, creating a chain reaction that blocked everything. Emergency equipment couldn't get to us, etc. A foot of snow had accumulated on our cab before we were able to work our way near the first exit ramp. The people ahead of us pushed their cars up the exit ramp to get off the highway. So I got out to push the cab.

Surprisingly, I stopped myself before putting my shoulder to the cab's trunk. I say surprisingly, because my mind-set has always been that I can do anything to which I put my mind. Despite being pregnant, in high heels and wearing a skirt, my reflex was to push. Fortunately, my maternal instinct kicked in. Though I didn't articulate the words, my subconscious was telling me that pushing the cab was a risk to the life of my unborn child. It went against my grain to be cautious, but I was slowly learning that at times, my accountability to others took top priority. I came to see that, when it came to my kids, I couldn't play the odds. I vowed not to put myself in another situation like this one. I was done traveling for a few months. My life priorities became very clear. Someone else's needs were more important than mine, and I was accountable to him.

Susan Hogan put this succinctly when she said, "Pregnancy made me understand that my life was important. If I die, it's a big deal."

RATIONAL RISK TAKING

Does *rational risk taking* seem counterintuitive? Especially in light of all the articles and books advocating more risk taking, you might think that pregnancy decreases rather than increases leadership effectiveness. Actually, if you are naturally predisposed to taking risks, learning how to reign yourself in increases the odds that the gambles you take will pay off. No doubt, you've taken risks in the past that have enabled you to succeed in your career and help your company do well. It's likely that you consider your risk taking a strength. Overuse of a strength, though, turns it into a weakness. Off-the-chart risk takers need to learn to be conservative in certain situations. Typically, quick decisions get many risk takers into trouble. Should I sign this financial report with just a cursory glance? Should I hire this person? Should I approve a new product for delivery? Should I ask for more data?

Pregnancy usually catalyzes a change in risk-taking attitudes, as evidenced by what happened to Toni, a top executive with a major corporation. Toni has always prided herself on bringing an "entrepreneurial" perspective to the world of big business. Brilliantly creative and able to cut through bureaucratic red tape, Toni has earned a reputation for getting things done and getting results. Her record of risk taking hasn't been without blemish—she got herself into hot water a few times when projects she green-lighted failed or when she oversold products to her customers. Toni didn't suffer any serious repercussions, until she decided to move the assembly of her product overseas.

While everyone on her team agreed that moving overseas would generate goodwill and ultimately lower costs, her colleagues advised her to wait until the company established a high-quality manufacturing facility. Toni moved prematurely, and it turned out she was wrong—the factory couldn't consistently assemble the products on time and with quality. Consequently, even costs went up—and Toni's reputation went down. With hindsight, she should have taken more time to put all the processes in place and listen to her team.

Shortly after this snafu, Toni became pregnant, and over the nine months of her pregnancy, her approach to risk changed subtlety but significantly. She was less aggressive when opportunities presented themselves, willing to engage in discussions and research before making a decision for which she'd previously lacked patience. Though she still relished her end runs around the bureaucracy and her ability to move quickly while others analyzed the data to death, Toni was a little more cautious and a little more willing to consider options before acting. Though these changes were small, they made a big difference in the way Toni was perceived within the organization.

The dash and daring that many women leaders such as Toni bring to their jobs is terrific, but they need to develop the instinct to think before they act. Making a cavalier investment or acquisition can cost people their jobs; you may be spared termination because you made a bad decision, but other people in the company or your customers might not be so lucky. Replacing your impulse for risk taking with an impulse to consider those to whom you are accountable will help you take more thoughtful risks.

The best risk takers in organizations are not the ones who take the biggest or most risks but the ones who take the right risks at the right times. Maternal leaders have an uncanny ability to achieve the latter goal. During pregnancy, they become more sensitive to consequences that affect others. It is one thing to take a risk that only involves you, something else entirely to take a risk that endangers your child. Leaders who hold themselves accountable to others are more savvy risk takers.

BALANCED PERSPECTIVE

While pregnancy awakens your protective instincts, forcing you to balance your innate, charge-ahead nature with a degree of caution and a sense of accountability, you can also think of it as a nine-month course in broadening your perspective. As these women became responsible for another person's life, concerns about their career became less relevant and decisions at work became less monumental.

Anita Beier, senior vice president and controller of U.S. Airways, said, "Pregnancy put everything into perspective. If I were to lose my job, it would be awful, but not the end of the world. The worst thing that could happen is something with my child."

Elizabeth Buse, an executive vice president with VISA, said, "I gained a much healthier perspective on my career. I realized that everything takes time. And the relative importance of my rising in the company changed. When your life is no longer just your job, it changes your perspective."

Once they stopped agonizing over decisions, some of these executives actually started taking more risks. While some women need to temper their risk taking, others need to embrace risk, and a broadened perspective helps them achieve this objective. After becoming pregnant, they saw that they took certain things too seriously that, in the larger scheme of things, were actually not that serious. They realized that small failures were relatively insignificant and felt more comfortable forging ahead.

Many of the women changed their style as this new perspective took hold. Some found that they worked less, and others found they handled crises more in stride. Ruth Ann Gillis, a president at Exelon, said that work had her attention 90 percent of the time before her pregnancy, but once she was pregnant, things changed. She said:

During my pregnancy, I saw a shift in my priorities. I remember it vividly. I was asked what the most important thing I was doing now was, and my reaction was "having a baby." My pregnancy put my life balance into perspective.

Shelly Lazarus of Ogilvy & Mather described an event that helped her put a crisis at work into perspective:

I was in my boss's office when the media planner walked in and started pacing in circles. We were supposed to be in a client meeting in an hour to present a media plan for the year, but the computer was down. Back then, that was a disaster. She couldn't pull the numbers and prepare the plan and was really upset. My boss stopped her in her path. He actually shook her and said, "What do you think they are going to do to you—take away your children?" Right then, I realized how the importance of children gives perspective to everything else.

Pregnancy starts the process of developing a balanced perspective, but all stages of motherhood contribute to this development. As you'll discover, everything from a toddler's trip to the emergency room to a teenager's rebelliousness helps maternal leaders gain balance and emotional maturity. One executive mother noted that managers who aren't parents sometimes lack this balance and maturity, saying:

I often think in the back of my head, "So and so would be dealing with this really differently if he or she had kids." I strongly recommend that if you plan to be a leader without being a parent that you actively get involved on a meaningful level with something that you care about more than yourself.

CLARIFIED VALUES

Becoming a mother added a new dimension to these executives' lives. Their view of the world changed dramatically and started some positive changes in their leadership style. Not all of it happened overnight, but pregnancy started the process. The president and COO of

The Pampered Chef, Marla Gottschalk, said, "When you get pregnant, you begin to really see the miracle of life. It drives a lot of things into perspective. It makes you think about your own life and your relationship with others. And you value things that you had not paid attention to."

These nine months are also a time for reflection, not only about work, but about what really matters to you. Many leaders in high-stress, high-activity positions lack the time or inclination to take a step back and consider what really matters. Women who are pregnant naturally are inclined to contemplate what they value. Great, well-thought-out values make great leaders. Knowing that you believe in treating people with kindness and respect, that you want to make a difference in the world, and that trusting relationships are of great importance translates into being a principled leader.

Some of these women were true pioneers, and as such, they received a certain amount of flak. When they became pregnant, some colleagues judged them harshly—they said they were ruining their careers or had chosen the wrong time to become a mom—and these judgments caused them to reassess their values.

One of the maternal leaders I interviewed said:

> I never had mother as a mentor. The other women leaders in the company hated me—they felt they gave something up, while I felt I didn't have to make the same sacrifice. The men I worked with and their stay-at-home wives were harsh judges about what kind of mother I would become. They thought mothering while maintaining a high-powered career was a terrible thing.

This bombardment of negative reactions gave these pregnant mothers cause to pause and clarify their values. They knew they had the desire to do both, and some said it was such a strong desire that they knew they could not *not* do both. While they were pregnant, many of these women began assessing their childcare options, and they thought about them from a values perspective. They were determined to find caregivers whose values matched their own.

While a few women relied on husbands or grandparents, most employed nannies or another type of outside caregiver. For all these women, this selection process involved more than just finding someone who would cook for and baby-sit their children. Searching for someone with shared values meant defining their own values. This is not something that many people do consciously; it takes a specific event such as becoming pregnant to catalyze the process.

Though they all didn't follow a formal process of writing their values on a piece of paper and using them as the specs for hiring a nanny, they considered what type of person would be acceptable to them, given their own beliefs. They determined that being trustworthy, respectful, loving, and honest were extremely important to them, and consciously or subconsciously, they looked for caregivers with the same qualities.

As Jocelyn Carter-Miller, president of TechEdVentures, observed:

> I researched all sorts of childcare, like I've never researched anything before, and it was fruitful. The effort of finding the right person for us paid off. You have to know what you want and be extremely resourceful to find the right person. Our nanny loved Alexis as much as we did. She was always there, always trustworthy. She nurtured Alexis and treated her with love and respect. She took care of all of us like a grandmother. After our second child was born we hired a new nanny, who has moved across states with us and become part of our family.

When leaders hire direct reports, they tend to search for people with the right mix of experience and expertise. They focus on the specs, on finding individuals who have the knowledge and skills that a given job demands. Certainly no one would hire a caregiver who didn't know how to cook or drive (assuming cooking and driving are key parts of the job), but the nature of the search requires women to focus on the whole person. This holistic perspective carries over to the workplace, where values are factored into hiring decisions.

Hiring caregivers enhanced these executives' people-selection skills; they became more resourceful, more analytical in their evaluations, and better able to assess an applicant's values. In terms of this last attribute, maternal leaders are often much more astute than others about the importance of values such as trustworthiness and compassion. Long-term relationships, in childcare and business, are crucial, a truth that often escapes nonmoms.

"If my nanny leaves, my life falls apart," said Priscilla Lu, the chairman and CEO of InterWAVE, who moved her nanny from China to New Jersey to California.

According to another maternal leader, "You start by wanting the perfect person and realize that you are not even that person, so you have to prioritize what you're looking for."

Nayla Rizk, a partner at Spencer Stuart, added, "You have to define your goals and find a nanny who can share your goals. It is more important to align on goals and values than agree on how they go about things."

Searching for a nanny clearly pushed these women out of their comfort zones. Though they were veteran executives who had seen and done just about everything within the world of business, pregnancy forced them to do things they had never done before, such as look for a value-consistent caregiver for their baby. Being pushed out of one's comfort zone can be a great learning experience, especially for high-powered women executives who need to adapt their style to move to the next level. As we'll see, pregnancy also creates healthy discomfort in another way.

EMERGING SOFTNESS

At some point early in their careers, many women have been told they were too emotional. Deidre, now a top executive in the pharmaceutical industry, remembered being no more than three years out of business school, working as an assistant product manager, when she went into her boss's office to protest his firing another person in her group. In a quavering voice, Deidre defended the fired individual, suggesting that this person had many strong qualities even if she didn't always get her work done on time. "Can't we give her another chance?" she asked. Deidre's boss told her that her defense of a coworker might seem admirable, but that if she wanted to move up in the organization, she would start putting results first and people second. He said that another boss might hold this request against her and assume she was too "soft" to do well in a managerial role.

Most executive women learned early in their careers that, just as there is no crying in baseball, there is no crying in the office. Typically, a tough male boss conveys that crying or any similar emotional display signals weakness. As a result, women learn not only how to shut off the tears but how to avoid turning red, acting frustrated, or speaking out of turn. This isn't all bad. Learning to control bursts of emotion helped them become more effective leaders. At the same time, however, it hardened them. In response to this early career lesson, some went too far in an emotionless direction. They adopted an overly stoic style and lacked the warmth and passion that characterizes powerful leaders. Pregnancy triggers women to soften their hard stance, to a certain extent forcing a happy medium between crying and being stone-faced.

Ellen Kullman, a group vice president at DuPont, started out as a mechanical engineer and has worked in a male-dominated industry her whole career. She said:

> You grow up thinking that toughness is a prerequisite for the job. For us type-A personalities, emulating the masculine style is easy. But by my mid-30s, when I got pregnant, I lost my harshness. I learned you can be softer and still be tough and demanding and have high standards. I just make sure that I don't lose my edge. Because I need that edge to see the landscape and understand where we need to go.

Pregnant women cry often, and their tears don't always have a discernible cause. Pregnancy also brings unpredictable mood swings that are very hard to suppress. Mirian Graddick-Weir, executive vice president at AT&T, said, "You have all these different ranges of emotions and you don't know where they are coming from. I tried to figure out where the highs and lows were coming from, but I didn't have a clue. These nine months cause women to experience joy in the midst of physical discomforts like nausea, hair loss, dry skin, constipation, heartburn, and feeling fat. Some were feeling "nurturing" for the first time in their lives. Given these myriad feelings and experiences, maintaining a stoic demeanor is a challenge. As a leader, people will appreciate that you have a full range of emotions and that you are confident enough to express them in the work environment.

In my second pregnancy, I found out that I had an ectopic pregnancy and headed into emergency surgery. When I heard the news, I was upset and didn't listen carefully to the surgeon's summary of the procedure. It was a Friday morning, and I called my boss, Neil Whittington, to let him know what was happening. Neil, who had a military background, possessed a command-and-control style that encouraged getting results and following orders. When Neil answered the phone, I immediately adopted my work persona and matter-of-factly told him that I had an ectopic pregnancy, was having surgery, and wouldn't be in until Monday. To my surprise, Neil responded with sensitivity and gently dove below the surface. When I allowed myself to express my fears and sadness, he communicated that he felt privileged to be there for me. It was a great sharing experience and it strengthened our relationship. Neil also had experience with ectopics, understood the surgery was pretty invasive, and let me know that I wouldn't be back Monday.

He also encouraged coworkers to support me. I was inundated with visitors in the hospital, and they saw me as they had never seen me before. It wasn't just that I was in an unstylish hospital gown or that I lacked makeup, but that I was far less guarded when we talked. It had been too long since I talked with bosses, peers, and direct reports from my heart rather than just from head, and it greatly strengthened our relationships.

Sometimes women appear softer just because they are pregnant. Donna Lee, the CMO at BellSouth, said:

> I received mixed reactions when I got pregnant. A number of people were shocked because my wanting children didn't fit with their view of my personality. Their mental model was that I was going for the brass ring and nothing else mattered to me. After the initial shock, they viewed me as much more approachable. Being pregnant softened my edge. It gave people a richer view of me—opened up avenues. They saw the human side.

Dawn Lepore, the vice chairman at Schwab agreed. She said:

> I have been at Schwab for 21 years. When you grow up in a company, people have pretty set perceptions of you. People didn't think I ever wanted kids. My husband and I spent ten years trying to have children. No one knew I was going through all that. When I announced I was pregnant, people were shocked. It changed their perspective of me. Knowing there was something else in my life made a big difference to them. Later, they couldn't get over seeing me cooing at my newborn.

Leslie Donovan, a senior vice president at Targetbase Marketing, said:

> Pregnancy was the single most interesting experience for me. When I told a few people in my office, their reaction was, "Thank God. We will finally have someone in senior management who has children." Even though I was already pretty approachable, I found people engaged with me more than before.

Most women also become less inhibited when they are pregnant. It starts in the doctor's office. Then, once you start to show, people react to you differently. They offer you their seats, open doors, and become more caring toward you. Mirian Graddick-Weir said, "People do view you differently." And several women commented that strangers would come up and touch their stomach. Although their personal space was invaded, these women understood those gestures were empathetic and welcomed the world's new way of seeing them. Coworkers were often making a fuss by throwing showers or taking bets on the baby's birth date, sex, and weight.

All that affectionate attention encouraged these women to respond in kind. Beyond their attention and affection, they felt their children kicking and saw ultrasounds of their curled-up little bodies with thumbs stuck in their mouths. If all that doesn't soften you up, nothing will.

A PREGNANT PAUSE
Taking Stock of Your Leadership Life

In lieu of pregnancy, you can assess your own behaviors in the areas of risk management, values, softness, and perspective and be aware of where you come up short. Both men and women fail to embrace and develop these leadership strengths, because they mistake them for weaknesses. They believe that "the more risked, the more gained," that "you have to be tough as nails to succeed," and "if you get results, values don't matter." While all these leadership adages contain a grain of truth, they also distort the truth and cause potentially great leaders to fall short of greatness; they discourage people from taking smart risks, displaying their soft side on occasion, and balancing values with results.

To help you determine if you've learned the lessons that come with pregnancy, I'd like to offer three tools, starting with the Cold-Hot Comparison Chart. This chart is a result of questions I asked both men and women leaders about "ice queens" and why certain women executives are viewed as being cold. On the left are the cold traits, and on the right are the warm ones. Look at both lists and determine which traits fit you best.

Remember, the key is to find a middle ground between cold and hot; it's unrealistic to expect that a woman who has led coldly for years will suddenly become warm and cuddly, whether or not she becomes pregnant. Moderating your cold traits a bit can make you a better leader, and this assessment can start you in that direction.

Cold Impression	Warm Impression
Serious body language and posture	Smile and laugh often
Critical	Give positive strokes
Overly sophisticated power clothes	Wear softer clothes
Uninterested	Give honest compliments
Overly sophisticated and articulate	Tell jokes, kid positively
Annoyed, rushed, distracted	Engage in small talk
Bold or arrogant	Modulate strong opinions
Disagreeable, countering	Agree where possible
Aloof, indifferent, don't care	Affirm, be inquisitive and attentive
Above it all, executive air	Act as an equal

The second tool involves a Values Assessment. The following questions will give you a sense of whether you have thought about what is important to you and if you've incorporated these values into your life as a leader.

1. If you had to list three values that govern your decision making at work, could you name them?
2. Do you observe the same set of values in your personal life as in your professional one?
3. Are you working for a value-based company? If so, are their values aligned with yours?

4. Does your company give more than lip service to values? If so, how do you apply them in your role?

5. If you are a mom, have you become more aware of your values since you had a child; do you remember the approximate time that you became aware of them?

6. If you are not a mom, has there been another highly emotional, significant event in your life that caused you to think deeply about your beliefs (e.g., the death of a loved one, a spiritual journey, etc.)?

The third tool involves examining your risk behavior. Consider how your subordinates perceive you (ask them directly if you can) and order the following list of skills according to your greatest strengths.

- Action oriented
- Decisive
- Troubleshooter
- Expediter
- Follows through
- Weighs consequences
- Is accountable
- Change agent
- Risk taker
- Influencer

Examine the list. Where do *Is accountable* and *Weighs consequences* fall in the list?

There are no right answers. For high-powered, fast-track women executives, the goal is to recognize if your behaviors are extreme and, if they are, moderate them a bit. Pregnancy often has this effect naturally, but if you aren't a mom or if for some reason your pregnancy didn't have this moderating effect, you can make a conscious effort to soften your style, broaden your perspective, define your values, and manage your risks with more accountability.

5

BABIES

Nurturing Becomes Second Nature

"When I had Cecilia, I became more human."

Maria Martinez, *Corporate VP, Microsoft*

As unlikely as it might sound, many of the most powerful, toughest women leaders have natural nurturing tendencies. Their nurturing capacity isn't always apparent, though, because they are so focused on achievement. In their quest to achieve and excel, their nurturing skills may grow rusty from disuse. Both men and women are judged early in their careers on how they perform in individual contributor roles. Naturally, they focus on results over relationships, on achieving goals rather than communicating with people. Everyone receives the message that they will be rewarded for achieving rather than for nurturing.

Nonetheless, when women first become managers, they often are empathetic and caring. This is a natural response for women who become responsible for other people. Unfortunately, these neophyte managers receive precious little positive feedback for being compassionate bosses and for developing their people. Over time, their inherent competitive fire and results orientation emerges, and they pay less attention to nurturing responsibilities.

Martin B. Friedman, author of *The Leadership Myth,* points out how leaders are expected to be powerful and results oriented:

> You have to be big, you have to be strong. . . . Any sign of sympathy, compassion, or anything that suggests a warm, cozy feeling about other people—sensitivity, a willingness to be caught up in an emotional moment—suggests to the macho mind the existence of terrible weakness, a great fear that, perhaps, there is a side of the personality which is feminine. The big mistake here is that these qualities have nothing whatsoever to do with femininity. They have to do with humanness. And humanness in a leader is a great attribute. (Friedman, 61–62)

Babies promote humanness. Let's examine how and why.

THE OVERWHELMING IMPULSE TO LOVE AND CARE

Babies open up most women's hearts in a way they have never been opened before. Their innocence, their softness, their fragility, and their cuteness overwhelm new moms and tap into their tremendous capacity for love and nurture. This is not a temporary hormonal reaction but an ongoing awakening. Although it starts with birth and is most apparent when the newborn child is adorable and helpless, it continues throughout the child's journey to adulthood. As women watch their children grow, their connection to them becomes deeper and more complex. This emotional connection cannot help but soften even the hardest-seeming executive. In the vast majority of instances, when a woman executive has a child and returns to work, her colleagues comment on how she seems more patient, responsive, and "human."

Joyce Rogge, the senior vice president of marketing at Southwest Airlines, said, "Kids soften you as a person. They bring out that incredible nurturing side. For me, it wasn't tapped until I had my kids, but ever since, it has helped my career. Southwest Airlines is a pretty loving company, and nurturing is seen as a positive."

Women with leadership DNA usually have not received many kudos for their nurturing ability. This is not to say that they aren't nurturers—a number of women interviewed in these pages felt they had this quality before they became moms—but that this behavior wasn't rewarded. From the time they were little, most women leaders were organizers, competitors, tomboys, and academic high achievers. These women didn't spend a lot of time playing with dolls or acting like earth mothers. They were seen as achievers, and this perception placed an artificial limit on their nurturing behaviors. They didn't realize that they possessed a capacity to nurture far greater than the norm.

Maria Martinez, a corporate vice president at Microsoft and former CEO of Embrace Networks, is one of the most driven people I know. She said, "When I had Cecilia, I became more human." The idea of becoming more human upon giving birth was a refrain among interviewees. When I asked Maria what she meant by human, she explained that she became more compassionate:

> The minute Cecilia was born, putting her needs ahead of mine came naturally, instinctively. Though I am compassionate by nature, she ushered me into a lifestyle that triggers my compassionate and nurturing side more regularly. She brought a whole new dimension to my life, which created a whole new balance to the way I work.
>
> Before I had Cecilia, I didn't know what I was missing. I didn't foresee that motherhood would change me so profoundly, nor could anyone convince me back then that I needed to be more human.

Maria described how Cecilia's birth not only helped her achieve more than if she had been childless but how her reawakened desire to nurture played a role in this success:

> No, I would have stalled at a certain level [if I had not been a mother]. Looking back, I was too focused on my own achievements and the success of my immediate team. The higher up you go, the broader a view you need to take. My passion to make a difference, while still there, was overtaken by a passion to nurture others to make a difference. At the high levels, it is more than just personal or your own team's achievements; it's about taking on a broader corporate responsibility.

Nurturing is an umbrella term for the qualities that often emerge after women have babies. Specifically, these qualities are the following:

- Empathy
- Sensitivity
- Caring
- Warmth
- Patience

Before learning about these characteristics in detail, take a moment to do a self-assessment. Think about how your behaviors and attitudes at work relate to each of these qualities. To help in this assessment, answer the following questions:

Empathy.
- Do you regularly understand your people's emotional reactions at work?
- Do you take their particular situations—both personal and professional—into consideration when you provide them with guidance?
- Do you communicate that you understand how they feel about a given assignment or problem with which they are grappling?

Sensitivity.
- Do you notice when your colleagues are behaving differently from the way they normally do?
- Are you aware of subtle but significant shifts in what direct reports, bosses, customers, and others do or say?
- Do you pay attention and respond when someone you work with appears unusually sad or happy, disappointed or excited?

Caring.
- Do you usually respond compassionately when people tell you about their problems at work?
- Do you demonstrate to your people that you care about their needs by championing causes that will benefit them?
- Do you spend time servicing people at all levels and functions in your organization?

Warmth.

- Have you ever received feedback indicating that people consider you "hard to get to know" or words to that effect?
- Do you routinely display warmth in a variety of ways—through smiles, handshakes, a friendly tone of voice, acknowledging people when you see them?
- Have you found a balance between being overly warm and fuzzy and overly focused and serious?

Patience.

- Are you able to stop yourself from issuing demands and commands when your people need more time and space to do their best work?
- How do you handle bad news, like missed budgets or milestones?
- How often do you find yourself interrupting others in the midst of a crisis?

No matter how you answered these questions or how many of these five traits you already possess, you can benefit from knowing how each helps top women leaders be more effective. Let us look at each quality and determine how babies contribute to their acquisition.

EMPATHY
Responding to Feelings besides Your Own

Empathy is the capacity to grasp another person's feelings. Many times, however, organizations create environments where there is no time or motivation to be empathetic. Under the crush of deadlines and the pressure to raise your group's performance level, you may not notice that a subordinate seems unusually quiet and distracted. Or you notice but don't feel you can spare the time to deal with the situation. Or you notice but think that it's not your responsibility to "coddle" a grown-up.

As naturally empathetic as most women are, like their male counterparts, they often succumb to these environmental factors and fail to pay attention to what's going on beneath the surface. As a result, they come across as hard-nosed and myopically focused on goals and careers. More significantly, they fail to help their people develop as quickly or as fully as they might, and they lose people to other organizations with bosses who are empathetic.

A senior human relations director of a well-known company said:

> Executive women without children have no sense of balance. No boundary lines. There's nothing else in their lives, just a 150 percent dedication to work. There's not nearly the degree of empathy about other people's needs as there should be. We refer to them as corporate nuns. They have the devotion of a nun, but there's no understanding.

Becoming empathetic isn't easy; you can't turn it on like a light switch. Even women leaders who are aware that displaying more empathy would be in their best interest—they have received formal and informal feedback to this effect—find it difficult to display a side of themselves that they have long suppressed. It feels awkward to reach out to other people when you rarely act this way. You believe that people will view your effort as phony or manipulative. For this reason, some women executives may make sporadic attempts to empathize and communicate but eventually revert to their old form.

This is why having a baby facilitates the transition to a more empathetic leadership style. When you are taking care of an infant, it no longer feels awkward or phony to respond to how another individual is feeling; empathy becomes a very natural reaction.

Certainly childless women and men can be empathetic, but they must overcome the image of leaders as driven, numbers-oriented people. In fact, many women executives attribute their success in large part to their hard-charging, results-focused leadership style. No doubt, they are right. But being driven and being empathetic aren't mutually exclusive. Many of the country's top women leaders have found a balance between the two, and often this balance has been achieved right after they had babies. Intellectually, these women may have always recognized this balance was possible. Caring for a baby, though, helps women make the emotional leap to make empathy come naturally.

Let's hear what three maternal leaders have to say about caring for babies and how it impacted their leadership style.

Amal Johnson was an executive at IBM when her daughter, Hannah, was born. She said:

My child became the office's child. I had lots of young women in my operation when I had Hannah. [Before having Hannah,] I had no empathy for people who didn't work long hours if work required it. The minute I had Hannah, I thought about that differently. Mothers are required to go home and nurture. I became much more empathetic to my coworkers' situations. They appreciated that.

Doris Jean Head, an executive with Marconi Communications, said:

My children taught me empathy and the value of recognition and communication. I have to acknowledge that, although I had been trained, I really learned from my kids the value of recognition and communication. Their faces brighten when you shower them with love or come to see their school activities to cheer them on, acknowledge a school paper or report card, or take the time to *listen* to their thoughts or experiences. Similarly, every employee wants to know they have value and that you respect them as individuals. Children help teach you the habit of focusing on others . . . they seldom hear the "not right now" discussion in their enthusiasm to get your attention. Seeing the rewards of time spent listening, acknowledging, and rewarding helped me grow in empathy and led me to better decision making.

Lorene Steffes, the former president and CEO of Transarc, said:

My empathy scores on a recent personality test came out off the scale on the high side. I was a teacher before I became a businesswoman. Between teaching and mothering, I learned I am a better motivator if I know where people are coming from. The 14-year-olds in my lab sciences class could be wowed by science itself, but the 18-year-olds were harder to impress. I had to see things from their vantage point and figure out what was important to them. This became the way I relate to people. I don't do this because I want to be a nice person. There's a business reason. Results are only sustainable if you care about and motivate people.

SENSITIVITY
Being Visually and Emotionally Perceptive

It is one thing to be empathetic; it is another thing entirely to pick up on the sometimes subtle signs that signal that a direct report needs help or that a colleague's confident exterior is a disguise for uncertainty and doubt. Leaders who are acutely observant of other people's behaviors are much more effectively empathetic, and the care and feeding of babies provides women with greater sensitivity to tone of voice, body language, and inferred but not stated requests for help. As a busy and stressed executive, though, it isn't always easy for women to display their natural sensitivity. A number of maternal leaders talk about how their babies heightened this sensitivity to other people.

Mindy Meads, the president and CEO of Lands End, said, "You go through so many issues and changes, but the one that sticks out for me is that Griffin taught me to be more sensitive." Babies are like emotional tuning forks. If you raise your voice, the harshness in your tone can send them into a crying fit. If you smile, they can reward you with a look of joy that will make your day.

Before having children, if I were focused on something, I could walk past people in the hallway and not even see them. Afterwards, my emotional antennae were raised. Just as a tiny cough in the middle of the night would wake me, a pensive look on the part of a peer would warn me that something was going on.

Being a mother of a newborn is an exercise in deciphering nonverbal communication. Moms are able to figure out by the pitch or decibel level of babies' cries whether they are hungry, wet, tired, bored, or hurt. They become sharply observant of the little things.

For example, one of my sons had trouble falling asleep when he was a baby. Oddly, though, some nights he'd drop right off, while other nights he would toss and turn. I noticed that on the nights he went right to sleep, he wedged one finger in his belly button—I suppose it was his version of sucking his thumb. From that night on, we made sure his sleeping clothes gave him access to his belly button, and his sleep problem disappeared. Being sensitive to this small, telling detail was part of being a mom; I was so concerned about his discomfort that I noticed something I otherwise would have missed.

One of the great challenges for leaders is dealing with talented but troubled employees as well as difficult bosses, customers, and colleagues. The phrase "He needs to be handled with kid gloves" is one every executive has heard. Moms learn how to be skillful kid glove handlers. They become adept at finding ways to work effectively with prickly customers and mercurial bosses for the same reason they can deal with sleep-challenged babies. They pay attention to what is troubling them and respond appropriately.

Sensitivity isn't limited to perception. Most women who succeed in organizations have to be perceptive to do well. Instead, they are emotionally as well as visually perceptive. There's a difference between noticing that a baby is crying and knowing what the cry means. You have to care a great deal about another individual to be emotionally perceptive. You tune in to the nuances of the other individual's behaviors, and this helps you figure out what is troubling both a baby and an employee.

CARING
Demonstrating Your Compassion

You can be a successful individual contributor or manager without really caring about your people. Plenty of technocrats and bureaucrats are experts in their fields but exhibit all the compassion of a snail. Top leaders, on the other hand, care about the people they work with, and this caring allows them to build strong relationships—relationships that provide them with everything from networking opportunities to intensely loyal customers and employees. As much as most women value meaningful relationships in their personal life, they may adopt a strictly professional attitude to relationships at work. Though the militaristic reporting relationships of an earlier era have largely faded away, many cultures still frown on leaders who become too close to their people. Women, who are more likely to be viewed as soft than men, respond by not letting their caring side emerge.

In an increasingly relationship-driven world, however, projecting an uncaring attitude can be detrimental. Leaders who care aren't just touchy-feely types. Caring can mean leveling with a subordinate about their weaknesses and insisting that they work on them. This task is painful, but if a leader really cares about another individual, she is willing to raise this difficult subject for the other person's sake. Caring can also mean taking the time and making the effort to help others with their problems. People gravitate toward leaders known as compassionate people who are willing to listen and help; their caring causes people to stop in their office rather than in someone else's.

Once women have babies, they are more likely to show their caring side in the office. Jocelyn Carter-Miller formerly of Mattel said, "My children taught me to put others before myself." Carol Evans, the president and CEO of Working Mother Media, put it this way: "It's a deep, deep, deep feeling—it's an, 'I will throw myself in front of train for this kid' feeling." Babies teach women that it is okay to put someone else first, that showing you care for another person can be a rewarding experience for both you and the other person.

Marilyn Seymann, who prior to her corporate climb was one of the first female professors at Columbia, had three kids in three years. Her first child was very sick, and she slept under the oxygen tent on his crib for a long time. Marilyn became a very compassionate person and made promises to God about helping children in distress. As an activist against child abuse and a foster parent of over 50 children, she has fulfilled these promises. Putting her compassion into perspective, Marilyn said:

> Prior to kids, I wasn't a big nurturer. I grew up with all younger brothers. I didn't play teacher. I was always set on having a career. Having children is a huge life event and it doesn't go away. There is such a transformation. It makes a profound effect . . . taking in all these stray children was a real incongruity to everyone but me.

While men may view most women in business as being too soft, they also may label powerful women leaders like Marilyn as too hard and uncompassionate. As Marilyn said, "There's still a stereotype out there. It's not ubiquitous, but some men do not perceive women at the top, mothers or not mothers, as nurturers, period."

Yet mothers who care for their ill babies nurture out of necessity. Nothing is more heartbreaking than caring for an ill baby or small child.

When my son, Michael, was little, he could not lie horizontally without coughing. This went on for five years until the doctors thought that Michael had a lung disorder that carried a very low life expectancy. We went to Children's Memorial Hospital in Chicago for exploratory surgery. I will never forget handing him over to the lung surgeon and watching him disappear into the operating room. I sobbed and prayed and worried and felt utterly helpless.

Although I recall making numerous promises to God like Marilyn, it was the event itself that had a lasting effect on me. It was as if I had flicked on a compassionate switch that had been in the off position. My emotions really poured out, especially afterwards when it turned out he did not have the dreaded lung disorder.

Although I always had a soft spot for people who were struggling, since that time, I've found myself responding even more compassionately whenever I encounter anyone who is suffering. At work, I discovered that I gravitated toward both people in trouble and worthy causes. When a direct report was upset and struggling, I tried to help. I became a champion for a variety of diversity groups and spoke out when people were treated unfairly because of their gender, race, age, or role in the organization.

A caring leader can also excel in situations where colder executives might fail. Linda was a top executive at a major technology company and a member of an extremely competitive management team. Because of the organizational structure, there was tremendous friction between business units. The executives who headed these businesses fought constantly, waging internal wars over resources and for recognition. As the only female business head and as a relatively recent replacement for a popular male executive, who had been demoted, Linda was in a tough position. The other business heads resented that she had taken a well-liked peer's position, and they questioned whether a woman could survive in an intensely competitive environment.

Linda, though, not only survived but thrived. Having returned to work after having a baby less than two years earlier, Linda had become a truly compassionate, caring leader. People loved working for her, in part because she clearly valued, listened to, and developed her subordinates. In fact, the executive who Linda had replaced told her, "I have to apologize. I was working against you when this move went down, but watching you has made a believer out of me. You really do have every-one's best interest at heart."

It was not that Linda was the only one of the business heads who cared about people. Most of the other top people at this technology company were compassionate people. As a result of being a mother, however, Linda was more consistently and demonstrably caring. Unlike during her prebaby style, Linda went beyond the occasional kind word to express her compassion and concern. She made it her business to know what her subordinates needed from her to grow and succeed, and she made a sincere effort to give it to them.

For example, when a group of people complained that the compen-sation system was unfair, she demonstrated that she cared about this bread-and-butter issue by seeking the board's approval for bonuses tied to stretch goals. This was a bold move, and Linda's people appreciated that she was willing to risk censure for making it. It was a clear demon-stration that she cared about them. As a mother of a baby, Linda under-stood the importance of making compassionate gestures. Babies respond to being held, carried, smiled at, and sung to. In the same way, Linda's people responded to her gesture on their behalf.

WARMTH
Allowing Your Natural Friendliness and Feelings to Emerge

You can't manufacture warmth. If you're a cold fish, you can't turn yourself into a warm-blooded mammal without everyone seeing through your act. Many executives, however, adopt an emotionally neutral stance in the office, giving the appearance that this is their natural state. In re-ality, they are suppressing who they really are.

The early stage in a child's life, however, prompts women to let their natural warmth shine through. An analogy here involves a baby's bath-water. If it is too cool, a baby will shiver; if it is too hot, a baby can be scalded. Moms become expert at finding exactly the right amount of bathwater warmth for their babies, and in the same way, they communi-cate warmth without overdoing or underdoing it. Smothering a baby with affection will elicit screams from an overwhelmed child, while treating a baby with the formality reserved for adults will leave the child feeling rejected. Displaying just the right amount of warmth requires a mother's instinct, and this instinct serves women leaders well in the workplace.

Many women start their careers too warm and then become too cold. Motherhood brings out a mother's authentic warmth, which is a natural balance between the two. Melinda Brown, the controller for PepsiCo Beverages and Foods, said:

> Growing up, I spent more time on my emotional self and generally was very sensitive and empathetic. Once I joined the workplace, I became increasingly fact based and focused. I work for a company that's highly competitive, and I quickly learned to put on my game face. I became less emotional. Even my mother noticed and asked me, "What happened to the sensitive girl that was my daughter?" Happily, I've been able to relax and allow my emotions to surface again.

The right degree of warmth can make a leader both approachable and respected. Finding the right degree, though, can be especially tough for women. In an article titled "Mindful and Masculine: Freeing Women Leaders from the Constraints of Gender Roles," the authors noted: "Female leaders face a paradox: If they emulate a masculine leadership style, their male subordinates will dislike them. If they adopt a stereotypically warm and nurturing feminine style, they will be liked but not respected." (Kawakami, 1) To translate their conclusion into our concept of warmth, being overly cold creates dislike, while being overly warm creates a lack of respect. As a possible solution to this problem, the authors suggest that women leaders be more "mindful" or "genuine," explaining that their experiments reveal that being genuine garners more favorable evaluations than just being warm.

Genuineness or mindfulness is another way of finding a middle ground between warm and cool. After having a baby, strong women leaders tend to find this middle ground naturally. Trying to find the right degree of warmth in a more conscious manner, though, can be tricky. It is easy to display too much warmth inadvertently, and women should be prepared for negative consequences if they do.

I worked in a predominantly male environment with many male engineers, some of whom could be generously described as Neanderthalish. When I was consciously warm and fuzzy in my interactions with them, these guys would entertain romantic fantasies. I was shocked when my boss told me that his wife, who was pregnant with their third child, was upset with him because he'd told her he was in love with me. With hindsight, I realize I erred on the side of nurture. He was always struggling with his boss and his boss's boss, so I would try to build up his confidence and encourage him. Other times, he was depressed, and I would try to pump him up by being funny, even silly. Obviously, he was misinterpreting my warmth for something I hadn't intended to convey.

Another tricky aspect of warmth involves consistency. If you are warm toward someone one minute and blow them off the next, you will be considered colder than if you had never acted warmly. Warmth has to be consistent, steady, and genuine. Intensely driven, focused women leaders often make this mistake.

For example, I was astonished when people referred to me as an Ayatollah. I knew I had acted in a warm and caring manner on numerous occasions. But I had not been consistent. One day, I was all smiles and friendly greetings, but the next day, I was curt and walked by people without acknowledging them.

PATIENCE
Recognizing That You Can't Control Everything

Nayla Rizk was working for McKinsey when her oldest son, Peter, was born. She said:

> I think having kids was one of the best things that could have happened to my personal growth. My first son, Peter, was easy, and I started thinking I was a good mother. Then I had my second child, Andrew, who was very active and not to be controlled. I learned to be a lot more patient. I can't imagine anything that could help you grow as a person more than having children.

Both of my sons were colicky. Brian, in particular, was an off-the-charts screamer for most of my six-month leave. One time, he cried for 26 straight hours. Given my history of impatience before having children, I was very worried that I would be an impatient mother. To my surprise, that turned out not to be the case. Despite being utterly exhausted, I didn't scream at Brian to stop crying or run out of the house telling my husband I couldn't take it anymore. Instead, I felt so bad for him, I did everything I could think of to comfort him through his pain and tears and reassure him that I was there. After cutting all possible foods out of my diet that might trigger colic, I knew the "cure" was a matter of letting nature take its course. And I learned to roll with it.

I will admit that sometimes, in the middle of the night to get a moment of relief, I would run the vacuum. It would startle Brian at first but then calm him down for about a minute. I also baked over 1,000 Christmas cookies that year, with Brian wrapped around me with a snuggly because the sound of the mixer had a similar effect.

Any strong, dominant leader tends to be impatient. To a certain extent, this impatience has a positive impact, in that it compels leaders to demand excellence, to demand it all the time and with all due speed. It becomes a problem for women leaders, though, when it creates the perception that they are unreasonably intolerant or that they act before they think. In certain business situations, though, patience is a virtue. Truly wise leaders wait just the right amount of time for events to unfold and trends to reveal themselves before taking action.

Patience requires you to give up control of the wheel. Children are naturally uncontrollable. One executive mom had just returned to work after having her first child. At a cocktail party attended by employees and their spouses, she introduced her husband to her new boss. One of the first questions her boss asked her husband was, "Who wears the pants in your family?" Her husband replied, "Well it used to be me, but our son seems to have taken over." He explained that their baby boy was uncontrollable; he usually was impervious to cajoling, compliments, commands, and other tools that businesspeople use to get what they want when they want it. He went on to share, "My wife has done a better job at figuring out we can't control him and is a lot more patient with him."

As Nayla Rizk put it: "You get comfortable not being in control, and it helps you to open up to other possibilities, to analyze more." This is the key to the wise use of patience: becoming comfortable with not taking control all the time.

KNOW YOUR NURTURERS

How many people do you know who possess the five nurturing qualities I've described? I've found that doing the following assessment helps people appreciate the positive leadership traits that come from taking care of babies—and recognize the negative behaviors when these traits are absent.

In the column on the left, you'll find the names of famous people, both real and fictional. Listed horizontally are the five nurturing traits. Your assignment is to place a checkmark for each trait a given famous person possesses (just skip people with whom you're unfamiliar). After you've done this, think about how each individual might perform as the CEO of a Fortune 500 corporation and how their nurturing traits (or lack thereof) might help them succeed (or fail).

	Empathy	Sensitivity	Caring	Warmth	Patience
Hillary Clinton					
Carmela Soprano					
George Steinbrenner					
Richard Nixon					
Oprah Winfrey					
Mary Tyler Moore					
Martha Stewart					
Michael Jordan					
Dr. Laura Schlesinger					
Dr. Phil McGraw					
Mister Rogers					
Coach Bobby Knight					

6

THE TODDLER YEARS
Managing Chaos

"I would argue that I am one of the most efficient people on the planet.
I am also potentially the worst cook."

Cindy Christy, *Mother of four children and President, Lucent Mobility Solutions*

Executive life has become incredibly frantic. Unexpected crises frequently disrupt carefully planned daily agendas. As downsizings, restructurings, global competition, and technology breakthroughs change traditional practices, our business pace accelerates. More than ever, leaders need to function effectively in confusing, fast-paced cultures.

Moms become skilled at getting things done even when the household is in chaos. Toddlers, of course, are adept at throwing things up for grabs. Their mobility is a shock for moms used to a relatively stationary child. Suddenly, they're wandering off and endangering fragile objects as well as themselves. The period between first steps and starting school can be wild and unpredictable. From the terrible twos to the frenetic fives, moms must deal with what often seems like constant chaos. During this time, women become adept and creative at handling child-related crises as well as unpredictable events that make a mishmash of plans.

Dawn Lepore, the vice chairman at Schwab, is a relatively new executive mother. She has a two-year-old and a six-year-old, and described her return from a recent vacation in Hawaii as follows:

> The long trip home had even lengthier delays and turned
> out to be very tiresome. Both children developed ear infections

and were struggling the entire trip back. When we got home, they couldn't sleep, so we had to take them to an urgent care facility. I had to catch up when I returned to work the following day. I was so tired, I couldn't think.

Somehow, she made it through the day and attended a board meeting that night. Dawn said that she doesn't have the juggling act down pat quite yet but added, "There are days when it's tough, and there are other days when you get in a zone and you are on top of things in a very positive way and realize you are doing it all. That feels really good."

Handling the chaos and crises that sometimes accompany vacations with toddlers prepares leaders like Dawn for the chaos and crises that crop up at work. Linda Wolf, the CEO of Leo Burnett, has been heralded in the press for her crisis-management skills. She shared how she acquired these skills:

> Balancing work and home forces you to become more efficient. You attain efficiency because your family helps you keep everything in perspective, including business. Our business is highly competitive and very intense. I actually became more in control after having children, because I learned not to let events take over. Things come at you in all directions. I stopped dwelling on things, made decisions, and moved on. Over time, after years of juggling everything and managing to do it all, I learned that I could handle an awful lot at a time. I became attuned to the work crisis, the babysitters not showing up. I realized that managing chaos became a behavior. I got good at it, and I learned how to not get rattled.

I would bet that, earlier in their careers, Dawn, Linda, and most top leaders took crisis-management courses. My first management course at Bell Labs was called the New Supervisors Seminar and included classes in managing chaos and ambiguity. Most leaders, therefore, have had some training in managing change and chaotic situations. A number of women I interviewed were good at handling crises before they had children. Still, some of them noted that they often responded to chaos with anger and frustration rather than cool reason—or with dogged determination and time-consuming effort rather than efficient, pragmatic solutions—until they had a chance to mother a toddler.

Before having children, they would get to work at the crack of dawn, go through their e-mail, and update their to-do list before most people arrived at work. Then they would head into meetings that were booked for ten hours a day and, between meetings, handle numerous, unexpected interruptions. Around 6:00 PM, they would review their upcoming schedule with their administrative assistants and try to stuff new meetings into their calendar. If a crisis disrupted their day, they just stayed later. In fact, they routinely worked into the night or until all the important items on their to-do list were checked off. On weekends, they would put in as much time as necessary to catch up on the little things.

Once their kids were born, many of them committed to spending dinner, evenings, and a good chunk of the weekends with their families. Staying at work as long it took was no longer a solution to chaos and crises. Something had to change. Deb Henretta, the president of Global Baby and Adult Care at Procter & Gamble, was like this. She said:

> I used to let work expand to the time allowed. The difference now is just that the time allowed is a whole lot less. I have always had a huge capacity for getting things done. Now I am not putting in as much time to get results. I have become more efficient and make different choices.

Their toddlers helped them evolve their leadership style in ways that gave them alternative—and more effective—ways to manage the unpredictable emergencies and occasional madness of the business world. Instead of working harder, they learned to work smarter. Being the mother of toddlers helped them develop the following traits:

- Hyperdrive
- Being appropriately organized
- Clear priorities
- Creative problem solving
- Adaptability
- Letting go
- Being calm

HYPERDRIVE

This first trait of toddler motherhood is best described by Carol Evans of Working Mother Media, who said:

> I was pretty much of a workaholic. So I pulled back a little. The cool thing about kids is that they have their own demands. In a way, you get to a higher level of hyperdrive. And even though there's a lot to do, it was very fun. I was passionately excited to face the challenge to create the family life I wanted. It triggered increased energy on my part.

Hyperdrive is the ability to summon a higher level of energy. Both at home and in the office, hyperdrive is critical in chaotic situations, in that any major snafu or surprise demands tremendous amounts of focus and effort. You need to concentrate with intensity and make a big effort to deal with hairy situations. I found I had to exhibit hyperdrive when dealing with my toddlers, especially when I returned from extended work trips. I traveled regularly when my sons were young, and I was on the road for 11 days during one trip. When I returned home jet-lagged and exhausted, the first question one of my sons asked was, "What's for dinner?" My husband looked at me, pointed to the boys, and said, "They're yours." Excited by my return, the boys ran wild for the next few hours. I told myself, I could not afford to have jet lag. I willed myself to have energy. My family needed me to take charge. My self-talk worked, and I found that I could ratchet up my energy level not only at home but also when it was needed in work situations.

All of the 50 maternal leaders interviewed for this book had such a strong will to be great mothers and great executives, that they pushed themselves to new levels of energy, focus, and organization, much like an athlete has breakthroughs in strength or agility during crucial games.

Soon some of this boost in performance will likely be attributed to biological changes that begin with pregnancy. Research with animals shows that the changes in hormone levels associated with maternity enhance brain functioning in the areas of memory and learning, and that these changes are long lasting. (Craig H. Kinsley, et al., 137–38) Whether through sheer will or enhanced brains, these women surpassed their original level of high performance when they became mothers. They discovered reserves of energy that they didn't know they had until their children began walking. Summoning this energy to be a good mother taught them to apply this same hyperdrive to being a good leader. They learned that they could focus and get things done in a relatively small window of time in a way that had never before seemed possible, even when their toddlers were bouncing off the walls and they had a to-do list as long as their arms. They discovered that they could apply their energy with great passion and creativity rather than just "grind it out."

Everyone has experienced hyperdrive at some point in their lives. Typically, it emerges during a speed-based test in school when you really have to focus. Maternal leaders display this ability to focus intensely many times during the course of a workday. They have an almost Zen-like ability to block out distracting thoughts and external demands and zero in on a critical issue.

Lorene Steffes, a former president and CEO of Transarc, shared that she was able to block out all distractions when she needed to. She said, "I would get so focused, I wouldn't even notice considerable commotion all around me. I'd just set priorities and focus on what had to be done at the time. "

Kate Ludeman, now the CEO of Worth Ethic Corp., wrote her first book in the evenings. Here's one of her favorite stories:

> I found an old typewriter for my daughter, and we typed together. She still has her books. They are so adorable. Anyway, I wrote my entire first book taking interruptions every three minutes. I learned how to not get irritated by her questions or interruptions, and I learned how to keep a lot of threads intact in my head. I could take the interruption and go right back to my train of thought. And when she needed my head back in her book, I was able to pick right up where we left off. I became much more adept at multitasking.

Hyperdrive not only allowed these women to get a lot done in a very short time, but it gave them the ability to change gears frequently through the day.

Leslie Donovan, the senior vice president of sales and marketing at the marketing firm Targetbase, said, "Having children caused me to get even better at shifting gears. If an hour frees up in my calendar at work,

I can process dozens of very diverse action items in that very short period of time."

Colleen Arnold, the general manager of IBM's global communications sector, said:

> Lots of people ask me how I do the balance thing. I got laser focused on what mattered. I am always in the moment. I can cut through issues very quickly. I got protective of what I was going to waste my time on. My coworkers learned the value of my time and what was important. They learned to come in prepared and focused. It's made my whole team more efficient.

As all these women discovered, it is difficult to be a mom to toddlers if you are unfocused or make poor use of your time. Toddlers demand attention. They test a mother's endurance and ability to switch from one task to the next instantly. To get everything done when you are caring for a toddler—even talking on the phone is difficult when your child is darting about the house—calls for an intensity of focus. Some women learn how to hold intelligent phone conversations while their child is slamming blocks on the floor and singing songs. Other women perfect the art of composing intelligent e-mails while their children are fighting over a toy. After these experiences, creating a strategy to cope with a volatile market becomes child's play.

BEING APPROPRIATELY ORGANIZED

I borrowed the term *appropriately organized* from Karl Albrecht, who wrote the book *Executive Tune-Up,* because top leaders not only have to be well organized to deal with time demands, but they must learn to work effectively within the constraints of a tight schedule. Karl describes some people who "go to the extreme, compulsively arranging, cataloguing, labeling, filing, and storing things, without necessarily increasing their ability to do practical things effectively." (Albrecht, 81) Tighter organization is not a solution for every problem. Finding a balance between being organized and being spontaneous is often the challenge for senior leaders. Managing chaos isn't just a matter of being organized. In fact, it's futile and frustrating to try and put everything neatly into boxes when everything is constantly flying around the room. In organizations, the best managers of chaos are the ones who occupy the middle ground, who know when to rely on structure and when to go with the flow.

Most of the women I talked to felt they were well organized before their children were born. Nevertheless, each child caused them to take their organization skills to a new level. Those with the most kids seemed to have acquired the greatest skills, and they often acquired these skills when their kids were toddlers. During this period, kids don't know the meaning of picking things up or putting things back. In the blink of an eye, a toddler can create a huge mess. They also expect their mothers to remember where they put their favorite toy or stuffed animal and grow frantic when mom can't find it.

Everything going on at home and work needed to be streamlined for efficiency's sake. Even those with live-in help had a lot more arranging to do at home and less time at work. Deanna Oppenheimer, president of Washington Mutual's consumer group, said, "I became a much more efficient prioritizer. I worked differently. I worked smarter. I had the early shift; my husband had the later shift. I would go in early and get organized."

They also organized their lives differently. First, they took more off their personal plate. They didn't get their nails done, unless they could find someone to come to the office and do them during conference calls. They went to low-maintenance hairstyles. They rarely shopped for clothes, but when they did, they power shopped (i.e., purchased all their clothes for the season in an afternoon) or used a personal shopper. They caught up on the news during their commute, and they hired people to help with household chores they normally would have done. Most of them exercised before their long day started or after everyone was in bed, and they read work-related material while riding the exercise bike or climbing the stair master.

They also organized their families. No matter how significant a role their husbands played in parenting, these moms had the lion's share of responsibility for organizing the family and ensuring that it ran smoothly. Whether dealing with meals, clothes, schedules, doctor appointments, childcare, celebrations, or scrapbooks, they made sure everything got done. Many of them, like Patricia McKay, CFO of Restoration Hardware, moved their residences to be closer to work. She said, "I picked homes that were close to work so I could jump to school for an important event and not waste time commuting."

At work, they took steps to organize themselves and their associates to save time. They made sure that they had extremely talented administrative assistants. They moved the relationship building and mentoring that they typically did after hours to breakfast and lunch meetings. They took the stairs instead of the elevator to get in a little exercise. Whenever possible and weather permitting, they combined one-on-one talks with walks so they could get out of the office and get some fresh air.

Marion McGovern, the president of M Squared, said that she needed to be much more organized after becoming a mom. "I know that I cannot keep track of everything, so I overcompensate with planning, scheduling, and reminders. You have to plan your time efficiently, or you are not going to survive." Jo Anne Miller, the former CEO of Gluon Networks, who is a very free spirit, said, "My kids taught me planning. I couldn't just be spontaneous."

Dealing with toddlers helps many executive moms find this middle ground between planning and spontaneity. Murphy's Law dictates: What can go wrong, will go wrong. No matter how much you plan and organize your toddler's life, something will make havoc of those plans. You may put together the best-organized birthday party ever for your four-year-old, but the clown doesn't show up and, 30 minutes after the party starts, three kids get the stomach flu and have to go home, while another child has a bad reaction to the peanuts in the candy bars. Or you may take a day off of work because you've promised your child for weeks that you would take him to the zoo, but when you arrive, he is frightened by the growling tiger and insists on leaving.

Adjusting to these changing circumstances and making the best of them is a skill that moms can apply directly to the workplace. As organized as senior leaders must be, they cannot mindlessly adhere to their plans and schedules when events conspire to make these plans and schedules less than ideal.

Nayla Rizk, a partner at Spencer Stuart, recalls, "I always planned vacations way in advance. After my children were born, I became more spontaneous. I had a whole bunch of friends in the same boat, and we all let go of that need to plan everything ahead."

Donna Lee, the CMO at BellSouth, said:

The number-one thing that I feel good about that has really made a difference was that I have integrated my home and work calendars. People would ask me all the time, "How did you make it to the school play?" The trick for me was running a seamless life. The world wants to compartmentalize things, and most don't think home activities should be interspersed in my work calendar. But luckily, my assistant and I clicked on this, and we built one outlook calendar. Anything that is important to me, we build in. It helped things run better on the job because I could see conflict early on. For instance, tomorrow my boss has a 9:00 AM meeting—but I knew in advance my daughter has a meeting at school at 8:00 AM and I'd probably be late. So I arranged the agenda so that my team could handle the first agenda item without me and got his agreement in advance. He's okay with that. My kids are so aware that I am able to make these things.

CLEAR PRIORITIES

In today's chaotic times, most leaders find themselves engaged in a multitude of mission-critical matters. It is quite common to hear employees complain that everything seems to be high priority or that leadership keeps changing their priorities. Leaders often talk the talk without walking the walk. Employees are clamoring for leaders who are consistent or at least predictable. Leaders who react to chaos by sending mixed messages or churning their organization can create highly negative situations.

In these turbulent times, executive mothers in leadership roles are admired for their dependability and clarity. Coworkers of the 50 executive moms echoed the same sentiment: During tough, confusing times, these women provided clear direction and focused everyone on primary objectives.

Executive mothers agreed that they became proficient at establishing priorities and sticking to them when their children were still relatively young. As they experienced the joy of their toddlers taking first steps and suffered with them through illness and injury, they became less likely to sweat the small stuff and more likely to identify and stick to priorities that made sense. They learned to identify what really counts and subordinate the rest.

Caring for toddlers means dealing with a multiplicity of responsibilities and interruptions. It means resetting your social schedule and assigning your time based on not only what you want to do but what is most important to you, your child, the rest of your family, and coworkers. Prioritizing is no longer a matter of determining who is screaming the loudest or what you feel like doing most. As a mom, you prioritize and reprioritize in real time based upon your goals, controlling chaos in a way that is meaningful rather than arbitrary.

Lori Craven, the COO at Tekelec, said:

> I got a lot better at prioritizing and figuring out what was important. And it wasn't just the big priorities, it was the little ones, too. For instance, I changed old routines. At home, it was more important to go the park than to cook from scratch or straighten up the house. At work, I shortened the long conversations with people popping in my office after hours. I became a lot more efficient with my time.

Priscilla Lu of InterWAVE discussed how she developed a way of working with nannies that carried over to business prioritizing.

> When my children came along, my life seemed to be in a state of constant chaos. I eventually adjusted both at home and at work. To make it work, I had to set very clear priorities and parameters with nannies. And in return, I had to let go of the "how." This is very relevant to work. I had to set priorities for myself and my teams. And I had to let them manage the how. I was able to do this because my children put everything I was doing into perspective. They stabilized my priorities.

Kathryn Kimura Mlsna, who leads McDonald's marketing and intellectual property group, told me that, when her children were toddlers, she received a last-minute request to complete a negotiation shortly before she was supposed to leave town and work on a key overseas deal.

Kathryn, though, wanted to see her children before they went to bed, so she agreed to the scheduled meeting time, running home to have dinner with her children before returning to work. Later, when she went back to the office for the meeting, the other individual didn't show up. Kathryn waited until late in the evening, unable to reach him but unwilling to leave in the event he did appear. The next day, he called Kathryn and explained that his plans had changed and he'd gone out to dinner with his wife. Kathryn learned a good lesson: What seems like a high priority at first glance may not be so important upon further investigation. From that moment on, she started putting requests like this through a more rigorous priority check, rather than reflexively sacrifice time with her children.

Colleen Arnold of IBM believes that her clarity about the importance of family has created an atmosphere that fosters trust, horizontal collaboration, and high productivity. She said, "I work very long hours and travel a lot, so I do not feel the least bit guilty for leaving the office in the middle of the day to participate in an activity important to my children. And I don't hide it. I tell people where I am going, so that they know they can do the same."

Colleen truly walks the walk when it comes to the importance of people's life outside of work. Perhaps surprisingly to some, by integrating people's personal priorities into work teams, Colleen has gained increased productivity. When she was CEO for a joint venture in Australia, the issue of work-life struggles was of great concern to many of her employees. She helped the second and third shift find ways to take time off for high-priority activities outside of work. Members of teams were asked to share their needs for time off at work with each other. Some wanted to coach their kids' ball teams, some needed to take off for childcare or eldercare emergencies, and some really wanted to catch the surf. The teams were given the flexibility to cover for each other. Not only did their productivity go up by 20 percent, but the company was recognized as the best company in the country for working women.

CREATIVE PROBLEM SOLVING

In addition to helping you stay focused on the most important tasks, kids bring your creative problem-solving skills to the surface. Toddlers, especially, present parents with dilemmas that sometimes require Solomon-like wisdom. Just figuring out all the ways you can make time to be with your kids and still do justice to your job can be a creative challenge. It requires the type of ingenuity we alluded to earlier—using outdoor walks as ways to hold one-on-one conversations with colleagues, for instance—and a willingness to revamp routines. Parents are also motivated to get creative to avoid hysteria or tantrums. They may have been good problem solvers before having kids, but toddlers provide them with skills that take their problem solving to a higher level.

Lorene Steffes said, "Problem solving my kids' issues definitely carried over to work. When things weren't going well on a project, I learned to stay positive, and I would figure out a way to make things work. In most cases, when your employees see how hard you work to find creative solutions, they do likewise and come through for you."

When faced with a problem, just about all maternal leaders reflexively consider a broader range of alternatives than nonmoms. One of the women I interviewed noted how she, like most executives, used to rely on what had worked in the past when confronted with a tough decision or ticklish situation. In recent years, however, she discovered that decisions and situations had become much more complex than in the past—that, sometimes, what had been effective before was no longer as effective. As she explained, "With three children under the age of six with very different temperaments, I had to get pretty creative to keep them all distracted for a half-hour so that I could hop in the shower. In fact, my creative energy seemed to be flowing 24/7. I had to broaden my alternatives for action, and I found myself doing the same thing at work."

Procter & Gamble's Deb Henretta shared, "I actually wanted to be a graphic artist when I was a young girl, so I have always been a creative type. But I learned the knack for fearless creative problem solving from my children. Children don't have a fear of trying new things. I see that every day. . . . Before I had children, I would tend to overthink when I walked into unknown territory. The constant day-in and day-out reminder that children try things without fear has really been good for me."

Executive mothers also acquire another problem-solving skill from their toddlers, one that is atypical for most leaders: They learn to ask for help.

When babies become toddlers and start moving around, having temper tantrums, and demanding more of a mom's time and attention, asking for help is often a necessity. For some women, this represents a leap, in that they have always prided themselves on their independence and ability to solve problems on their own. Many of the women I talked to said this was the first time in their adult lives that they asked someone else for help.

At first, it was awkward. Whether they asked their husbands, their own parents, their in-laws, or siblings, they had to swallow their pride and admit they required assistance. They soon realized, though, that people usually liked being asked to help, that it made them feel valued. Just as significantly, their efforts really made tough situations easier. It became natural for these women to experiment with asking for assistance at work when they were confronting a particularly difficult problem.

Gradually, as they saw how the ideas and information others provided helped them deal with vexing situations, they became more comfortable requesting assistance from others. They also found that their admission of fallibility created better relationships with their peers. Being Wonder Woman might have helped these women achieve their leadership positions, but acknowledging their own vulnerabilities helped other people relate to them as human beings.

ADAPTABILITY

These women didn't just wake up one day after their children were born and start changing. They really didn't have a clue about what they needed to change, when they would need to change, or how they were going to change. All they knew in advance was that everything was going to change. Certainly, they experienced some of these changes when their babies were born, but when their babies became toddlers, their world turned topsy-turvy. They found themselves adapting almost every day to the unpredictable needs of their kids, husbands, caregivers, and coworkers. They juggled their personal and professional schedules and routines to keep everyone else's activities on track. Routines that they had held sacred—exercise routines, eating routines, weekend social routines—all had to be scrapped or revised as their toddler took precedence. These executive moms all became skilled at changing on a dime, able to adjust their plans to a child's illness or sudden need for attention without trepidation or bitterness.

At work, these maternal leaders adapted with greater speed and effectiveness to everything from new ownership to revamped organizational structures. Rather than fighting the changes, dragging their feet, or complaining about them, they accepted things had changed and found a way to make the best of the new situation.

One top executive with a large packaged goods company, Jan, had to adjust to a new CEO, who had been hired after an extensive search. This CEO possessed a style that clashed with the company's culture; he was less open and communicative than their previous CEO. At times, Jan and other executives found him abrasive and secretive. Yet he was also a great strategist and extremely knowledgeable about what it took to become a successful global company, an area where Jan's company had been weak. Two of Jan's fellow executives quit after working with this CEO after less than a year, and a few others seemed to be just biding their time until they could get out.

Jan, however, made an effort to adjust to his style and create a good working relationship. Once he trusted her, he became receptive to her feedback. She said, "Before I had kids, I would have been bent out of shape over this and probably resigned, too."

LETTING GO

The best leaders let go of the mistakes, confrontations, and other emotionally charged events that come with the territory. In today's highly stressful, fast-paced environment, there will be unpleasant exchanges and second-guessing. When executives carry around this emotional baggage, they are not as effective as they could be, especially in a chaotic environment. They are still dwelling on the previous day's confrontation when another confrontation occurs. Consequently, their normally razor-sharp thinking is dulled. When they can't let go of negative feelings, they aren't operating at full cognitive strength.

I'm not suggesting that leaders should be automatons. Emotional intelligence is obviously critical to good leadership. Becoming stuck in a particular emotional moment, however, is counterproductive. Leaders need to feel it, acknowledge it, and let it go.

The vast majority of women leaders keep a tight rein on their emotions, at least to the outside world. Inside, though, they are churning up a storm that can cloud their judgment. Many of the women I interviewed talked about how difficult it was to shed negative emotions that built up at the office. Some said that it could take days to overcome the emotions attached to making a mistake, losing a big contract, firing an employee, or being harshly criticized. Some of these women admitted that they wanted to be more like their male peers, who seemed to be good at shaking things off and just "forgetting about it."

Quite a few of the executive moms said that their toddlers helped them learn to let go of emotional baggage in a variety of ways. First, letting go is easier when one no longer has much time to dwell on emotions, be they negative or positive. Keeping up the pace of an executive while managing a family is so time consuming, that when they finally had a few spare seconds to examine an emotional wound, it had practically healed. Second, their passion to be fully present with their children motivated them to get past the negative events of the day. Shoving aside these hot-button feelings allows them time to cool. When these women returned to work, they still thought about them but without the heat of the moment. Third, being greeted by an excited, cheerful toddler screaming "Mommy, mommy!" while showering them with hugs and kisses often obliterated work stress.

Carol Evans shared her insights about this phenomenon: "Kids have a way of grounding you, so that when you walk out of the office, you don't carry it with you. They require you to shift your concerns quickly. When things are not going well at work, I let it go when I go home. I learned to put my emotions aside for a while. In order to excel at work and home, you have to have the mind-set to shift your emotions and let go of the stress."

Susan Hogan, a principal at Deloitte Consulting LLP, said she has learned to let go of stress and guilt. She said, "I am not as stressed because I am able to turn off things a lot easier. I can flip that switch that has me just thinking about work or just thinking about home. And I learned to stop feeling guilty about turning things off for the moment."

Many of the mothers agreed that just being with their toddlers helped them forget about problems at work. Even the simplest of activities, such as coloring with crayons or playing hide-and-seek, distracted them, lured their minds away from work, and allowed them to have fun. The ultimate soother seemed to be putting toddlers to bed. Many women had wind-down rituals with their kids that helped the moms, too, let go of the day. Later in the evening, peeking in on a two-year-old sleeping peacefully and innocently carried over to the next workday, making these women less likely to obsess about something that wasn't worth obsessing about.

Our family followed my dad's tradition at night; we'd say our prayers and tell God what we were thankful for. Then I would make the sign of the cross on my child's forehead and say, "Good night, I love you, God be with you." When the kids reached talking age, they would offer me a similar benediction. To this day, when we go to bed, we make three signs of the cross on each other's foreheads and say, "Good night, I love you, God be with you. Good night, I will love you and like you all the days. Good night, you are precious and good to me." Whether they were toddlers who could barely talk, or now 220-pound athletes, no matter how tough the day was, their tender touch and words help me let go of emotional work baggage faster and more completely than ever before.

Certainly, toddlers can add stress to your life and cause you to feel upset or guilty, but moms can do something about these emotions. If they feel guilty because they were away from their children on a business trip, they can make an effort to spend more time with them. If their children have temper tantrums, the mood will soon pass, and they will do something adorable to make moms forget that they just threw a handful of oatmeal at them.

BEING CALM

If you can remain calm when your toddler has to be rushed to the emergency room after swallowing a coin or when the house has erupted in chaos because one child is screaming and the other is demanding your attention, then keeping your cool in chaotic work situations becomes a no-brainer. Toddlers test the patience of saints, and there are times when moms feel so frustrated, they lose their cool.

Amazingly, most moms learn the art of being consciously calm. They quickly realize that they need to make a concerted effort to control the anxiety that both their children and their work push to the surface. To function effectively at home, they must red flag themselves when they feel about to lose it. They become practiced in the art of being calm, and this skill carries over to the workplace.

Peggy Johnson, president of QUALCOMM Internet Services, said:

> Early in my career, my manager told me that I got too stressed out over things, and I did make a conscious effort not to get rattled. But ultimately, it was my kids that helped me learn to stay calm. Once I'd lived through a few child emergencies, I learned how to take a deep breath, stay calm, and start taking steps toward resolution. I use this same "stay calm through the storm" approach at work during chaotic moments.

Amal Johnson said, "I learned that, regardless of the depth and breadth of the crisis, if you can just calmly deal with it, there are answers." Motherhood teaches you to take things one day—and one crisis—at a time. Childhood emergencies show moms that they cannot control every situation. There is no way to prevent bee stings, ear infections, and other maladies and mishaps. As painful as it is to see your child suffering, you also realize that sometimes all you can do is be emotionally supportive and call the doctor.

Executive moms who are accustomed to being in control recognize that, at times, all they can do is comfort and wait. They recognize that remaining calm, assessing the situation, and taking action only if things deteriorate is often the best course of action. As difficult as it is to hear your child screaming, you can't go rushing off to the emergency room every time they get a scrape or a fever. Every time your child spills ketchup on the newly cleaned (usually white) carpet, you can't holler and threaten in the belief such a demonstration will prevent it from happening again. These emergencies force moms to confront their need to control; mothers recognize that managing chaos doesn't necessarily mean taking immediate action.

In a world where change occurs at a lightning pace, sometimes the best response to problems at work is to remain calm. This doesn't mean refusing to make a decision or never becoming worked up. Wisdom is often gained by keeping your wits about you and observing, taking in information and ideas, and then making a decision. Not only does this posture often result in increased effectiveness, but a calm demeanor in the midst of chaos often reassures the people who work with you. People tend to put their trust in calm leaders rather than ones who are spinning out of control.

Marilyn Seymann of M One, Inc., stays calm because she has let go of her perfectionism: "People who do not have anything pulling them tend to make a huge mountain out of things. Three kids in three years forced me to let go. Letting go reduces the chaos. I am not sloppy; it's just that certain things don't matter as much. Your priorities really change with kids. What matters changes."

Several years ago, Motorola hired Kaplan DeVries, Inc. to do a leadership assessment for me. It was an incredibly thorough analysis. They interviewed everyone in my life, including my childhood friends and family. They also interviewed my sons. I have to admit, what my sons had to say mattered to me more than what anyone else had to say, and I was a little nervous about it. Your family knows your faults better than anyone, and kids have such an innocent, yet blunt, way of pointing them out. I prepared myself for the worst. So I was a little surprised to learn that the first thing Brian had to say was, "My mom stays calm."

While I learned to control what I referred to as my double-whammy, Irish-Croatian temper, I always had to be aware of it. It was such a battle for me to stay calm early in my career that I was shocked to realize I no longer had to make an effort to control my temper. With two wild, toddler boys, I had endless practice at not only staying calm but creating calm. I realize now that the greater the heat, the calmer I became.

One of the executive moms said, "I am a type-A driver. Once my children started repeating everything I would say, I became a lot more aware of my knee-jerk reactions to bad traffic or drivers. In order to keep from reacting, I would take a deep breath. Before I realized it, I didn't get disturbed at all by bad traffic or drivers."

Doris Jean Head of Marconi Communications had a wake-up call when her daughter's first words were "Hurwy, hurwy, hurwy." She realized that she was constantly rushing her daughter and needed to slow down, with a focus on prioritizing the *important* over the urgent, not only at home but also in the workplace, and in helping her develop her organization to do the same—see the forest for the trees.

Staying calm isn't always an inherent quality of ultrahigh achievers. It is, however, a key requirement for any top job in a modern company. The day of the mercurial, warrior-leader is over. In a diverse, litigious society, CEOs who rage and react will soon find themselves on the receiving end of resignations and lawsuits. Perhaps more importantly, they will be viewed as overreactive dinosaurs and lose the respect of their people. Obviously, no one will remain calm all the time, but leaders who are poised and thoughtful during crises gain everyone's admiration. The vast majority of these executive moms are admired because they appear in control when events are out of control.

Mirian Graddick-Weir, an executive vice president at AT&T, remembers when the head of her daughter's school brought the parents together and said, "Your daughters are going to be on a roller coaster. Your job as parents is to not get on the roller coaster with them." Mirian said this was excellent advice. She said:

> Your kids know more than anyone how to get to you. I learned to detect my daughter's moods as I walked in the house after work. In the event she was having a bad day, I would prepare myself for her volatility. When she would start getting emotional, I would step back and not get on the roller coaster with her. I would get calmer and calmer. My calmness would disarm her. It helped us both avoid unproductive battles.

As a result, Mirian found herself becoming calmer at work. She said:

> People at work often remark about how calm and even-keeled I am. Work is competitive and volatile. We are all under pressure. When people are under stress, they can be irrational. They are not always logical and thoughtful. It's easy to react to emotional people with emotions. I learned how to spot if my people were on the edge. When I could spot it, I could be ready for it; this helped me enormously. By staying calm, I was able to help them calm themselves, which ultimately leads to very productive outcomes.

Staying calm allowed Mirian to absorb her coworkers' anxiety. This skill is extremely helpful during conflicts and crisis. In his book *Organizational Culture and Leadership*, Edgar H. Schein said, "Leaders often absorb and contain the anxiety that is unleashed when things do not work as they should. The leader may not have the answer, but he must provide temporary stability and emotional reassurance while the answer is being worked out." (Schein, 318) Emotional reassurance becomes second nature to mothers. Bridgette Heller of Chung's Gourmet Foods shared a story that illustrates this point.

Bridgette was an executive at Kraft at the time, and her CEO asked a question that filtered down two levels and then over to her office. When the question was asked, Bridgette was at the dentist and could not be reached. So one of her managers, aware that the CEO had asked the question, deployed ten different people to start working on it with all due speed. When Bridgette saw that she had missed three calls, she called the office. Her manager was wound up about the CEO's request, but Bridgette did not overreact:

> I kept asking her what question she was answering, and it ended up, after I calmed her down and she thought about it, she realized she wasn't really sure. It was like the game telephone. The message was so garbled, it didn't even make sense. So I went back up the chain to check up on the question. It ended up that the CEO just wanted to make sure I knew that a customer had complained. He hadn't intended to start a flurry of activity.

It is not unusual for people to become anxious and jump into action before thinking when a big boss twitches a muscle. Moms have learned that their toddler's cough is not a death knell and that a temper tantrum will vanish as suddenly as it arrived. Therefore, they focus on identifying core issues rather than jumping through hoops.

TRANSLATING TODDLER TRAITS INTO LEADERSHIP LEARNING

I'd like to conclude with a fun exercise that will help you appreciate how being the mother of a toddler confers skills that are especially relevant in a chaotic workplace.

On the left, you'll see a list of 15 toddler traits or situations. On the right, you'll find a list of our six chaos-managing leadership skills. Moms who deal with these toddler traits and situations regularly frequently develop corresponding leadership skills. See if you can match the situation with the skills it requires.

1. Temper tantrums
2. Constant movement
3. Whining
4. Missing pacifiers
5. Earaches, colds, other minor illness
6. Need to visit hospital emergency room
7. Emotional separations
8. Huge messes
9. Lightning-fast mood swings
10. Needy of your time
11. Asks why constantly
12. Fussy eaters
13. Toilet training
14. Sleeplessness
15. Repetitive entertainment (books, movies)

A. Creative problem solving
B. Being calm
C. Adaptability
D. Hyperdrive
E. Being appropriately organized
F. Clear priorities
G. Letting go

The top two skills I found that mothers claim to practice most often with each situation are:

1. (A, B)
2. (C, G)
3. (A, B)
4. (C, D)
5. (B, C)
6. (B, F)
7. (A, G)
8. (E, G)
9. (B, C)
10. (F, G)
11. (A, C)
12. (A, F)
13. (A, E)
14. (A, B)
15. (C, D)

7

ELEMENTARY SCHOOL
Developing and Motivating Teams

"People will do what you ask them to do for the most part. But if they are not happy
about it, they are not going to bring passion to it and the work will not be their
best. I learned this from my children. I can see how they pursue things they
are passionate about and the results that come from this."

Deanna Oppenheimer, *President, Washington Mutual Consumer Group*

Olga Kharif at *Business Week* re-
cently wrote an article about Anne Mulcahy, the chairman and CEO of
Xerox and the mother of two teenage boys. In it, Ann said, "I believe
strongly that my success as a leader is driven by my commitment to understanding and meeting customers' requirements, as well as developing and nurturing a motivated and proud workforce. With the right
amount of focus, the two combined have the potential to drive exceptional results." (Kharif, 2)

How often do you hear a CEO attribute her success to "developing
and nurturing a motivated and proud workforce"?

All the mother leaders I interviewed were passionate about developing and motivating their teams. Contrary to what you might think, this
focus on teams was not second to financial growth or competitive dom-
inance. In fact, these women all talked about their teams as if they were
their children. During the early school years, these moms found that
they acquired the following team-building skills:

- Empowering others
- Embracing differences
- Showing tolerance
- Inspiring personal growth

EMPOWERING OTHERS

While women are somewhat empowering by nature, they also may be strong, dominating leaders. At times, the latter trait overwhelms the former one, and they become overly controlling. Some operate their teams like puppets on strings and become dependent on them. Consequently, these teams fall apart when their boss takes time off or moves to a different role. On the other hand, when executives consistently delegate tasks and responsibilities to their subordinates, their people learn, grow, and step into leadership positions sooner rather than later.

When women have children, they naturally want to spend more time with them, especially when they are young. Empowering others makes spending more time with kids feasible, providing motivation for women to delegate more responsibility to their people. Just as significant, moms of elementary age kids discover that they can entrust their children with an increasing amount of responsibility. They can send them to schools within walking distance, give them household tasks, and ask them to watch a younger sibling. When they see that their children take these responsibilities seriously and execute them properly, they realize that they are worthy of empowerment. This recognition carries over to work, where they are more willing to entrust people with assignments that they previously were reluctant to delegate.

Lori Craven of Tekelec said, "Along with delegating more, after I had kids, I truly handed off responsibilities to others. My desire to get home in the evening forced me to be less involved and less directing. I truly empowered others and held them accountable. And not only did it make me more efficient, my employees liked it. They enjoyed working for me more."

Nayla Rizk, a partner with Spencer Stuart, shared Lori's sentiment: "I learned how to delegate more. Delegation requires trust. So . . . I had to find people who I could trust. I learned how to empower people by letting go of the 'how' so long as they got things done."

These leaders didn't just delegate tasks. They often delegated their own job. For instance, many maternal leaders treasure their vacation time with their kids, and the only way they could take their school-aged children on a long overseas vacation was to have strong backup in the office. Recognizing this fact, they actively recruited rising stars for their team. They would groom and then empower them, then be able to take extended family vacations. Several of the women I interviewed mentioned that their children would demand that they leave their cell phones back home—the kids anticipated long, work-related conversations—and because of their confidence in their teams, these women could honor their children's request.

Leslie Donovan, who leads the business team for Targetbase, offered another empowerment benefit from motherhood:

> I was always a delegator. My having children has made it easier on my team. They used to arrive for work in the morning and have their inbox stacked with action items generated by me from the night before. I didn't realize that my working late made everyone else's mornings pretty rough. I did that to a much lesser extent once my kids started staying up later and needing help with homework. I don't check up on them [the team] as much. And I don't bother them with the little things.

Amal Johnson, a former president with Baan Corporation, said, "True leaders are the ones who enable all sorts of people to have moments of leadership. If you give people a chance, they are capable of making decisions, if they feel enabled and it is expected of them. Being a mother gives you plenty of practice at this." Having said that, she also shared that there can be too much empowerment:

> Our nanny was so good, we relaxed a bit and let go of some responsibilities that should have stayed with us. There's a fine line between enough empowerment and too much. My experiences with motherhood helped me learn to walk the fine line. If a CEO has a world-class CFO, she can easily fall into the trap of giving too much responsibility to the CFO. But the buck stops with the CEO, as many have learned the hard way recently.

Many of the executive moms make the point that empowering others is more complex than just saying, "Here, you do it." Some male leaders miss the subtleties of empowerment, subtleties that motherhood confers. Doris Jean Head pointed out one of these subtleties, when she noted that leaders must empower their people even though they know they will make mistakes:

> With my children, I learned that I had to let them learn on their own. They all learned how to ride a bike. And even though

they were not going to get results right off the bat, and they would likely fall and hurt themselves, I had to give them a bike and let them fall. This correlated to work. I had to let my people learn, even though they wouldn't get everything right all the time.

In some companies, leaders talk a lot about empowerment but unwittingly sabotage their own efforts to grow and develop people. Part of the problem is that many executives reflexively argue with or criticize subordinates' decisions, undermining their confidence. Cindy Christy, the president of Lucent's Mobility Solutions Group, is a 38-year-old mother of four young children and explained how motherhood helped her deal with this reflex. She said that since she has had children, she disagrees less and empowers more:

> At home, I could take the approach of forcing my children to put their toys away right after they use them. But with four children, I would be spending my whole day just telling them to put their things away. So instead, we have an agreement that all things must be put away by bedtime. This empowers my children to choose when they put their toys away. They take more responsibility, and I am not on their case all day. And so long as the goal is achieved at the end of the day, I view it as success. For me, I had to learn to live with clutter. I am okay with clutter now.

Cindy pointed out that this experience directly impacted her approach to empowerment. She said:

> Before my children were born, if someone did or said something that I didn't fully agree with, I would give my input and often argue my point of view. Perhaps back then, I felt a need to prove myself. Now I have a much broader perspective on work and life. I do not need to demonstrate my intellect. If a person's decision or perspective doesn't change the outcome of what we are trying to achieve, and it doesn't affect the customer, even if I disagree with it, I let it go and I let them be. I no longer need to voice my disagreements. I'd rather avoid needless negativity and empower others as often as I can.

EMBRACING DIFFERENCES

It's not that leaders consciously reject differences among team members, but rather that they unconsciously favor those who have backgrounds and points of view similar to their own. Though few leaders would admit to being part of an "old boy's network" today, many still retain a preference for people who share the same schools, companies, and clubs as they do. Male leaders, especially, who moved up through the ranks when these networks were strong, are more likely to create an inner circle of like-minded confidantes and rely on them to the exclusion of other points of view. In today's diverse culture, however, such behaviors can easily disempower teams and stifle creativity. Not only can women and minorities come to feel like outsiders, but anyone whose ideas are different may feel excluded. Though women are less guilty of rejecting or subordinating people who are different, they too may fall into this trap. Fortunately, motherhood provides some good team-building lessons in this area.

Ellen Kullman of DuPont discovered the importance of considering other points of view after she had children:

> DuPont is a very personal culture, which is conflict free and built off long-term relationships. When I first went to work for our current chairman, who was an executive vice president at the time, he kept trying to get me to be less unilateral and more embracing (of differences). Although I was pretty inclusive, if there was disagreement, I would go ahead and make the decision the way I thought was best. In retrospect, I didn't always take the time to see the issue from other people's perspectives. Luckily, my kids got my attention on this issue. I saw how my behavior affected them. It made me put myself in others' shoes and understand the world from the other side. While I do not always alter my beliefs, I did alter my behavior. Now, I think about disagreements, understand them, and then make clear choices. . . . Your arsenal when you get higher has to be more than a direct frontal attack. While I didn't think that was my style, it was. My kids helped me take a broader view. My arsenal with dealing with conflict and disagreement has grown tremendously. I am much more inclusive.

Ava Youngblood, president and CEO of Youngblood Executive Search, started her corporate climb at Amoco where she was often tapped to kick off their weeklong Valuing Diversity class for management. Ava understood that the typical white male was a reluctant participant. As a result, she always started the kickoff with the question, "How many of you have more than one child?" A good majority would raise their hand, and she would follow by saying, "You already know more than you think about valuing diversity." Ava recognized that parents are brought face to face with valuing differences right in their own homes.

Unfortunately, not all male executives benefit from the diversity lessons that parenting confers. Many times, they simply don't put in as much time with their children as moms do. In other cases, they are not as emotionally invested in being parents and therefore don't reap the same benefits. Moms, on the other hand, often referee feuds between elementary school-age siblings and figure out how to deal with the particular sensitivities and idiosyncrasies of each child.

Mirian Graddick-Weir of AT&T said:

> I believe I am a much better manager of people as a result of having children. You learn so much with your kids, especially if you have more than one. Each person's style is different, and you learn from your children that one size doesn't fit all. They learn differently, and their reaction to things is very different. My older daughter can be defiant at times and requires firmness; my younger daughter is extremely sensitive and requires more of a gentle approach. I have to motivate each of them differently, while still being fair and showing that I love them the same. I face the exact same situations in the work environment. My coworkers all learn differently. I try to understand them on an individual level. I learn about their needs, their background, their strengths and weakness. Like a teacher trying to connect with a class of 30 very different children, I had to learn to differentiate how I treat them or connect with them while being fair.

For leaders to embrace differences in people, a powerful emotional experience is usually required. Diversity training generally doesn't have much impact, nor does a boss's insistence that everyone must learn to get along better. A strong emotional experience, on the other hand, forces people to reexamine their beliefs and prejudices and makes it possible to change. A woman who is a CEO talked about her experiences with her young son, who has a learning disability involving sequential memory. She said:

> I had to put myself in his shoes and change my success criteria. And it didn't always come naturally. He was really struggling with his foreign language classes. I was encouraging him to try harder. It ends up that it's almost impossible for someone with that disability to learn a second language. I didn't recognize that at first. I had to keep his perspective at the forefront of my thinking. This helped me a great deal at work. I learned how to get on the same page as people who are different.

Bridgette Heller, the CEO of Chung's Gourmet Foods and a former executive vice president at Kraft, spoke passionately about valuing her daughter's differences. She shared a story about her daughter:

> Her Montessori teacher told me that I was going to have a difficult time parenting this child: "She learns by touching and observing. She likes to sit back and take it all in." Her teacher could tell I was a trial-and-error type of learner. But she explained that my daughter would be mortified by this approach. She needs to master things before she tries.

Bridgette said that she never imagined that she would be tasked with raising a creative type, explaining:

> My husband and I are straightforward, logical thinkers. My child is a painter. There were signs that she was different from us very early on in life. I recall one time when we were at the beach and she said, "Let's collect shells, Mommy." I said okay and got up and started heading down the beach to find shells. She asked me, "Where are you going mommy?" And I realized she wanted to sit where she was and dig in the sand to find shells. And she found beautiful shells, right at her feet. This was wonderfully eye-opening for me. Her thought processes were so different from mine. I have always considered myself to be very open-minded, but she took me to a different level. And as a result, I became much more aware of the different learning styles across my work teams.

Cindy Christy found that her diverse group of children helped her deal with a global marketplace:

> I have an overachiever, a smart laissez-faire child, a socially adept child, and a special needs child. My children all need different support structures. The same is true in business. I outsource manufacturing to China and India. I sell sophisticated products to sophisticated countries and basic products to emerging economies. They all have different business models and need different support structures. My kids gave me a good appreciation for the value of diversifying my approach to support very different business models.

To demonstrate how moms facilitate accepting differences, try the following exercise. Choose two leaders in your organization, one a mother and another not (it can be either a man or a woman). You can fill one of these slots with yourself if you wish. Then place the initials of the person after each of the following statements if it applies to them:

- Has assembled a diverse team in terms of age, ethnicity, and gender.
- Does not rely on an inner circle of pals to make important decisions.
- Appreciates diverse viewpoints and encourages people to air them, even if they differ from his or her own.
- Does not have "pets" who share the same background/thinking as he or she does.
- Makes an effort to manage and develop direct reports as individuals rather than as interchangeable parts.
- Is aware of the distinctive backgrounds, talents, and styles of each team member.
- Takes other people's opinions and ideas into consideration before making a decision.

The odds are that you wrote the mom's initials next to more of these statements than the nonmom. Motherhood may not foster an ideal form of inclusiveness—everyone falls off the wagon at times and plays favorites or rejects an opposing point of view—but it certainly encourages leaders to be more receptive to the differences inherent in any team.

SHOWING TOLERANCE

When children start school, parents often expect them to follow in their footsteps. Moms who received straight *A*s in school and never misbehaved expect the same performance from their kids. These expectations often aren't met. Some children struggle at certain subjects at which their parents excelled. Some kids misbehave. Some find it difficult to make friends or have trouble with sports. At the same time, these children often develop personal skills and academic strengths that their parents lack. As a result, parents must learn to be tolerant of their children's ways of doing things, at least within reason.

Obviously tolerance doesn't extend to granting them carte blanche to avoid homework or be ornery, but most moms and dads recognize that they must give their children room to develop and grow in their own ways. In addition, kids have numerous activities during the elementary school years that parents attend. Suddenly, there are parent-teacher conferences, open houses, and chaperoning responsibilities; kids join youth soccer leagues and other sports teams, and parents go to their games; children need and often want everything from computer games to clothes, so someone has to take them shopping.

Moms generally are the ones who drive their kids around and attend their various activities (though an increasing number of dads are taking on these responsibilities), and they are the ones most likely forced to make compromises in other areas of their lives. As a result, they learn to be more tolerant of everything from missing regular hair appointments to accepting a messier-looking house.

Pam Lopker, the chairman and president of QAD, said:

> I was a very meticulous housekeeper. I started letting go of stopping in my tracks and cleaning a spot on the wall. I got to be much more tolerant and casual. I didn't get upset over things that didn't matter, like when something broke. My plants didn't always get repotted. You see what's important and what's not important. That's something that probably comes with age, but being a mother has certainly increased this capability. With tolerance, age, and kids, I have learned to let go of business nuances and avoid unnecessary conflicts that I might have otherwise taken seriously, wasting my energy and that of my team. I

might have headed down a punitive route over some things before, which I tolerate now.

At the same time, leaders need to draw a line between being tolerant and being overly accepting of all types of mistakes and negative behaviors. As Pam said, "Some people view teams as a large family. I don't. I look at the company as a large team. Weak links weaken the team. You need to set the parameters and hold people accountable if they don't stay within them. Pam learned to set parameters for her children and hold them accountable. If they didn't maintain decent grades, they didn't receive certain privileges. As a result, they were motivated to perform in school.

As a mother, your kids force you to be more conscious of what you say and do. Even in elementary school, they are proficient at challenging your opinions and decisions, and these challenges result in self-assessment. Many of the women profiled in these pages are ultrahigh achievers who have set such a high standard for themselves, they don't always realize they are holding others to this impossible standard. They can be intolerant of disorganization, mistakes, and opposing views. One executive mother said that her children helped her moderate these tendencies. "I was being overly strict and applying pressure on things I wanted a little too strongly. My kids pushed back and questioned why I was so strict. I realized some of my reactions to things were knee-jerk reactions, and I became more tolerant. I realized that some of my responses to people were no longer appropriate."

One senior mother said she was intolerant of poor performers:

> My feedback in my early career was, "Does not fools suffer lightly." I was pretty judgmental. With my special needs son, I had to become a different person. I had to learn to accept what the moment gave me and adopt a completely different time horizon. I had to slow down and become a more patient person. I very much wanted to accept him for who and what he was and love him for that. The biggest epiphany for me was I learned tolerance. At work, I now control my propensity to be overly judgmental.

Deb Henretta said:

> One of the things I learned watching my children develop is recognizing they are a work in progress. It reminds me that I, too, am a work in progress, and it helps me understand that so are my team members. My people are learning, and I have learned to tolerate their mistakes. Mistakes can occur despite the best of intentions. I was reminded of this by my children. With kids you have to watch from the wings. You want to be an advisor and help them rather than orchestrate or dictate their lives. You know they learn from mistakes, and so you don't interfere. This has rubbed off on my approach to teams. I now say, "It's better to be a guide from the side than a sage from the stage." The degree to which a leader can be an advisor from the wings, versus the dictator taking all the credit, the better a team can achieve their goals.

INSPIRING PERSONAL GROWTH

Inspiring individuals within a team to grow and develop is a challenge that every leader faces. Some respond to this challenge by cracking the whip, assuming that pressuring subordinates to work harder and longer will help them grow. Other leaders do very little to inspire this growth, focusing instead on results.

Most of the maternal leaders, though, explained that prior to becoming moms, they did try to help their people grow. In some instances, however, they didn't do as good a job of it as they felt they should have. When their kids entered school, they realized that they couldn't inspire their children to achieve by wielding the carrot or the stick. They recognized that, if they wanted their children to become more responsible, to develop good values, and to do well in school, they needed to communicate that they trusted and respected them. Only when they learned how to show their kids how much they valued and cared about them, did their sons and daughters start to make strides in school and in life.

Deanna Oppenheimer of Washington Mutual's consumer group said:

> I have two terrific kids. And I tried the approach a boss takes at work. Just do it because I said so and I am your mother.

And that didn't work. You have to tell your children what you are trying to accomplish. You have to ensure they know they are part of a team. Building a team with my family is important and much like building a team at work. People will do what you ask them to do for the most part. But if they are not happy about it, they are not going to bring passion to it, and the work will not be their best. I learned this from my children. I can see how they pursue things they are passionate about and the results that come from this.

Mirian Graddick-Weir ran a sales and service center for AT&T and was appalled by the way some managers gave feedback to their reps; this unproductive feedback negatively impacted the team's motivation. She said:

I drew from experiences in my home to train my managers. I told them that it's one thing to give a rep feedback in a constructive way, but it's another to do so and keep their self-esteem intact. At the end of the day, before you send them back to interact with customers, think about how you may have impacted their self-esteem. If you have chipped away at it, that could impact how they deal with customers. It's important to send them back to their jobs with a better understanding of how to improve the calls with each customer, yet feeling confident and good about themselves. It's equally important to discipline kids in a way they can learn yet continue to strengthen their confidence and self-esteem.

Sophie Vandebroek, Xerox's chief engineer, said:

The key thing I have learned from my children was how to influence without direct control. To get my children interested in something, I had to learn to grow their confidence, create the right environment, and show them a vision. I can sense when my children are hesitant about trying something. I try to create possibilities in their minds and grow their confidence before they ever say no to something. I plant seeds that ultimately spring into their own ideas. For instance, my second son likes to read, so I use books to help guide him. At work, I use the same three concepts. I build confidence, create the right environment, and show the team a vision.

Sophie went on to say:

> Inspiring others is all about connecting with them at a deep human level. The 5,000 engineers across Xerox report into many different organizations. To influence such a disparate group, I needed to quickly connect with others. My life-enriching experiences, such as having children, gave me the ability to quickly connect with others. I didn't figure out the relationship piece until my children were in elementary school. For some reason, it just dawned upon me one day. Perhaps it was because I realized work was like home. I couldn't walk in the door in the evening and start giving out orders to the kids. I needed to start the evening by finding out about their day. Getting them to talk and learning to truly listen helped me understand what was on their minds.
>
> I realized that at work, I was so focused on keeping up a frantic pace, that I was all business. In order to create more solid relationships, I forced myself to start every meeting just checking in with my coworkers. I would ask them how they were or how their child's ballgame went the night before. In the first week I did this, I learned more than I had learned about my people in ten years. Then I had to learn to remember what each of these people shared with me. But it made such a huge difference in my working relationships. I created a much stronger fabric, bred loyalty . . . this led me to better relationships, and I improved results. I used to think it was inappropriate to bring your feelings to work. Now it would feel awkward if I didn't do it, and I am a strong believer that personal relationships are key to business success.

Earlier, I talked about how many executive moms had a velvet-glove touch, meaning that they inspire gently rather than harshly. Meg Whitman, CEO of eBay, was recently featured in a *Business Week* article that pointed out: "The collegiality that created and sustained eBay also shows in Whitman's management style, according to those who see her at work. 'She has an amazing velvet-glove touch,' says Sun's CEO, Scott McNealy, who worked closely with Whitman to fix eBay's site crashes. 'Instead of making me angry, she made me want to do just about anything we could to solve her problem. And that's what we did.'" (Hof, 2)

Kids teach you the velvet-glove touch. During the elementary school years, especially, these mothers constantly tried to preserve their children's spirit and self-esteem. As a result, they learned to use a velvet glove.

The velvet-glove touch often requires deep insight and creativity. Fran Keeth, the president and CEO of Shell Chemical, found a very gentle way to inspire her son:

> My son Russell is very creative. So we would sit at our kitchen table and create stories to get him to think about his challenges with math and science. I would start the story by saying something like, "There's a boy in the lab . . ." He would build on it, and we would go back and forth. We would paint stories about boys studying science who would struggle to get their work done but would ultimately invent a cure for some disease. This would inspire him to keep at it.

She went on to share how important this approach is at work. She said:

> Leadership is about painting a picture of the art of the possible and creating an environment where employees are excited about pursuing the plan. That is what raising kids is all about.

VELVET-GLOVE TEST

Determine if the velvet glove fits your style. Score yourself on the following questions as follows:

1 = Rarely
2 = Sometimes
3 = More often than not
4 = Almost always

Column A

1) Speak rapidly and in short sound bites.
2) Feel that I am smarter than those around me.
3) Am impatient when people waste my time.
4) Appear opinionated.
5) Find flaws in other people's ideas.
6) Check up on competent people's work.
7) Use a direct frontal attack.
8) Place people issues before financial issues.
9) Use the same motivational style with everyone.
10) Have knee-jerk reactions or outbursts.
11) Convince others that I am right.
12) Resist process change.
13) Appear dissatisfied.
14) Attack the messenger.
15) Interrupt others.

Column B

16) Start meetings with personal inquiries.
17) Allow others to have moments of leadership.
18) Communicate enthusiasm.
19) Respond positively to mistakes.
20) Get buy-in to my decisions.
21) Put myself in other people's shoes.
22) Comprehend the other person's point of view.
23) Listen to the eccentric creative types.
24) Tolerate or ignore unimportant nuisances.
25) Look interested.
26) Advise from the side.
27) Show curiosity about my coworkers' priorities.
28) Consider my employees' self-esteem.
29) Show appreciation.
30) Motivate teams

Your score equals (75 minus the sum of Column A) plus the sum of Column B. See below which category you fall into, and think about the items above where you can show improvement.

30– 60	Tough as Nails
61– 90	Have an Edge
91–110	Velvet Glove
111–120	Pathological Liar

8

TWEENS

Listening at a Higher Level

"The conversations you have with your children are the most high-value conversations in life. They have the highest stakes—your child's development is at stake, and your relationship with your child is at stake."

Joan Gulley, *CEO, PNC Advisors*

Contrary to expectations, you won't find many CEOs or other senior executives of large companies who lack basic listening skills. Some still assume the myth of the arrogant CEO who talks but never listens is reality, but the truth is that becoming CEO of a large company is difficult without absorbing ideas and information from other people; forming two-way, supportive relationships; and doing other things that require listening. At a time of evolving gender roles, the old stereotype of men being better talkers than women and women being better listeners doesn't always hold. In general, though, women tend to be good listeners, and this skill helps them form alliances and build relationships, two essential leadership traits.

Taking listening skills to a higher level, though, is a hallmark of maternal leaders. They don't just hear, but they see. In other words, they use what others tell them to be more perceptive about people and policies, politics, and processes. They leverage listening to establish rapport with key people, provide valuable feedback, and demonstrate that they want and need to hear their peers' and subordinates' viewpoints.

Many of the women I talked to noted that they ratcheted their listening skills up a notch when their kids were in middle school (or between the ages of 11 and 14). During this transitional period to adolescence, kids start shucking off the shell of childhood, changing in ways that demand a parent pay more than casual attention.

Joyce Rogge, the senior vice president of marketing at Southwest Airlines, said, "I became a much better listener. Before, I tended to be impatient—let's cut to the chase. When you pick your children up from school, though, they want to tell you all about their day in their roundabout way, and it is important. Now I listen attentively out of habit rather than forcing myself."

Joan Gulley, the CEO of PNC Advisors added, "The conversations you have with your children are the highest-value conversations in life. They have the highest stakes—your child's development is at stake, and your relationship with your child is at stake."

Tweens are very vulnerable. They are straddling the worlds of childhood and adolescence, an extremely awkward stance. They start being influenced by their equally immature friends, experiencing tremendous hormonal changes, and breaking away from their parents. Their behavioral and emotional shift from fifth to sixth or seventh grades gives them a lot to say, and moms are all ears. As a result, mothers can develop the following leadership attitudes and skills:

- Operating at full attentiveness
- Reading between the lines
- Biting your tongue
- Matching wavelengths
- Being open to others

OPERATING AT FULL ATTENTIVENESS

In this hectic, multitasking world of ours, many people listen without paying full attention. At some point, you've probably talked to your boss, a customer, or a colleague and intuitively understood that, though their head was nodding and they were saying, "Yes . . . uh huh . . . yes," their mind was elsewhere. At best, this type of listening is irritating; at worst, it communicates that the listener doesn't care about you.

The ability to listen fully and deeply is a great leadership talent, in that it tells people that a leader truly values the other person's ideas. Leaders who are full-attention listeners earn the respect and trust of their people in ways that other leaders don't. People work harder and longer for these leaders because they hold their bosses in great esteem.

Given the pace at which women executives move, it's not surprising that they aren't always as attentive as they should be. For maternal leaders, though, tweens remind them that being tuned in is one of the keys to communication. They learn that the more attention they pay to what their teenagers say, the easier it is to help them with their problems. They also learn that if they don't listen carefully, they can miss clues that their child is in trouble or is asking for help. These women naturally apply such lessons to people at work. By being more attentive, they are in a better position to receive and respond to critical pieces of information. In the course of a hectic workday, it is remarkably easy for even the best leaders to overlook an important topic that a direct report raises or to miss a colleague's hint that a project is in trouble.

Intellectually, these maternal leaders understood that being attentive was a good leadership trait even before their children were born. Afterwards, though, it became second nature. They didn't have to think about trying to pay more attention; this trait became part of their work routine, and it paid off with greater awareness and understanding of direct reports, peers, bosses, and customers.

Deanna Oppenheimer, president of Washington Mutual's consumer group, leads over 35,000 people but still recognizes the need to be attentive to as many of those individuals as possible. She said, "While I am still very driven and expect a lot from my employees, my attentiveness toward my kids resulted in my being more attentive to my employees as well. I listen better, and I take more time to understand what is important to my associates."

Colleen Arnold, who leads IBM's global communications sector, shared a story about how her son Jack was testing the importance she placed on their goodnight ritual. They would usually talk through the day's events when she went to his room to say goodnight. One night, the phone rang as she was talking to him during this bedtime ritual. Jack said, "You better get that phone, Mom." Colleen ignored it. Then it started ringing again. Jack's next comment was, "Mom, it's Sam [Sam Palmisano, IBM's chairman and CEO]. He's calling you to offer you the CEO job. Don't you want to get it?" Colleen still ignored it. Then Jack added, "Okay, because you are not answering his call, he's going to go offer it to someone else." Colleen didn't budge despite Jack's teasing.

Colleen understood how important it was to pay attention to her son when he was most likely to talk about what was on his mind. This experience rubbed off on Colleen's work behaviors. She said, "Now, I always ask everybody what's going on. I will start meetings with questions about people's children or hobbies. The meetings flow into a much more collaborative session than they otherwise would have. They succeed because my coworkers know that my interest in them is sincere."

For many executives, learning to pay close attention is almost counterintuitive. To cope with the multitude of responsibilities every leader has, their minds have to be going a million miles a minute, sifting through numerous issues and concerns. Focusing on just one thing for an extended period seems like a bad strategy, given all the other problems that must be addressed. Tweens help moms balance the need to address multiple issues with the need to pay attention to the individual.

Kate Ludeman, now the CEO of Worth Ethic Corporation, switched jobs, thinking she would have more time to spend with her daughter. It wasn't working out that way, and she acknowledged this to her daughter. Catherine's response was, "Mom, I don't know why things would be any different. You took your same self with you to the new job." Kate said, "She got my attention. I realized that, despite my career change, I would get very passionate and overinvolved at work. I made more conscious choices after that about my time with my daughter."

Middle school kids live in constant crisis, and parents learn to be extremely observant and responsive. One of the executive mothers said:

> My children taught me to pay attention to my people more. And I found I needed to not just pay attention to the inexperienced managers and poorer performers but also the stars. Everyone that works for me needs some level of my undivided attention. I look around and see my peers who haven't learned this lesson. They don't attract the caliber of talent that I can, because either they don't pay attention or they don't know how to tune in.

Paying attention requires time and commitment. You can't just turn attentiveness on and off, but you must be consistently accessible to others and tuned in when they come to you. In this way, you end up being the first to know what is worth knowing. If you establish a reputation as someone in an organization who pays attention to others, people are likely to come to you first with ideas and news.

Moms often develop this consistent attentiveness by making an effort to be as accessible to their children as possible, especially during the difficult, preteen transition years. This isn't always easy to do, especially given the extensive travel schedules of many women in top leadership positions. Still, a number of women I've talked to discovered that cell phones allow them to stay involved in and informed about their children's lives, even when they are on the road.

When one of my sons was in the fifth grade, he called me one day after school when I was in India. It was 3:00 AM. I answered the phone, and he said "Hi mom, what's up?" I could immediately sense he had something on his mind, but I let him take his time getting around to it while I tried to wake up. Finally he asked, "Mom, do I have a big butt?" I almost giggled, but could tell he was serious. So I said, "No, why do you ask?" He went on to tell me that Lizzy, a girl in his class, told him that Allison, another girl in his class, gave up looking at his butt for Lent. But Lizzy also told him that Allison was not keeping her Lenten promise and was sneaking looks at his butt. He wanted to know if there was something wrong with his butt.

I realized that he was clueless about Allison's motivations, and we had to have our first serious conversation about the birds and the bees right then. While I wished I had been home with him for this conversation, I was grateful that he thought to pick up the phone and call me about it.

From that moment on, I became a believer in accessibility. Despite all the headaches that being accessible to people can bring, I learned that the benefits were huge. I was rarely caught by surprise. My male peers and bosses were always amazed that I knew about things, good and bad, before they did. To them, my access to the latest information was a mystery. I suspect it wasn't as much a mystery to other moms in the organization.

READING BETWEEN THE LINES

Like employees, tweens aren't always forthright about what is bothering them, so moms are continuously learning to read between the lines. During this time, girls are sometimes prone to crying, and one of the women I interviewed said that, by the time her daughter was 12, she could discern the subtle shades of meaning when she cried. She could tell the difference between a "serious" cry that indicated something really was wrong versus an "I'm just having a bad day" cry. This mother emphasized that, "You have to know the difference. If you react to every cry, you are reinforcing her crying and dependence. On the other hand, it's not uncommon anymore for preteens to have serious emotional issues. You have to know the difference. It isn't always easy." Another mom said, "They (her sons) don't really talk, they grunt. You have to read their grunts. I must say, there were times I needed to use some grunt deciphering in the boardroom."

Catherine West, the president of Capital One Bank, said:

> If I listen with intent, I can tell when my son Will says one thing but really means another. I can figure this out, because I know what is in his head and his heart. Because I know what he really means, we can figure out things better. This is so applicable at work. I listen intently, watch their body language, and read between the lines, and I am able to unlock the issues on the table.

Ruth Harenchar, the CIO at Bowne, reflected on how she picks up on things happening all around her and not just in front of her. She said:

> Mothers have eyes in the back of their heads. My antennas are on all the time. Some people will do their management by walking around and be clueless about what happened in their wake. I watch just as much as what's going on behind me as in front of me. I get better information that way. If something I said didn't go over well, I will pick up on it and cycle back around. Almost every cliché about the strength of mothers relates to the office. I have come to absolutely value those eyes in the back of my head. My staff will frequently say, "I can't believe that you picked up on that."

Cindy Christy of Lucent said that she constantly observes her four kids' moods, postures, sleeping habits, and eating habits so she knows what is really going on inside their minds and hearts. She said, "Now I watch industry trends like I watch my kids. I don't wait for big announcements; I recognize the subtle signs and see things coming."

Without children to remind them to read between the lines, leaders can fall into the trap of being overly literal minded. They focus on exactly what is being said and ignore the context. In business today, ambiguity and complexity are the norms. Being able to spot subtlety and nuance helps leaders interpret what really is going on. On an individual level, this means paying attention to facial expressions, tone of voice, and posture. On a broader scale, this means being aware of everything from significant shifts in the marketplace to emerging industry trends. Certainly, some childless and male leaders can read between the lines with the best of them. Being the mother of a tween, though, increases the reading skill level. To help you see the connection between the two types of experiences, try this exercise.

The following is a typical comment made by a 12-year-old, followed by five interpretations of what he really means. Choose the one that you think is right.

> You arrive home from work and find your son sitting on the couch staring into space. You ask him if anything is wrong, and he replies, "Everything is fine." Does he mean:
>
> A. Everything is peachy.
> B. Everything is great except he's just tired.
> C. Everything is fine, but he's bored.
> D. Something is bothering him, but he doesn't feel it's significant enough to talk about.
> E. He has a big problem, is struggling with it, and wants you to push him to talk about it.

You had only a 20 percent chance of getting the answer right. Without being in the room with the boy, you can't tell how he said, "Everything is fine." Without practice at reading him, you will find it difficult to know what he is actually saying, even if you are in the room. Therefore, here are some more details that a mom would naturally take in.

> You arrive home from work and find your son sitting on the couch with a faraway look in his eyes; he doesn't even look at you when you walk in the room, and you have to say his name twice

before you get his attention. You've noticed that during the past year, he has tended to drift off into his own private world when something is bothering him. When you ask him if something is wrong, he refuses to look you in the eye and says in a monotone, "Everything is fine."

With this information in hand, you're in a much better position to read between the lines, and you can reasonably guess the correct response is E. Now let's look at a similar work scenario:

A subordinate returns to your office after meeting with your company's largest customer. You ask how the meeting went, and she says, "Good." Does she mean:

A. The meeting was terrific, and she accomplished all her objectives.
B. The meeting generally went fine, but one issue came up that needs to be addressed.
C. The meeting was okay, but she feels like she has no chemistry with the customer and that this could spell trouble in the long run.
D. The meeting was okay, but she's afraid that you'll come down hard on her if she says anything less than good.
E. The meeting was a disaster, but she wants to cover her mistakes before she tells you what really happened.

Again, it's tough to know the right answer unless you had observed this subordinate perceptively. Therefore, here is what you would have observed:

When the subordinate returned to your office from the meeting, she seemed calm. You've observed this person in the past when things didn't go well, and her anxiety has been transparent. When you asked her how the meeting went, however, she hesitated before saying, "Good." You also detected a catch in her voice. When you called her on it, she admitted that one issue had surfaced that might become a problem, but she didn't want to talk about it until she had more information.

BITING YOUR TONGUE

People who listen well don't just know the right thing to say, they know when (and when not to) say it. Children teach their parents that when it comes to conversation, less can be more; that extending a conversation past a certain point can be counterproductive; that saying nothing at all can provide more support than a long-winded, well-intentioned speech. Many of the maternal leaders related experiences in which they started lecturing their 13-year-olds about something and realized that their words were falling on deaf ears. They also recalled incidents when they voluntarily cut themselves short, realizing that anything they might say would only hurt their children.

Bridgette Heller of Chung's Gourmet Foods said:

> I was never so concerned about someone else's self-esteem until I had my own children. It's so important to me that they feel good about themselves and have strong self-esteem. As they grew up, my listening skills grew tremendously, because I learned to stop talking, and I learned to pick the right moment to speak. I also found that my daughter listened better if she was fidgeting. I learned to let her fidget. By doing these things, I helped open up a lot more sharing on their part. I wasn't really paying attention to other people's self-esteem prior to having kids, and now it's on the top of my mind at home and at work.

Gail Evans, a retired executive vice president with CNN Newsgroup, is now a consultant for senior executive women and an author. She said that women need to put more trust in their ideas rather than in convincing others about the worth of these ideas. She explains, "So many women keep repeating their points when their male colleagues don't respond to them, and they become too pushy. If the men didn't value what they said the first or second time, they are not going to value them the third time; they are just going to see them as pushy."

Biting one's tongue is another trait that is counterintuitive for many leaders. Executives often feel compelled to use their considerable verbal prowess to persuade. They are extremely confident in their ability to win people over to their point of view. Certainly, maternal leaders are frequently articulate and even eloquent, but they also recognize when people are not receptive to what they have to say and aren't going to be receptive. The sudden and seemingly inexplicable bad moods of tweens help moms identify times when it's more effective to remain silent.

Kira, for instance, was a top executive in charge of her organization's sales function when one of her children was 12. As someone who had come up through the sales ranks, Kira was nothing if not verbal. She was especially adept at communicating with customers, creating powerful arguments that helped both sell the company's products and maintain strong customer relationships. Kira's sharp mind, combined with her charm, made her a favorite not only of customers but also of her own people.

At one point, though, the company was in danger of losing a major customer. As the senior vice president in charge of sales, Kira was asked to use her talents to repair the relationship. Though she had met and worked with the customer company's CEO in the past, she didn't know him well. As she got to know him, however, she found him to be pleasant but preoccupied. His company was going through many changes, and he was working long hours trying to help ease his organization through this transitional period.

At first, Kira tried to work her verbal magic on him, but she quickly realized that, not only wasn't she having an impact, but he resented her taking up his time with discussions on issues he believed were of secondary importance. Kira backed off, in no small part because of what she had learned about her 12-year-old: "There are times when I talk to her [Kira's daughter] and I know anything I say is going to irritate her. It doesn't matter what it is or how I say it, she's going to take it the wrong way. Now I'm pretty good at sensing when she is in one of those moods where the best thing I can do is say nothing." This same strategy paid off with this particular customer. Kira waited until he seemed more receptive to talking about the customer service issue that was weakening the relationship—the company had implemented most of their change initiatives by then—and she worked with him to solve a number of major problems.

MATCHING WAVELENGTHS

Listening can also help leaders and parents to communicate on someone else's wavelength. Too often, we rely exclusively on our own wavelengths, assuming that they will work for other people. When kids are in middle school, parents quickly discover that their child is tuned to a different frequency. When they really listen to their children and pay attention to their evolving communication styles, they find that they can connect with them better.

Melinda Brown, a controller at PepsiCo and a rapid-fire communicator, has a teenage daughter who is "laid back." She said:

> My 13-year-old daughter thinks differently than I do, which makes communication difficult. The first step toward open communication was intellectually understanding our differences. The harder step for me was ensuring I related to her on her terms. It can be very challenging, but I am so motivated to value her and understand her that I work hard at this. My kids have benefited from the training I received at work, but my co-workers have also benefited from my experiences with my children. I put much more effort into understanding the individual needs of the people I work with.

Lori Craven, the COO at Tekelec, said, "Our kids are facing different situations than we faced. To understand their issues you need to be in tune with their situation. You have to proactively figure out where they are coming from. Everyone came from somewhere. In my business, it's mostly Nortel, Cisco, or Lucent, and all three have different industry perspectives. I make it a point to know where my employees came from, so that we can communicate more effectively."

Unlike in the past, most leaders today are surrounded by people who come from different backgrounds and have different perspectives. Success as a leader depends upon being able to see the world through your customers' eyes or through your coworkers' frames of reference. Mothers are passionate about understanding their preteens, and they make the necessary effort to see the world from their kid's perspective. They ask experts, read books, watch their children's favorite TV programs or movies, and listen to their favorite music. They also network as much as possible with their children's friends, teachers, coaches, neighbors, and other parents.

Through this information gathering, they are in a better position to interpret what they hear their children tell them. When they listen to their kids talk, they have a context through which they can make sense of it and communicate with them on their wavelength.

The leadership benefits gained from this particular maternal behavior seemed quite diverse. In making the effort to get on their children's wavelengths, some women discovered the value of networking. One mother said:

> I thought networking was a waste of time, until my children got too old for a nanny and I didn't know exactly where they were or what they were doing. I found the best way to keep abreast of their issues and thought processes was to network with the other mothers. We all had the same goal, which was to keep our kids safe and out of serious trouble. The more I networked, the more grateful I was and the more rewarding I found it. I became much more supportive of networks at work. Their value sunk in. Among other things, they really help you decipher where people are coming from.

Linda Wolf of Leo Burnett, on the other hand, found her efforts to understand her sons provided insight about sports, a topic she had never been particularly interested in but one that many of her male colleagues were passionate about. "My sons are into sports, so I got into sports. I went to all of their soccer games and Little League games and learned about the sports. This has helped me build a rapport with the men with whom I work. In business, it's all about relationships. My kids have helped put me on the same page as most of the people I work with."

Jocelyn Carter-Miller, a former executive at Mattel, derived perhaps the most direct and applicable benefit from her attempts to understand her daughters' points of view. When her daughters were preteens, the Barbie campaign was, "We girls can do anything, right, Barbie?" Jocelyn, who was responsible for the Barbie brand, said:

> Well, there's nothing that my daughters think they cannot do or anything they cannot be. From their perspective, the cam-

paign slogan was no longer relevant, and they told me so. They helped me realize that the times and kids had changed a bit. So we changed the Barbie slogan to, "I'm into Barbie." This slogan exuded confidence. Girls could experience anything they wanted. The world is about opportunities, and we made Barbie astronauts, businesswomen, and doctors. People questioned us, but it was a hit. Barbie's sales doubled, all because I was able to see the world through my daughters' lenses.

BEING OPEN TO OTHERS

Many executives claim to have an open door policy but really don't. I remember moving into an office building at Motorola, and the executive offices were spread out around the building to foster open communication. Each of our offices, though, was protected by administrative assistants' offices. You couldn't even see into our office unless you walked through their room. When we were each given a budget to redecorate our office, I used mine to reconstruct the entrance, so that people could see into my office as they walked by. This did not sit well with some of my peers, who liked their privacy and didn't want to be pressured to follow suit.

Being open and receptive to all types of individuals in an organization is a distinct leadership advantage. Before I had children in middle school, I'm not sure I would have reconfigured my office as I did. Afterwards, however, I understood that projecting an open and receptive demeanor often determined whether my children would make the effort to speak to me about something that was going on in their lives. Because of this awareness, I knew that the more receptive I seemed to people, the more likely they would be to tell me things I needed to know. Whether it was bad business news, a daring idea, or a career issue they were struggling with, I wanted them to feel free to talk to me.

I also knew that if they wanted to talk, they would take a test stroll down the hallway past my office, trying to see if I was there, if anyone else was with me, if I was in a good mood, or if I was busy. I can't count the number of times I'd see someone passing by and just know that something was up and there was nothing random about their stroll down the hallway.

I learned from my kids that you have to go out of your way to encourage them to initiate difficult conversations. You might only get one chance to hear them tell you something important, so you better make sure you are ready, willing, and able to listen.

Not only do leaders need to be open to news and ideas, but they must also be open to criticism. For ultrahigh achievers, criticism is often the last thing they want to hear. Kids can make this criticism more palatable. Anne Showe from Sun said, "Unlike work colleagues, kids tell you how you really are. Their feedback can be humbling." Too often, a senior executive's position precludes her receiving much difficult feedback. As a result, many top organizational people develop a false sense of infallibility and, consciously or not, discourage criticism.

Kids, on the other hand, don't care about your position. Generally, if they have a bone to pick with you, they'll pick it. They certainly aren't interested in softening their remarks or telling you about your faults in a constructive way. They just blurt out whatever is on their mind, especially when they're in their tweens. Mothers learn that not only is there some valuable self-learning in what their kids are saying, but that to keep communication open, they must be receptive to their children's criticisms.

Joan Gulley, the CEO of PNC Advisors, said:

> I learned to set a context to listen to my son. I tell myself that, although he doesn't have the skill yet to be constructive, he is trying to make a contribution. I try to really hear what he is trying to tell me without getting defensive. I avoid thinking to myself that someday he'll know better. It made a huge difference. And this is exactly the same skill set I needed at work. Hearing through the poorly chosen words and really getting to the person's point, instead of preparing my defense, benefits everyone.

Donna Lee, the CMO of BellSouth, said:

> One of the things that my kids brought into stark reality for me was my tendency to be aggressive and not take no for an answer. One day, we were in a restaurant, and I was aggressive about getting the appropriate level of service. My son asked me,

"Mom, why are you being like this? You are not treating them very well." He's helped me see myself as others sometimes would see me. I realize now there are softer ways to do things. I need to sugarcoat some things I say or find different ways to couch things. He wouldn't think of himself as a coach, but he is.

Nayla Rizk, a partner at Spencer Stuart, said:

My sons point out my weaknesses directly. My coworkers would be much more hesitant in their approach. My sons figured me out and have me down pat. I have to acknowledge my weaknesses to them. I had to accept their feedback and also learned to take myself with a grain of salt.

Joan, Donna, and Nayla were all conscientious leaders before their children were born and attempted to improve their listening and interpersonal skills earlier in their careers. Nevertheless, their children caught their attention in much more powerful ways than the formal and informal feedback mechanisms at the office. Anita Beier, U.S. Airways's controller, tried to explain this process:

My children's feedback can get to me like nobody else's. That amazes me, because I have worked with lots of different people and received constructive and overly critical feedback. But my kids have a deeper impact. They make me realize that I have to pay attention to their input and I have to be responsive, because I really want them to respect me as a mother. I am so emotionally attached to them that I would do anything to strengthen our relationship. Being open is a must.

Not only do their children give mothers tremendous practice at being open, but they also help them understand their weaknesses and motivate them to improve their skills. Kids can get through to moms about their weaknesses in ways that even the most trusted of subordinates or coaches can't. Once they do get through—generally sometime in middle school when their powers of observation and articulation have been developed sufficiently—women realize the areas where they need to improve. They understand that, if they had not been open to criticism from their children, they would never have benefited from their kids' perceptive observations.

All this is not to suggest that preteens come up with brilliant observations that immediately result in revelations and behavioral changes. They are not going to observe you as a professional coach would and point out weaknesses and strengths with clarity and illustrations. Instead, the lessons learned come from the small truths they tell about us. For instance, tweens are often obsessed by physical style—whether it is our hair or clothes or makeup, they have something to say about it. Pam Lopker, chairman and president of QAD, said:

> My daughter is famous for telling me to go back and change, my outfit looks bad on me. She taught me that shoulder pads are out, nylons with sandals are out, and my comfortable shoes are ugly. She tells my hairdresser how to do my hair. She is blunt, but she's right and I accept her advice.

All this fosters openness. Almost without exception, maternal leaders are more willing to hear what others have to say, be it good or bad news, compliments or criticisms. They make their willingness to listen clear, not only by telling people they want to know the truth or hear a dissenting opinion, but by their demeanor after they hear what others have to say. Just as they don't bark at their kids when they tell them a dress makes them look fat, they don't shout at their associates when they tell them their strategy was flawed. Their tweens have taught them that the truth is worth whatever pain accompanies it.

Kids also teach moms that people communicate in different ways and to be open to different forms of communication. When M One founder Marilyn Seymann's son was ten, she was headed to a meeting at the White House. She said, "I was nervous, and my children knew it. They all said goodbye and knock 'em dead. My one son left a note in my shoe, which I found when I unpacked. He couldn't say he was proud of me, so he left a note."

In the same way, some people at work may favor e-mails over the spoken word when they really have something important to say. Maternal leaders like Marilyn learn that key messages come in a variety of forms.

LISTENING AUDIT

If you are a mother of a preteen or older child, you may not even realize how your listening skills have improved. It's only when you take some time and think about the conversations you have with your child that these skills become apparent. If you're like most moms, you've learned how and when to hold these conversations so you gain maximum information; you've discovered when to back off when you hit on a sore subject or your child is just not in a mood to talk; you know when to shut up because you see your child's eyes glazing over; and you know how to convey your willingness to hear what the child has to say through your body language.

These skills carry over to the workplace, and if you're a mom of a preteen, you probably will be able to provide positive answers to many of the following questions. If you're a man or a woman without kids, though, you may have more difficulty with these questions. In either case, they're designed to make every executive more conscious of their listening skills.

Before answering, take a moment to reflect on the most important conversations you have at work (other than those with your boss). Who are they with? What are the stakes? When and where are they held? Now answer the questions below with respect to these conversations.

1. What percentage of these conversations do you spend listening? Talking?
2. Do you start with sincere inquiries to how the other person is doing?
3. How often do you successfully realize anything you say will do more harm than good? How often are you unsuccessful in this effort?
4. Do you take interruptions during these conversations? If so, why?
5. Are you fully attentive? If not, what distracts you?
6. Do you pay attention to nonverbal cues?
7. Can you read between the lines?
8. Does your conversation partner usually sit with an open or closed style (crossed arms and legs)?
9. Do you usually sit with an open or closed style?

10. How do you make it easy or hard for them to share negative news?
11. If they use poorly chosen words, how do you react?
12. If they criticize you, how do you react?
13. How often do you find yourself preparing a defense while they are talking?
14. How soon do you follow up on the issues raised in difficult conversations?
15. Are you able to get on other people's wavelengths? Do they agree (or do you think they would agree if you don't know for sure)?

9

TEENAGERS
Coaching with Unconditional Love

*"As a working mother, I really had to instill trust. My children earned
a lot of freedoms and handled their growing independence pretty well,
largely because they understood that if they chose the wrong path,
life as they currently knew it would end."*

Doreen Toben, *CFO, Verizon*

The vast majority of the executive
mothers in this book had their children in their 30s and were middle
managers at the time. Many of them reached senior levels in corporations during their children's teenage years. The timing was perfect, in
that as they were learning to let go, stay calm, not sweat the little things,
tolerate pink hair, and listen openly, they were being asked to apply
these same behaviors to the job (with the possible exception of tolerating pink hair). As a result, they took on senior roles armed with knowledge and abilities that their nonparent peers may have lacked.

Just as senior positions are the ultimate test of a leader's skills, teenagers are the ultimate test of a parent's skills. The maturity, wit, and patience acquired from raising younger children are put to the test at
senior corporate levels. At these levels, direct reports are very bright
and independent with sizable egos, self-confidence, a fearless assertiveness, and strong opinions. Despite their talent, they need to grow into
their roles, improve interpersonal skills, and get with the plan, even if
they disagree with the boss's direction. These leaders are called upon to
exhibit subtle and refined skills; they have to coach even when their
managers do not feel the need to be coached.

No doubt, many top executives try to coach their people. Some of
them, though, are coaching without the necessary training or experi-

ence; a significant percentage of executives reach top positions with limited skill sets in this increasingly important area. Nonetheless, with the current emphasis on growing people and grooming a successor, these executives give it their best. Unfortunately, in difficult situations, they often struggle—unless, of course, they happen to be mothers of teenagers.

SHIFTING GEARS INTO ADVISOR MODE

Mothers of teenagers receive a great deal of practice as coaches. Their kids are in the process of breaking away, yet they aren't quite skilled enough to make all the critical life choices facing them. To make matters more complicated, moms aren't quite ready to let them go, even though they have had practice with letting-go behaviors when their kids were little. Donna Lee of BellSouth said:

> We [my son and I] are in the break-away-from-mom phase. I was very independent, so I can appreciate there is need for separation. But it's still hard. Intellectually, I say I am dealing with this well, but emotionally, I am struggling with no public displays of affection. If we go to a meeting together, I get the look that says, "You are not going to dare ask a question, are you?"

The separation process is not a smooth one. Teens are on a roller coaster. One minute they are receptive, the next minute rebellious. One minute they are happy, the next minute angry. One minute they care about school, the next they don't. Their driver's licenses also provide them with newfound freedom. Parents must relinquish some control over their kids and their environment. They also have to deal with their teenager's belief that mom is stupid or naíve as well as their child's resistance to advice.

Perhaps it's coincidence, but many executive moms seem to have teenagers who are as strong-willed, confident, and independent as they are. Consequently, they have their hands full as parents, which also provides them with opportunities to acquire the skills that are needed to coach other strong-willed, confident, and independent executives.

Amal Johnson, a partner at ComVentures, said:

Teenage years are the ultimate challenge. It was a particularly significant challenge for me, because my daughter was a reflection of me. I was very independent. I came to this country at age 17 by myself. Hannah is 15 and is trying to be just as independent. Her struggle for independence reached crisis levels and forced me to face the fact that I was still too controlling. It wasn't easy to work our way through this transition, but we did. I learned that it is okay for me not to be on top of her all the time, and I take very different approaches to coach her. . . . My struggles with Hannah have helped me at work, too. I have learned to coach people through transitions to greater responsibility much more effectively and much less authoritatively.

Doreen Toben, the CFO at Verizon, said:

It is hard to shift gears into the coaching role. My son spent his junior year in high school abroad. I went over to see him seven times. He didn't mind but joked that he saw me a lot more than most of the local kids saw their parents. As it turned out, my son was pretty worldly and ready for the independence that comes with teenage years. As a working mother, I really had to instill trust. My children earned a lot of freedoms and handled their growing independence pretty well, largely because they understood that if they chose the wrong path, life as they currently knew it would end.

Though Doreen was talking about being a parent, her words have an almost uncanny parallel with the coaching responsibilities of a leader. The best leader-coaches instill trust in their people and allow them the freedom they deserve. It can be risky to give a direct report responsibility for a major project, but leaders are willing to do so, knowing that it is a great opportunity for the subordinate to grow and gain confidence in themselves.

The letting go aspect of both coaching and parenting is tremendously difficult. With teenagers, parents fear that they will misuse their freedom and become involved in drugs or alcohol or fall prey to depression and eating disorders. Demanding edicts, threats, and punishments that worked in younger years become a parent's last resort and are reserved for only the most serious problems.

Parents learn to take on more of a coaching role, because that is the best role to help their children become responsible young adults. They help them problem solve without solving problems for them. They try to connect with their teenagers on their teenagers' terms, speaking their language. If they find themselves failing in their coaching role, they bring in an outside professional (such as a therapist) to assist them.

Leaders do the exact same things with their people. They recognize that giving their people resources and ideas is better than giving them answers. As tempting as it is to tell a struggling direct report what to do, they step back and provide direction rather than the answers. When problems spiral out of control—when they fear a direct report is in danger of failing in a significant way—they bring in an outside coach or some other individual to help get them back on track. Coaching, therefore, is more art than science, and the trial-and-error process of raising teens helps mothers practice this art.

Let's examine the following traits that moms exhibit with teenagers and how they translate into business-coaching behaviors:

- Earning receptivity
- Connecting on their terms
- Establishing rules of engagement
- Becoming a positive influence
- Being indirectly effective

EARNING RECEPTIVITY

As most parents learn, adolescents are not particularly receptive to their advice; they learn to build a foundation of trust and respect and wait for that receptivity to emerge. Waiting is an especially good lesson for high-achieving executive women who are used to being in control and getting results quickly. Once they realize that blind obedience doesn't work with teens struggling to be independent, they discover how to earn their children's receptivity through more effective means. Specifically, they use the following tactics:

- Build trust
- Cut them slack
- Respect their loyalties and their point of view
- Praise their good behaviors
- Show they care
- Use diplomacy

Pam Murray, an executive vice president and general manager at Marriott, has a 19-year-old son. She said:

> Fifteen and 16 were the really tough years. While we managed to have discussions, there was rebellion, and when he was around me he was negative. I didn't know what path he was going to take, and I worried about what the future would hold for him. I kept thinking, "So long as he is still talking to me, I can help him." I did everything I could think of to keep the doors of communication open. You want so badly for your child to be happy, that you find a way to stay connected. Well, now I tell people we got to the other side. We are happy to be together again. And ironically, he seeks out my advice often.

Cindy Christy, the president of Lucent's mobility group, said:

> One of the things I learned from my kids is that they don't always talk to you. I have to do more than just tell them, "If you are having a problem, come see me." They have to trust me. I have proven to them that I will give them the benefit of the doubt at first. I assume they do the things they do for the right reason. They know if they make a mistake, that I will cut them some slack. I have found this to work well in the office. I deal better with the 20 percent of things that don't work out. I assume positive intent, and it keeps the doors to communication open.

Being considerate of children's hot buttons or sensitivities also builds trust and receptivity. Ruth Harenchar of Bowne & Company, who has a blended family, said:

> Valuing my stepchildren's loyalties to their mother was very important for me to build trust. I would not criticize their mother. In essence, my stepchildren created the mental model I use at work. When I join an organization, I don't criticize the previous managers. I just say what I prefer and get buy-in that my ideas are sound. There's always bait to criticize your predecessors, but I learned to sidestep those questions and gain receptivity by avoiding negativity.

Ruth Ann Gillis, a senior vice president and president of Exelon's Business Services Company, pointed out that praise for good behavior goes a long way. She said:

> I remember reading a book that talked about catching them [teenagers] being good, and I started putting that into practice. It worked much better than focusing on the poor behaviors and constantly triggering attention flares. It doesn't mean I turned a blind eye. But I noticed a lot more of their good behaviors, like helping, sharing, and getting along with their siblings, because I was looking for it. And I found that they remembered the praise and repeated the rewarded behavior. And it stimulated more positive conversation than negative, which helped them be receptive to me when dealing with the tough issues.
>
> I was able to bring this to bear at the office, too. I realized that we didn't make an effort to call out enough positive examples of good performance, and we didn't celebrate success enough. Making a habit out of recognizing people's good work gave me a great deal more positive contributions to share come performance review time.

Picking their battles also helped moms earn receptivity. When they criticized their teens every time they did something bothersome, they would engage in continuous battles. They learned how to ignore many smaller irritations, saving their battles for the big issues. When they stopped the constant clashes with their adolescents, their kids weren't as quick to raise their shields, and over time, their children were more willing to talk and listen.

This skill carried over to the office in significant ways. Pam Lopker, the CEO of QAD, has two teenagers. She said, "At work, I have learned to be less intense and pick my battles. There's a lot of battles that I used to get involved with, but I don't anymore. I still disagree with things—for instance, our new employee benefits plan—but it isn't one of the important battles I should be focused on right now."

Employees are more receptive to their bosses when they are not acting like Big Brother. Direct reports who feel their every move is being scrutinized and every decision challenged will not listen with open minds. Instead, they will be defensive, focusing more on rebutting criticism than in absorbing what is being said. When executives are more selective about challenging or questioning their people, however, they find their direct reports are more likely to hear and respond.

Ruth Harenchar added that diplomacy and caring are also keys to coaching coworkers and teenagers. She said, "With teenagers, you need a lot of diplomacy. If they see that you really care, they will respond. You can't force them to do anything, but because they value your input and you've maintained a bond, they will respond."

She shared a recent experience with her teams where she applied the skills she used with her teens:

> My staff was treating three of our deliverables as three separate projects, even though there was a great dependence between them. The leaders owned their separate pieces, but no one owned the whole thing. I told my team that this was a lot like a three-legged race. None of us will be successful if the three project owners were going to approach it separately.
>
> I noticed that each leader was getting bruised feelings. In fact the three leaders were bruising each other. I called them in individually, and my mental picture was, "Bring them in, kiss it, smooth their feathers, and make it better." Once they were sufficiently soothed, I pulled them together as a team. I treated them like teenage siblings. I suggested they stop the brawling. They were real uncomfortable, but because they trusted me, they hung in there. I was able to break the ice with humor and they eventually started to talk to each other.

CONNECTING ON THEIR TERMS

To coach someone, you have to connect with them on their terms. Your employees might find certain environments intimidating or distracting. They want analogies and anecdotes that are pertinent to their interests. They want to feel that you've met them halfway and that you've thought about the issues that are of concern to them rather than just what is of concern to you. When you identify and respond to their hot buttons, they become much more coachable. They look at you as someone who might know what she's talking about.

These work behaviors flow naturally from the ways that moms connect with their adolescents. Pam Murray said she always made sure she had one-on-one time with both of her children. She would go to breakfast with her oldest son, Christopher, every Saturday morning. When he became a teenager, she revised her schedule to be with him when he was most talkative:

> I noticed that when he'd get home in the evening after a long day at school and baseball practice, that I couldn't get a word out of him. Because he was a morning person, I switched my schedule around and had breakfast with him every morning. Those mornings were important. We'd be able to talk about upcoming decisions. I would be able to ask my probing questions, and we'd talk through consequences.

Cynthia Augustine, a senior vice president and president of the New York Times Company, said:

> Sometimes I just need to be around enough in order to hear what their issues are. I can't just schedule time and expect them to tell me what their problems are. I need to be around my employees as well as my teenage daughter when they are ready to talk. I need to be available on their time . . . I have to create relationships with people and earn their trust before they will share problems with me.
>
> Also, if my daughter is moody or snaps at me, which is part of the teenage experience, rather than react to her moodiness, I try to understand what's triggering her mood. Perhaps she had

a bad day at school or just got an instant message that upset her. This approach has helped me coach her and the people in the office. I find myself reacting to my employees' problems more positively. I consider what could have gone wrong with their day and maintain empathy rather than judging their moodiness.

In bigger households, it wasn't always easy finding the type of alone time that enables rich conversation. Several moms commented that they volunteered to teach their children how to drive. Most state laws require a significant number of driving hours with an adult to get a drivers license. Mothers not only were able to coach their child's driving skills, but they were able to get 50 or so hours of alone time with them when many things on their teens' minds surfaced. Carol Evans was one such mom. She also shared that teenagers don't find the same enjoyment with their parents as they used to, so she had to get creative to ensure enough connect time. She was able to get a movie club going with her daughter and her friends. Not only did this create time to connect, but the movies created the context for provocative discussions.

As a mother concerned about connecting with her kids, Trudy Sullivan, an executive vice president at Liz Claiborne, Inc., has worked hard to understand teenage culture. She said:

> I pay attention to their TV shows, their music, and their styles. Not only does it help me understand where they are coming from, it's been a huge help in my work in the fashion business. My daughters are cool and totally get the latest in fashion. One of them is a trend spotter for *Teen People* magazine. They influence me a lot and keep me up to date on what's trending. Customers and employees are like your children. If you connect with them when it's conducive for them, versus when it's timely for you, they will be more likely to be open.

Connecting isn't just a matter of figuring out other people's interests and concerns but making an effort to communicate with them in language they understand. During the teen years, moms must make this effort if they want to get through to their kids. Adolescents naturally rebel against their parents, yet they also depend on them to be good listeners and advice givers (even if they would never admit this need). For a mother to fulfill this coaching role, she must figure out what communication approach works best with her child. Sometimes this means listening when she wants to deliver a lecture, and other times it requires figuring out what is really on her child's mind and addressing it rather than other, "easier" issues.

Moms become especially skillful at speaking in their teenager's language when disagreements occur. While dads usually raise their voices, say "This is the way it is. End of discussion," and leave the room, moms seek understanding and figure out what will keep conversations alive and constructive. Moms also grasp that, once their teenagers have opened the door to communication, the door can close quickly, and they need to communicate clearly and nondefensively. Unlike many dads, moms don't let their egos or impatience get in the way of communication. Leslie Donovan, the senior vice president of sales and marketing for Targetbase, said, "I speak quickly and in sound bites. I used to leave people at work and my daughter behind. She needed the reasons and more explanation. I learned how to give people fuller content. I learned to pause and take the time to explain things."

Moms become conscious not only of what they're saying to their teens but how their body language and facial expressions communicate their real feelings. Teens are very astute at picking up on nonverbal language and sense when they're being manipulated or when adults aren't really listening and understanding. Ava Youngblood's son said to her, "Mom, it's not what you say, it's how you say it."

Ava pointed out, "This was coming from my feeling child. He hears the emotions in things." Ava described herself as a "thinker" rather than a "feeler." Her other son is also a thinker. She said:

> One time, the boys came and asked me for something. And I went through the reasons why not with some emotion. But I ended up by saying that I would go along with their decision. If you guys want this, go ahead. My thinking child assumed that, because I said he could do it, they would do it. My feeling child heard my emotion and assumed that, because I didn't really want them to do it, they wouldn't. At Amoco, I found that my group members took away different messages. Because I am a thinker, I need to be sensitive to how the feeling types hear me.

US Airways Senior Vice President Anita Beier said:

> My daughter is a feeling type and is stuck in a family of thinkers and judgers, and we can easily hurt her feelings. I have to keep in mind that she is going to be sensitive. I learned to stop being honest and blunt to avoid upsetting her. My experience at this definitely carried over to work. One of my former project managers was also a feeling type. She said to me, "Of all the bosses I ever had, you are the first one that realizes that I am not like all of you."

A good exercise here involves imagining how you might communicate with your direct reports if they were your teenage children. Try putting yourself in the following scenario:

> You arrive at work to discover that a key member of your team has failed to complete a project by the deadline you both agreed to. This is unlike her; she is usually good at delivering when she says she will deliver. This is not an issue you can ignore, however, because you were chewed out by your boss—you had promised her you'd have the project report on her desk on a certain day, and you missed his deadline because of your subordinate's tardiness. You call the direct report into your office and ask her to explain what happened. She offers a number of excuses—she couldn't get her hands on a critical research paper, she was busy with another project—but the excuses don't really add up. You suspect that she's not telling you the real reason for missing the deadline.

The following provides two ways of handling this situation. One represents how some bosses would generally deal with it, and the other imagines how a boss would deal with it if the direct report were their son or daughter. Think about each response and determine which one is closer to the way you might respond.

The boss/direct report response. You find the excuses inadequate and chastise your direct report about her behavior, telling her that it's unacceptable and that you don't expect it to recur. You spend most of the meeting recounting how you were chewed out by your boss and focusing on the potential negative fallout of her action. You exact a promise from her that she won't repeat this mistake, and the meeting ends.

The boss/child direct report response. Your direct report enters your office, and you again ask her to explain why she messed up. She offers the same two excuses as before, but again the answers don't add up. There's something in her tone that suggests she's not being completely honest about her answers. Though you're furious at her, you hold your tongue and instead tell her that you think she might be underestimating the root cause of the delay. You share that it's important for both of you to really understand what happened, so that it doesn't happen again. You think something else is going on that she's withholding.

Though she says, "It's not that big of a deal," you disagree and explain the problems for her and everyone on the project of not meeting schedules. You acknowledge her positive intent about doing it on time, but you also reinforce that, unless something in her behavior changes, this will probably happen again. You give her options for getting to the root cause. She can explore them with you if she's comfortable, or she can talk to a coach that is not in a threatening position.

If she opts for a coach, you help her make the connection and ask her to let you know what she discovers. If she is willing to explore possibilities with you, you start with something nonjudgmental, such as, "Here are the top ten reasons why people in this department miss their deadlines. Do you think any apply to you?" In either case, you end the meeting by acknowledging her value and your commitment to help her succeed.

ESTABLISHING RULES OF ENGAGEMENT

One of the most challenging tasks for moms is setting and enforcing rules for adolescents. One of the most challenging tasks for leaders is setting and enforcing boundaries for subordinates. This is almost as much an art as it is a skill. You need to have a sense about when you're being too strict and when you're providing too much freedom. If you've never had to find the ideal middle ground with teenagers, you're likely to give your people too much independence and too little guidance; or you may go in the other direction and give them so little freedom to decide and use their initiative, they feel powerless. Adolescents have taught executive moms how to manage the paradox between independence and limits, and the skill has paid off in the workplace.

According to Deanna Oppenheimer of Washington Mutual's consumer group, "Children help you learn how to negotiate. You must set parameters and establish boundaries but allow them freedom within a box. They must know they absolutely cannot cross over. It's also important to have a united front as parents, and I make sure I line up with their dad." She went on to say, "This holds true with my business franchises. My employees have clearly defined roles and responsibilities, but I give them total flexibility on how to mange their departments."

Mirian Graddick-Weir of AT&T said:

> You have to let children know where the boundaries are. Kids want and need boundaries. As painful as it is, you have to hold them to these boundaries. Holding firm with my children while staying compassionate helped me at work. I learned how to be tough with people who are not delivering, yet do it in a compassionate way. It's really how you do these things, whether it's disciplining kids or firing people.

Trudy Sullivan, an executive vice president at Liz Claiborne, Inc., discovered that, as part of the rules of engagement, some issues are nonnegotiable while others are open to negotiation. "We have strict curfews, and one of my absolute rules is they have to have a charged cell phone at all times. There's a tremendous amount of talk about the rules. It's a constant negotiation and redrawing of boundaries. We have trials when we change the rules like extending their curfew, and we have lots of touch points."

One mom shared that her daughter taught her to stand firm. Her daughter was getting into serious trouble, like sneaking out with the car before she had her license and driving on a dangerous road near their home. This mom said, "I learned to stand down my peers at the same time [as I was dealing with my daughter's behavior]. Our CFO was doing something unethical. I laid out my rules of engagement like I did with my daughter."

Bridgette Heller of Chung's Gourmet Foods said, "It's a big balancing act to preserve your child's spirit, promote independence, and at the same time ensure she understands your nonnegotiable expectations. One of my greatest challenges at work was allowing other people the opportunity to express and contribute and be great, but getting them to fall in line with the plan. Parenting helped me learn how to balance the two."

Ruth Harenchar of Bowne & Company said:

> I took the philosophy with my teenagers that there's a playing field. I would draw a line in the sand. I would let them know that to the right of the line is unacceptable behavior. However, I actually would draw the line a ways before it was unacceptable. I did this because I expected them to cross the line and I wanted to keep them safe. If I saw them cross the line, without their knowing, I would ignore it. If they caught me catching them, I would have to inflict consequences, or they would learn that my lines were not the real lines.

At work, I will tell my teams what my real demand is. Sometimes the teams cross my line. I empower them to do it, because they are still within the limit I really hold. I make sure that if something at work or home doesn't work out, that nothing or no one is seriously hurt, because I only take this approach in safe environments.

Kathryn Mlsna, chief counsel at McDonald's, said:

> People are looking for leadership. They might not always agree with you. I learned at home that kids don't always agree with you, but they appreciate leadership and having goals. Here's the plan, here are the rules, let's do it. My kids gave me practice at saying no. Saying no is an important thing, but there are times we have to say no and explain the rationale. There are times when you cannot compromise.

BECOMING A POSITIVE INFLUENCER

The best leaders today recognize that they can no longer issue orders and expect to be obeyed. Even if they are obeyed, they grasp that their instructions won't always be carried out with energy and inspiration. They have learned, therefore, to be more creative with how they interact with their people. If they want something done, they are much more innovative than leaders of the past in motivating, providing resources, and establishing an environment that yields results. While many executives understand intellectually that command-and-control no longer is the best management style, they sometimes have difficulty integrating this understanding into their behaviors. Motherhood, fortunately, helps facilitate this integration.

Moms quickly learn that they can't order around their teenagers and expect unquestioning obedience. They discover that a better alternative is to be firm on a few key issues and flexible on less important matters. This discovery, however, may not come easily, if their own upbringing emphasized unquestioning obedience. One of the mothers of an executive mom I interviewed told me, "We didn't give our kids options. Here's dinner. The vegetable is green beans. You will eat the green beans."

Times, though, have changed, and parents no longer have as much control over their teenagers, a concern given the landmines out there—a wide range of available drugs, sexually transmitted diseases, eating disorders, and so on. For this reason, parents focus on coaching their kids to make good, sound decisions on their own. As coaches, they try to give their children the knowledge and confidence to make the right choice at the moment and create options for themselves when traditional paths don't work.

It's easy to know when teens, coworkers, or customers are headed down a path that is not acceptable to you. It's much harder to redirect them, because they don't always respond well to your directives. As an influencer, though, you can help them discover an acceptable path, one that incorporates your ideas but also takes their own needs and goals into consideration.

When I was at Motorola, I was involved with the 3GPP Global Standards Body, a group that included dozens of the world's biggest wireless telecom players. Three factions established different positions regarding the next-generation international, wireless telecom standard: NTT Docomo, the world's biggest operator from Japan; Ericsson, the world's biggest equipment vendor from Europe; and Qualcomm, the biggest technology vendor from the United States. For two years, Motorola tried and failed to convince them to establish a common standard.

Around this time, I had just facilitated a process that caused the warring tribes at Motorola to converge on their third-generation strategy, but it depended upon the existence of a common world standard. So I was sent on a mission to obtain convergence and obtain it fast. By the time I finished my second meeting, 3GPP settled on the first several layers of a common worldwide architecture.

It was very much like using influence to settle an argument with my children. This global body represented some of the world's most powerful companies, and they knew that going down separate paths would hurt the world markets, the consumers, and ultimately their businesses. Unfortunately, the companies involved tried to use power to bully their way to a solution, and after several years of convening for a couple of days every other month, few companies were even talking to each other.

I proposed the creation of a neutral task force and convened the most powerful of the neutral vendors, like Nokia and Nortel, to assess the sacred cows. I helped forge a proposal that took these sacred cows into consideration and gently nudged everyone in a common direction. The standards body accepted the proposal. Why? Perhaps it took the same skill sets I used day in and day out to settle arguments with my two teenage sons.

Moms learned to be positive influencers in many different ways. Ava Youngblood of Youngblood Executive Search said that her son, Lee, turned 13 and announced one Sunday that he didn't want to go to church.

> I told him that going to church has always been something we have done as a family and that I would hope we would continue to do it as a family and I really wanted him to go. But I said I would accept his decision—whether it's to go or not to go. He decided to go. At that point, it was his decision. It was about his expressing his independence. As a parent, you want your children to make their own decisions while they are still at home with you. At home, they can test out their decisions in an environment where they can experience consequences.

According to Ruth Harenchar:

> With kids, so long as I didn't say it absolutely positively has to be this way, we usually would find a compromise. If we got to

an impasse, I would try to explain my concern and share that it is based upon my experience. I would offer openness to alternatives. This approach works well with teens and at work, because it leaves people with the sense that they are empowered.

My teenagers have really helped me learn to put myself in someone else's position. Doing so helps me figure out options as well as ways to get my children to respond. In my last disagreement with my son, I spent a few minutes quietly in the kitchen to understand his view of a situation. I kept asking myself, "What can I possibly say that will influence him to take a different path?" When I figured it out, I went to talk to him. Because I was sensitive, he didn't get super defensive. He saw my concern. He came up with an alternate suggestion that I found acceptable.

At work, I recently received an e-mail. I didn't like the approach and needed to step in. I returned with an e-mail that clearly would get my associate's attention, yet I also made it sensitive. I simply stated that something different needed to happen. I opened the door for an alternative, and he came back with one that was okay with me. I got the change I thought was required, and he feels ownership.

Pam Murray at Marriott explained how her teenager taught her how to let go of control and coach with confidence, saying:

> I changed my coaching style. I now give people more rope. I don't make decisions that I don't have to make. Younger leaders need to get experience making decisions. They won't get great at it without practice. So I give them options. I make sure we agree on the goal and let them decide the path they want to take to get there. I hear them out and listen to their recommendations. Sometimes I don't agree, and I will tell them that I would do it differently, but because they have thought it through, I'll go with their approach. I'll monitor things and step in if there are big mistakes, but most often their choices work out just fine.
>
> Like with my son, I constantly reinforce how important getting off to a good start is, and I pay attention to interim milestones. If they get off track, I'll help them get back on. That's part of the teaching.

BEING INDIRECTLY EFFECTIVE

Many powerful leaders tend to attack issues head-on, charging problems the way that bulls charge red capes. Some get pushy and yell and demand their way toward solutions, while others simply take over by micromanaging. Sometimes, however, the problem is like the red cape; it's tough to attack in a normal way, because the person or team you need to influence is not receptive to you at the moment. For example, a customer can be unhappy with your product quality, but contacting them might make the situation worse. Or, in some cultures with very formal communication protocols, directly contacting someone other than your designated counterpart, or someone who is already debriefed on the issue, will not be productive.

The strongest leaders aren't always the most aggressive or direct. They learn how to use their power selectively, and sometimes an indirect method yields better results, especially when coaching is involved. Some dads deal with their adolescents' rebelliousness through bullying and controlling behaviors, or they steer clear of their kids as much as possible. Moms, on the other hand, are so compelled to help their kids, that when they can't achieve receptivity directly, they're willing to explore alternatives to their usual way of connecting. They sense that their teenagers want help, but because of their struggle for independence, they don't want it from them.

As Anita Beier put it, "They cry out but don't reach out." The high-achieving mothers who I interviewed were not inclined to lie down and play dead. Instead, they became creative and coached indirectly. To reach their children, they worked through friends, teachers, coaches, other parents, therapists, and even tools like the Myers-Briggs Type Indicator, a psychological assesssment. (Pearman, 1)

One of the mothers told the following story in which Myers-Briggs played a role:

> I remember when my daughter started driving. I lost control, and things became very challenging. I lost the ability to even understand how she was thinking about things. She didn't appear to think before she acted. Offering my own opinions on what she should or should not be doing just created power struggles and defensiveness. I got through to her by using Myers-

Briggs. She took the test, and it showed she was a max extrovert and a max feeling type. Myers-Briggs points out that extreme extroverts act before they think and extreme feeling types act on feelings. She received this input as factual and not judgmental. It got through to her that she wasn't anticipating her choices enough.

One night, she came home from a party, and her pride showed through. She said, "Hey mom, tonight when someone offered me a drink, instead of having it and then thinking about it, I thought it about it first. And decided I didn't want it. I'm thinking while I'm doing."

Interestingly, this mom began using more nonjudgmental feedback tools at work after this experience. Although this mother recognized that she brought Myers-Briggs home from work, she believed that applying it at home with someone she cared so much about motivated her to use such tools in the office. Though she still used her traditional, direct methods when necessary, she realized that indirect methods were more effective with certain people in certain situations.

Because we know our children so well, we can use our knowledge to develop highly effective, indirect methods of influencing them to do what's best. For instance, one executive mom noted that she is well aware of her 15-year-old son's rigidity, because it mirrors her own. At first, she tried to coach him to be more flexible, but in her words, "He blew me off." Then she switched tactics.

I reward him with praise when he exhibits flexibility, and I try to encourage him to be involved in activities where there will be more give and take on his part. He doesn't necessarily connect the dots, that the activity I am recommending involves training him in flexibility. If he did connect the dots, he'd definitely blow off the activity, too. Time will tell with him. I know for myself that one of the reasons I have been successful is that I have trained myself to be less rigid.

Backing off the direct approach and learning indirect methods is a critical leadership skill for very senior executive women. Egos at the top of corporations do not like "pushy" women. Many high-achieving women have trouble backing off when they think something is important and they know they are right. With teens, they learn quickly and painfully that, if they push too hard, their child will rebel and purposely head in the opposite direction. That is a very scary proposition at times—scary enough that they are willing to take another, less in-your-face approach. Over time, they discover that indirect tactics can be as effective as direct ones.

DO YOU INFLUENCE PEOPLE WITH A MOM'S TOUCH?

Executives can encounter a great deal of rebelliousness, moodiness, skepticism, and resistance at work. Rather than rely on traditional managerial approaches, moms have the benefit of dealing with these very same qualities in their teenagers. They have learned that sometimes they must fight their aggressive, hard-nosed instincts and consider alternatives.

To help you recognize these alternatives, I've listed ten typical situations that senior executives face. I'd like you to determine if you have used any or all of the five traits (A through E) discussed in this chapter to deal with them or if you've used any of the five traits (F through J) associated with driven, demanding leaders. Place the letter of the trait or traits used beneath each situation.

Mom Traits

A. Earning receptivity
B. Connecting on their terms
C. Establishing rules of engagement
D. Becoming a positive influencer
E. Being indirectly effective

Command and Control

F. Demanding compliance
G. Dictating terms
H. Relying on rigid rules of conduct
I. Threatening with consequences
J. Taking direct action

1. An employee three levels down glared at you throughout your last skip-level meeting.
2. Members of your staff are pointing fingers at each other for losing a recent account.

3. Your CFO has found irregularities in one of your staff's expenditures.
4. Your administrative assistant has taken an extraordinary number of sick days.
5. Someone in your organization, who has historically battled with you, is missing their deliveries.
6. Your boss is asking for constant status updates on a crisis that you are managing.
7. An irate shareholder is planning to create a stink at your next shareholders' meeting.
8. Your customer will not take your calls.
9. A job has opened up that you are interested in, but the hiring manager doesn't want someone with your background.
10. During you boss's staff meeting, your peers ignore your comments yet present your ideas as their own later on.

If you listed many of the F–J traits for these ten situations, think about how you might have achieved a better result if you employed the first set of traits, at least in certain instances. Ask yourself how people might have responded differently. Would they have become less defensive or fearful? Might they have had greater motivation to do as you requested? Would it have increased the odds that they really would have heard what you were saying and given it more credence?

Even the hardest-charging executive moms have found that their coaching improves when they have another "weapon" in their arsenal. Being a mom increases their range of responses to challenging people, whether they are independent-minded direct reports, bosses, customers, peers, or teenagers.

10

THE CHARACTER OF A LEADER

How Motherhood Brings Out the Best in People

With every little bit I give, the more I get!"

Deb Henretta, *President, Global Baby and Adult Care, Procter & Gamble*

Beyond all the age-specific learning that children provide, they facilitate character development. Over the course of 10 or 20 years, mothers grow and develop as people. As part of the "job," moms put their kids' needs before their own, gain confidence in their ability to handle unfamiliar and challenging tasks, and learn to "eat crow." Being a mom builds character in ways both large and small. From nursing a sick child back to health to chaperoning a third-grade trip to the zoo, motherhood tests the emotional depths and cognitive capabilities of women. As a result, they become wiser and more mature. They project the appearance of someone you would want to follow into battle or into a tough meeting with a customer.

Character has become an increasingly important leadership topic, especially in light of all the recent corporate scandals in which CEOs and other top executives have been accused of unethical behaviors. We need leaders who we can trust and who can restore our faith in organizations. More than ever, leaders must embody values that earn respect and build strong relationships.

In my informal surveys, managers refer to their own mothers as their best role model when it comes to ethics. Ajilon Office, a specialty staffing and recruiting services firm in New Jersey, surveyed over 600 professionals and found that 80 percent rated their mother's ethics stronger than or about the same as those of their company's chief executive. (*New York Times,* 1)

Motherhood doesn't transform immoral or even amoral individuals into saints, but it strengthens the character of good women. It deepens them. It broadens their view. It makes them more human. Though it's impossible to capture all the different ways motherhood builds character, let's look at how it strengthens moms in five areas:

1. Selflessness
2. Confidence
3. Humility
4. Groundedness
5. Honesty

SELFLESSNESS

For a mother to be selfless when it comes to her children is human nature. While moms can be selfish and nonmoms can exhibit selfless behavior, the 50 women interviewed here became more selfless after becoming moms.

Rita Kahle, an executive vice president at Ace Hardware, said:

> Without my children, I would be a lot more selfish than I currently am. I didn't necessarily learn it all with my first son, either. I had my daughter ten years after my son, and it was like a second wake-up call. As a result, I have become much more team oriented, and I more naturally put other people's needs ahead of mine.

Motherhood brings out the natural selflessness in people. It is not a conscious decision, but rather something that emerges from who they are as moms. Executives are used to controlling their reactions, but this selflessness is not something they control. The urge to serve and nurture is biological, and it spills over to all aspects of a mother's life. The executive moms I talked to agreed that they didn't plan to be more giving and self-sacrificing. Instead, it just happened.

Marilyn Seymann, president and CEO of M One, described it like this: "Having children is a huge, life-changing event, and it doesn't go away. It is the single most transforming thing in my life. My children are the joy of my life and the greatest source of love in my life. The more love you have in your heart, the more you have to give away. It rolls over into everything you do."

A mother's devotion to her children is usually intense and everlasting. She never stops giving, no matter what age her child becomes. Her generosity is a demonstration of her love and becomes an essential part of who she is. When my mother wants to show her love to her children or anyone else, she throws a party and cooks. She's in her 80s and still throws a dozen parties a year. She puts forth an amazing effort and acts like it's no big deal. She doesn't want anyone fussing over her. She feels good if we all enjoy each other's company and eat a lot. So we do.

Cynthia Augustine of The New York Times said, "My children have made me a much more complete and involved person. Devoting yourself to others makes you a deeper, better person. The give and take is huge. So is not needing to be in the center of it. To a great extent, it feels good to give and be helpful."

Motherhood opens the door to give selflessly in countless ways. Moms end up devoting most of their personal time and energy to their children, and giving to and serving others become routine behaviors, not only at home but at work. I don't want to make it sound as if maternal leaders are Mother Teresas. They do, however, become more generous of their time and emotional energy in the workplace.

Before having kids, some of the women I interviewed were so driven to succeed in the corporate world, they lacked the time or impulse to give to others. After becoming mothers, they retained their drive to succeed but not to the exclusion of meeting other people's needs, both at work and in the community. Ironically, their increased selflessness made them more successful. The most successful leaders today give before receiving. To create alliances, cement relationships, and inspire loyalty and increased effort, leaders must demonstrate that they are not just thinking of themselves. In today's environment, no one wants to partner with or work for a "taker." Selfless leaders don't just give their own time and effort, but they find ways to involve their companies in good works. They support and sponsor worthwhile causes, helping their organizations solidify relationships with various communities.

None of this is premeditated or calculating. These women strongly believe that giving unselfishly and wholeheartedly to others makes you a better person. While they may have harbored this belief before they had children, becoming a mother helped them translate it into action. Many of the women profiled here have expanded their philanthropic activities into different areas of their lives.

Deb Henretta, president of baby and adult care products for Procter and Gamble, for instance, has been very involved in supporting the children's hospital that took care of her daughter when she was sick. She said:

> Without children, the depth and breadth of what I am involved in at work or in life would have been much more narrow. Having children forced me to get involved in many activities. I feel much more connected to the community and have taken on greater responsibility in the community. I feel a much greater sense for the need to give back. With every little bit I give, the more I get.

You might find the following experiment helpful to assess the selflessness of leaders in your organization.

Start by writing down the names of ten people with whom you work who are at least on the managerial level—try to achieve a mix of men and women, moms and nonmoms.

Next, review the following list of selfless work traits and behaviors:

- Involves organization in charitable activities.
- Makes an effort to understand and support employee concerns (e.g., working conditions, discrimination policies, etc.) at all levels of the company.
- Is willing to take time out of busy day to listen to others complain, vent, or present problems.
- Regularly takes actions on behalf of others in the company without any political agenda or personal gain.
- Is willing to give others the credit when credit is due.

Place a checkmark next to the name of the person or people who best exemplify these traits. Though there certainly will be some exceptions, you'll probably find that the moms have more checkmarks than most.

CONFIDENCE

Executive moms receive great amounts of love and appreciation because of their selflessness. As Cynthia said, "The give and take is huge," and as Deb said, "Every little I give, the more I get." Being loved and appreciated builds confidence. Deb and many of the other women explained that their confidence in their work capabilities increased after they became moms. Self-doubt and uncertainty are greatly diminished in the wake of all that love. Executive moms go to work knowing that, no matter what goes wrong that day, their children's love and respect is something they can rely on. With this strong, positive sense of self, they can face all manner of obstacles and challenges without flinching.

Elizabeth Buse, executive vice president of product development and management at Visa, said:

> There's tremendous self-confidence that stems from having the three kids who you are raising adore you. I have been in meetings getting absolutely eviscerated, and my mind goes to the greeting I am going to get when I walk in the door that evening. My kids are nice, well adjusted, and loving. Knowing that you are raising children successfully is a so much bigger deal than achieving anything at work. So it makes the issues at work appear less risky, and I find I am willing to take more risks.

Now that my sons are past the breakaway stage, they are big huggers again. When they hug me, I think that I must be doing something right if these two wonderful young men love me so much. My son Michael is incredibly perceptive. He can tell when someone walks in the door if something is wrong. If all is well, he might choose to be a royal pain in the butt and announce that he needs his baseball uniform washed or that he's starving. If he perceives a heavy walk or a crinkled brow, though, his love and concern kick into high gear. He won't let me by until he knows what's dragging me down, and he seems to know just what to do to bring a smile to my face. Not only does this interaction diminish my work stress, but when I return to work, I feel confident about my place in the world. I know the relationship with my sons will endure no matter what else at work changes.

Throughout my interviews, many of the mothers expressed higher levels of confidence, so I asked a few of them to describe how confidence might manifest itself in an executive. Elizabeth painted a portrait that describes many of the executive moms perfectly: "If I have a confident boss, I know that boss will stick up for me and the business. They won't use people as human shields. Confident leaders are the ones who ask for forgiveness, not permission. They are more decisive and take risks. They are more innovative."

Gail Evans of Working Mother Media attributed this confidence not only to the love children give their mothers but also to the fact that these mothers are mastering an incredible juggling act between work and home. She said, "Once you are a mother, everything is possible, and you are not afraid to get your hands dirty. I had to learn how to be a mom in Moscow, without a doctor, baby food, or disposable diapers. I discovered the possibilities rather than the impossibilities, and it gave me confidence, and I became more powerful."

Many executive mothers shared the sentiment that confidence flows from successfully balancing the roles of executive and mother. They have gone against the grain and beaten the odds. Twenty or so years ago, when some of them started having babies, society was skeptical that they could be good mothers while holding down high-powered jobs with travel and long hours. Over time, they saw their children and careers flourish, and they realized that they made the right decision. Anita Beier of US Airways said:

> I love my family, my job, and my lifestyle. I know I wouldn't be happy if I backed off of either my work or my family. A few years ago, we were potentially going to be in a merger. I said to my son, "If the merger goes through, I might stay home and take care of you." He looked at me with horror. He liked his independence, and he knew if I stayed home, the house would have to be perfect. Knowing I am doing what is right for him and me gives me even greater confidence.

Leaders need all the confidence they can get, especially in volatile, uncertain times. Highly successful executive moms are remarkably able to forget about the skeptics who told them they couldn't juggle career and motherhood, overcome any lingering guilt because they aren't staying at home, and become more secure.

Fran Keeth, the president and CEO of Shell Chemical, described how her son built up her confidence from the time he was a little boy:

> My son Russell loved to help me get through the challenges at work. He was a base for me. I could talk to him even when he was little. It could be about work or about the world. He always wanted to hear my voice. It didn't matter what we talked about. My husband would respond to my conversations with practical advice. Russell would just sit in my lap and listen and pat my hair and tell me everything was okay.
>
> One time when I was doing law school at night, I got a C in a class. I had rarely gotten a B and had never gotten a C. I was beating myself up for incorrectly answering one of the final exam questions. Russell said to me, "Mom, to get into law school you have to be smart, right? So you are an average smart student. Isn't that good enough?" "Yep it is," I said.

I need to draw a distinction here between confident and competent. Many top executives believe that they are highly competent at what they do, but they often mask their lack of self-confidence with bluster and blarney. No doubt you've worked with people who were extremely talented and skilled, but they lacked the character of a leader. Perhaps they were overly boastful or overly quiet to cover up their self-doubts. Perhaps they expressed these self-doubts so often that it made others nervous. Perhaps they didn't inspire loyalty or effort in others; they appeared distracted or uncertain much of the time.

The self-confidence that motherhood confers diminishes these negative attitudes and behaviors. Moms usually can rise above the inner doubts and turmoil that plague others, gaining strength from being good mothers to their children. The combination of confidence with competence creates a dynamic leader.

Sometimes, though, we confuse competence with confidence, as the following story illustrates. I worked with Caryn, a very talented and powerful woman executive who appeared to be very confident. Caryn's CEO disagreed. He told me, "She's the most talented executive on my staff but also the most insecure. She lacks confidence and could easily self-destruct." My first reaction was to defend Caryn, because on the surface, she projected confidence, but the more I thought about the CEO's analysis, the more I realized he was right. Caryn always needed to be in the spotlight and was overly focused on getting others to pat her on the back. She strongly supported people who worked for her agenda, but she was not supportive of people who she perceived as competitors. She picked yes-people for her staff and was not receptive to pushback or feedback. Finally, Caryn always seemed to be in a power struggle with someone and rarely got behind other people's initiatives.

When the CEO confronted Caryn and told her she lacked confidence, she didn't accept the feedback. In fact, Caryn had difficulty accepting any negative feedback, because she had a neurotic fear of being wrong. As a result, she was unable to change and continued to fall short of her potential as a manager and as a leader. It's not surprising that Caryn was not a mother. She was devoted to her career, and it had helped her achieve a high level of competence. What this devotion hadn't helped her achieve, though, was true confidence and character.

HUMILITY

They may seem like incompatible traits, but confidence and humility go hand in hand. The former provides leaders with the ability to make tough decisions and inspire others, while the latter acts as a governor on this confidence, preventing it from turning into hubris. As Rick Warren wrote in his bestseller, *The Purpose-Driven Life*, "Humility is not thinking less of yourself; it is thinking of yourself less." (Warren, 148)

Mothers epitomize the concept of "thinking of yourself less." Helping others is deeply satisfying to them. Yet mothers aren't the only ones who come to this recognition. Jeff Caliguire wrote the following about humility in his book, *Leadership Secrets of St. Paul:* "It was a move from, 'It's all about me,' to a humble desire to make a difference for others. For some of us, this journey is a gradual and gentle process. With time, we recognize the importance of investing our lives in what will truly outlast us. We get the picture that it really is better to serve than to be served or to give than to receive. " (Calguire, 21)

Besides the benefits of being unselfish, humility is also useful for leaders who think that all is well when all is not well. Many leaders convince themselves that they can achieve anything or juggle innumerable balls if they put their minds to it, and while this trait is admirable, it can also be self-delusional. Just as motherhood helps women gain great confidence in who they are as people, it also offers ample evidence that they are fallible and vulnerable. Even the strongest, most successful women are knocked off their horse a time or two by motherhood.

I found it fascinating that many of the women I talked to were neither defensive about nor reluctant to admit that they had not always made the best decisions. Presenting a strong, invulnerable image to the world is a reflex of many leaders, and while this posture has its advantages, it also can result in an off-putting arrogance. These women, on the other hand, were quick to share vivid reflections of mistakes they made with their kids and the corresponding leadership lessons. Whether it was taking an eye off them for a split second and seeing them headed for the street or forgetting to pick them up from school, their mistakes were on the tips of their tongues. Joan Gulley, the CEO of PNC Advisors, said, "Parenthood taught me how to live with my own mistakes. The stakes are so high with kids. You want to kill yourself when you make a mistake as a parent. Learning how to give yourself forgiveness is a huge step toward happiness. It is a turning point."

When Joan's son was in the second grade, she discovered that he was struggling mightily in school and was not receiving the necessary time and support from her. She said:

> I felt so guilty and awful. How could I not have seen this coming? When you have something like that happen and learn that you have the ability to really blow it, there's a lot of learning about yourself. Owning fallibility was much more powerful than feeling guilty. And owning our screw-ups is a great thing for our children and our employees to see. When my son saw me take ownership, it made a difference for him. It was a big deal. Having the space for being less than perfect is very important for leaders.

Acknowledging humbling mistakes gives both moms and leaders the ability to focus on new ways of acting. No doubt you've observed a senior executive (or perhaps you've done this yourself) who stubbornly sticks with a strategy or other course of action for too long; this individual just can't admit that something went off course. Humility increases a leader's capacity to admit that her great idea didn't pan out and shift to a more effective approach.

Donna Lee of BellSouth, for instance, noted that as a mom, she realized that she was spending less time with her second child than she did with her first one, and her absence contributed to her five-year-old daughter's reading problems:

> I used to read with her brother every night, but because I traveled so much, I didn't do it with her. . . . So I changed companies and moved to a headquarters location. I made sure we read together every single night, and she's now as ferocious a reader as her brother. Moms are needed as part of the development process, and I needed to adjust my priorities.

Another executive mom acquired greater humility when she discovered that her daughter was anorexic:

> That was the toughest time of my life. I thought that the life that I enjoyed was over. If your child gets sick to the point that they could die, your life perspective completely changes. It shouldn't have taken so much for me to receive such a wake-up call. The situation got me to step back and reassess my whole life. Despite all of my great strides to let go, I was too controlling.

When you have a troubled child, ego doesn't matter anymore. You learn to accept your mistake and, for your child's sake, focus on solutions. Fran Keeth said:

> It really makes you humble when you hurt your child by some action you have taken. For me, it was moving my son to London his senior year in high school. I had turned down an international assignment three times already and was really feeling the pressure to accept this time around. I didn't think I could get another job easily, so we moved to London. When it didn't work out well for him and I realized I needed to get back to the States, I left Shell. In no time at all, I was offered a job with Mobil Corporation back in the States. And eventually, Shell hired me back. Realizing that I didn't have to disrupt his senior year in high school was more painful than any mistake I could make in the office. It has changed me as a leader. I know I don't always have all the answers. I create a support system at work to help me make

important decisions and keep an eye on key issues that have high stakes.

Not only did the executive moms I talked to have to face their fallibility, but they had to face their vulnerability as well. Motherhood spotlighted not only their external mistakes but their internal weaknesses. In a number of cases, they found out that they were more vulnerable than they had assumed they were. Marriott's Pam Murray's daughter, Stephanie, was born with Down Syndrome and a number of life-threatening problems. Pam said:

> We had to make life support decisions, and she was in neonatal care for a long time. Up until that point in my life, I thought I was in control of my destiny. With enough planning and perseverance, I thought I could do anything. It hit me hard. The depth of the pain and anguish was nothing that I had ever considered possible. At first, I overanalyzed the situation and questioned a lot. But then I learned to accept some things, especially that I was vulnerable. The people who worked for me before and after tell me I have changed. My intensity and passion is still there, but I channel it better. With some of my controlling behaviors, I know I wouldn't be where I am today at work if I had not made changes.

Sophie Vandebroek, who leads Xerox's engineering center, discovered her vulnerability when her husband unexpectedly died; she became a single parent of three little children. Though she may have felt vulnerable even if she had no children when her husband died, it's likely that the overwhelming responsibility of caring for three small kids on her own was crucial to her recognition of how vulnerable she really was. Sophie and her husband had immigrated to this country and had not built a support system. She not only learned that she was vulnerable, but she realized that admitting her vulnerability at work was powerful. She said:

> When my husband died, I realized that no matter what I had today, it could be gone tomorrow. I learned that we were so focused on work and our three young children, that we did not establish strong friendships in this country. I learned that I had

to pay more attention to relationships. One day, I realized that if I start sharing my feelings and some of my struggles with my team, people will respond in kind. Not only did this help me make more personal connections, but it helped my coworkers realize they were important to me. It was powerful.

GROUNDED

This trait is perhaps less tangible than the other three but no less important. In a very real way, it contributes to an individual's character and leadership ability. *Grounded* means being down to earth; it conveys solidity and rootedness. People who are grounded tend not to let praise go to their heads or fads sway them. As a result, colleagues, bosses, and subordinates depend on them and trust them. When I ask people to describe a leader who they thought was grounded, they described someone who had high integrity, was authentic, and was comfortable with people at all levels of the organization. In a world of characters, they possessed character.

Children ground parents directly and indirectly. Directly, they require you to do jobs that bring you down to earth: washing their dirty laundry, cleaning out their lunchboxes, and helping them blow their noses. Indirectly, they remind you of what really matters and help you put things in perspective. Moms tend to be the ones kids run to with problems as well as dirty laundry; they also come to moms with tales of their triumphs. The tasks of motherhood, combined with the parental role, anchors women at home and in the workplace.

Elizabeth Buse said that being grounded manifests itself in many different ways at work, explaining:

> Mothers do a lot of cleaning and dirty work, which really brings [them] down to earth. They stop being afraid of being stereotyped. For example, executive mothers are willing to pitch in and do everything in the office, even if it appears secretarial. If a group is trying to pull a presentation together, they will jump in and make copies or edit view graphs because they are down to earth. They are used to doing whatever is needed to get the problem solved. This is a direct consequence of having children.

When work is the only thing, it distorts your perspective. It sounds ironic, but having something more important than work in your life grounds you as a leader. Patricia McKay, the CFO of Restoration Hardware, said:

> Without kids, I believe the serious nature of what happens at the office can darken your whole attitude. When I go home and one son wants his back scratched or another wants me to lie down with him and chat before bed, or my third wants to stay up and chat in the late-night hours, it brightens up my day. This has a positive influence on how I go back to work.
>
> The unconditional love you get from day one is so fulfilling. When my kids are asking me, "Mom, what should I do?" or telling me their aspirations about wanting to be an NBA basketball player and baring their souls, it makes me feel better about life in general. It's because I have these great sons who I love and who love me to death, that I have life in perspective. This makes me a very grounded leader.

In each and every discussion, these women made it absolutely clear that their family was the most important element of their lives. They were not only secure in saying this publicly but passionate about it. Such clear, wholesome priorities also keep these women grounded. Their willingness to be forthright on this sensitive topic (in the face of some skeptics who might speculate that they are not dedicated enough to the job) sheds light on another strength of mothers—honesty.

HONESTY

As we see with many corporations, when the going gets tough, leaders sometimes resort to secrecy and deception. Even some of the most assertive and outspoken leaders avoid giving bad news, providing difficult feedback, or addressing sensitive topics. Tough issues are often ignored or glossed over, and bad news is sugarcoated to keep analysts happy or to give employees a false sense of optimism. Despite all the new laws, senior leaders still downplay or obscure poor results and forecasts.

Positive spinning takes place internally as well as externally. Executives who are trustworthy and ethical in most respects still fall victim to the white-lie syndrome, twisting the truth into a pretzel to avoid negativity of any type. Poor performers, for instance, are often told that they are doing fine, when in fact management has rated them below expectations. The false sense of security that develops because of false performance evaluations robs teams of their motivation to improve. Most managers don't recognize that, if they really cared about their people, they'd tell them the truth about their performance, no matter how uncomfortable it makes them feel. As a result, good people never realize their potential or even lose their jobs.

Motherhood changes how executive women deal with bad news or tough issues. As moms, they become more empathetic, sensitive, and compassionate. Their deep commitment for the well-being of their co-workers allows them to share the good and bad news more freely. Their experiences with their children drive them to arm people with the information they need to succeed, not a false sense of security.

Jo Anne Miller, now with Nokia, was the first mother to become a supervisor at my Bell Laboratories location. She was the most "tell it like it is" leader I had ever come across. She was direct, sincere, and totally open. You always knew where she was coming from, and you always knew where you stood with her. She often used humor and anecdotes from raising her kids to deliver bad news, which helped you process tough messages and gave you a feeling that she really cared about you.

Children give their mothers plenty of practice at being frank. Moms quickly find that beating around the bush is ineffective and confusing. Children are astute enough to see through false flattery and white lies, as Marilyn Seymann discovered. Her son told her that he was disappointed his dad wasn't coming to his guitar recital. When Marilyn assured him that she would be there, he said, "But how will I know how I played?"

In my own case, I had a tendency to exaggerate to make a point or embellish a story. I wasn't particularly aware of this tendency until my kids pointed it out. The first few times they mentioned it, I didn't pay much attention, but eventually I grasped that my exaggeration was a problem. I was embarrassed. I didn't want to be an exaggerator, nor did I want my kids to lose respect for me. So I added it to my ongoing "fix mom" wish list and trained myself to speak more precisely.

Peggy Johnson, a president of QUALCOMM Internet Services, said that her children helped her become more honest both at home and at work:

> My children have absolutely changed my character. I had to be more careful about sugarcoating in order to teach them honesty. I couldn't be anything but honest, and this has carried over to work. If I have to fire someone, it's ingrained in me to tell them like it is. I don't sugarcoat things. It's important that people know the truth.

Elizabeth Buse added,

> Motherhood has helped me be much more straightforward in business. I think that before I had kids, I was worried about how people would feel if I would give them bad news. My kids taught me to be direct. When I was disciplining them and started beating around the bush, because I was afraid they were going to cry, I didn't get the outcome I wanted because they were confused. Their life and mine became a whole lot easier when I used fewer words. The emotional breakdowns that I feared didn't happen.

To preserve their children's self-esteem, mothers learn to find the right time and the right words to deliver difficult messages. They learn to be precise and direct and to be truthful without being mean-spirited. As we've seen, you can tell the truth with a velvet touch or with a hammer to the head. Compassionate honesty is crucial at work. It's not just that people need to know the truth about their performance to improve, it's that honesty creates a bond of trust between a boss and her direct report. People appreciate and respond to frankness. Even though they might not like to hear bad news from their boss at first, in the long run, directness helps create respect.

CHARACTER IS THE SUM OF MANY PARTS

Most of us mature with age. Mothers don't have a lock on becoming better people, but children accelerate this personal growth process. Besides being more giving, confident, humble, grounded, and honest, executive mothers possess a wide variety of other qualities that build character. For instance, many moms change their behaviors to be better role models for their children. Some started going to church regularly and renewed their own spirituality. Some stopped using foul language. Some stopped drinking alcohol or reduced its influence in their lives. Most put in extra effort to keep their marriages strong and be more considerate of their partners.

Though your character is the sum of many parts, I'd like to concentrate on the main five traits in the following exercise, which will help you compare and contrast your leadership character with that of other leaders.

Start by writing the names of five leaders for whom you have great respect, making sure to include at least one mother. They can be people you work with now or with whom you've worked in the past. If you like, you can include a famous leader from politics or history that you know well from reading or observation.

Name		Leader 1	Leader 2	Leader 3	Leader 4	Leader 5	Sum of Scores
Selflessness	Absolute						
	Relative						
	Score						
Confidence	Absolute						
	Relative						
	Score						
Humility	Absolute						
	Relative						
	Score						
Grounded	Absolute						
	Relative						
	Score						
Honesty	Absolute						
	Relative						
	Score						

For each of the five characteristics, give an absolute rating to each of the five leaders as follows:

1. They exhibit it but only in moderation.
2. They clearly exhibit a characteristic.
3. They are exceptional when it comes to a particular trait.

Then, for each of the five characteristics, give them a relative rating as compared with yourself using the following criteria:

1. The leader is better at this than I am.
2. We are about the same.
3. I am stronger in this category than the leader.

Now multiply the two ratings for each characteristic and leader to get 25 resulting scores. Then add the 5 scores for each characteristic or row. Your sum for each row will be somewhere between 5 and 45. Compare your 5 different sums. Your highest sum reflects either your greatest strength or your role model's greatest strength, or both. Your lowest sum reflects an area of improvement for you and potentially your role models.

What does this exercise tell you about what you value in a leader? Most people value confidence over the other traits. Do you? If so, should the others get more of your attention? Why or why not? I recommend, mother or not, that you focus on your worst sum and resolve to work at being more mom-like in this particular area.

I suspect that the vast majority of you have good character; I doubt many moral reprobates would be motivated to purchase this book. The key, therefore, is to recognize that character counts in a leader and make a concerted effort to bring your character out, not just in your personal life but in your professional one as well.

11

APPLYING THE LESSONS OF MATERNAL LEADERSHIP

"If we are going to have systemic change in corporate cultures, we need mothers in the workplace."

Denise Morrison, President, Global Sales, and Chief Customer Officer, Campbell Soup

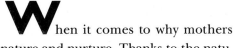hen it comes to why mothers lead best, it's a combination of nature and nurture. Thanks to the natural challenges of childrearing and the biological advantages of nurturing hormones, moms possess more leadership maturity and efficiency than others.

Mother leads best doesn't mean that others can't lead equally well. Both men and women without children can learn from and adopt the lessons of maternal leadership. In fact, executive moms can learn a lot from other executive moms. Just because you're a mother doesn't mean you're automatically a great leader. The key for everyone is to recognize that corporate leadership traditions need to change and that high-powered executive moms, like those profiled in these pages, provide a model for such change. When we need leaders with the strong character, clear purpose, compassion, and problem-solving skills of executive moms, every company's best interest lies in incorporating this model into their leadership development programs.

To use this model, both companies and individuals need to be aware of maternal leadership traits such as staying calm, listening effectively, adhering to clear priorities, inspiring people, and valuing differences. Awareness is a great starting place, in that it allows everyone to recognize the attitudes and practice the behaviors that have helped many women leaders succeed. Beyond awareness, though, there are a number of ways to put the lessons of this book into practice. I'd like to offer some specific advice to facilitate applying what you've learned depending on your particular situation. First, though, let's look at some general guidelines that will help everyone maximize the lessons learned from maternal leadership and minimize the mistakes.

GENERAL GUIDELINES

While interviewing the executive moms featured in this book and reflecting on my own experiences, I realized that people harbor preconceived notions about leadership, women's roles, and success. Some of these notions make sense, while others are just nonsense. It will be difficult to become a maternal leader unless you separate fact from fiction. Therefore, I'd like to provide you with four guidelines you can use in the real world of business.

1. Recognize that not all personal change is self-induced. While learning about maternal leadership and being inspired by other women's stories can help you change, you can't just depend on cognitive lessons to turn you into a great leader. Deep change often comes from deep experiences. Motherhood is a deep experience. From being pregnant to having a baby to taking care of a toddler to dealing with a volatile teenager, moms go through a lot. These passages change how they think and act in ways that even the best leadership training cannot approximate.

Therefore, if you're not a mom, watch for other, experience-based opportunities that foster meaningful change. As I've noted earlier, volunteer work can provide these opportunities, as can becoming a foster parent or a big brother/big sister. Spending a significant period living in a third-world country might be a life-altering experience. Similarly, taking a year's sabbatical from a job and becoming an inner city teacher or church minister may have a profound effect on how you view the world—and how you lead within it.

Training and development programs have taught too many businesspeople that change is a conscious, cognitive process. Leaders need to take a cue from the moms in this book and recognize that often, the most meaningful changes in how they think and act "just happen." In fact, sometimes changes take place against their will. Elizabeth Buse's friends became moms before she did. She said:

> I would think to myself, I am not going to become a dithering idiot like them and get excited because a baby blinked. And I became just like them. I couldn't help myself. I took this whole different view of the world. It reminds me of the Wizard of Oz. Before kids, life was black and white. When I had children, it was like I'd landed in a different world. Life was colorful and exciting.

2. Accept that the most powerful, leadership-changing feedback often comes from people you love rather than from people with whom you work. Given the popularity of 360-degree feedback and similar tools, it's understandable that leadership development programs use them extensively. Don't make the mistake in believing, however, that feedback from bosses, peers, and direct reports will sufficiently get your attention and catalyze monumental changes in how you manage and lead. Corporate feedback mechanisms are often too subtle to achieve this goal. It is all too easy to rationalize the feedback you receive from colleagues or to respond defensively (even while you pretend not to be defensive). This type of feedback doesn't always penetrate the outer layer like children's honest-to-goodness bluntness.

While many of the executive moms I talked to thrived on honest, open feedback at work, it did not cause the depth of transformation that motherhood triggered. When their children pointed out their flaws, they not only got it, but it affected them deeply, and their desire to earn their children's love and admiration stimulated them to change more profoundly than ever. The mother-child relationship is one of unconditional love, and this love makes it possible really to hear the other person; it also makes the recipient much better prepared to take the message to heart and motivates them to go about serious change.

If you're a mom, therefore, be as open and attentive as possible to what your children tell you about yourself. If you're not a mom, work hard at keeping the doors to honest communication open and pay very close attention to what the people you love tell you. It may be your spouse, your parent, or your best friend; whoever it is, they will level with you in ways that others might not be willing to do. Just as importantly, take what they're telling you to heart rather than merely listen.

3. Real leaders have real lives, so recognize that workaholicism detracts from rather than adds to your leadership ability. Spending too much time at work can hinder your leadership development. Even though you perceive that your 80-hour weeks demonstrate how devoted you are to your job and achieving company goals, the reality is that it detracts from your leadership character. To maintain balance, perspective, and humility, leaders must find a way to devote part of their lives to something besides work. Providing service to others, whether as a mom or in a volunteer capacity, helps achieve this objective. Many of the women I talked to were workaholics early in their careers and balanced leaders after they had children. Early on, they operated under the assumption that they would be rewarded for their selfless devotion to the company. Certainly, hard work is important for success, but maternal leaders recognize that nonstop work made them one-dimensional. Motherhood rounded out and matured their leadership style.

4. Embrace the possibility of excelling in more than one role. For years, women have been told to choose an area on which to focus all their time and attention, the assumption being that it was only possible to do justice to one area of their lives. Some working fathers also choose to focus on work to the exclusion of their family. Many of the leaders I've interviewed have proven otherwise. They are not only great leaders, but they're great parents, spouses, and community contributors. High-energy leaders often prefer doing instead of relaxing. Trudy Sullivan, an executive vice president at Liz Claiborne, Inc., said, "The huge epiphany for me was, 'Oh, my, I can do both.' It was such a huge rush."

Certainly they are not fulfilling all these roles alone; many have supportive spouses and corporations, and they have set clear priorities. Still, they have taken on ambitious goals in different spheres of their lives to synergistic effect. Though I've stressed how parenting helps men and women become better leaders, the reverse is also true. Leadership roles provide adults with so many tools for parenting, giving them a chance to recognize the value of accountability, the need to model positive behaviors, and the keys to good communication. Community roles also have a spillover effect into other areas of life.

I'm not suggesting that everyone become Superwoman, but I am saying that you can realistically believe that you can do well at more than one job and that, if you do become dualcentric, the impact will be far reaching and positive.

With these general guidelines in mind, let's examine some specific questions you might have if you're a parent, a young woman, childless, or a corporate leader.

PARENTS
Involvement Is the Key

Whether you've just become a parent or you've been a parent for years, embracing the changes that kids bring out in you is crucial. If you're a father, recognize that, while more and more fathers are fully engaged in the parenting process, most ultrahigh-achieving dads are not. An overwhelming majority of male CEOs have stay-at-home wives and delegate childrearing tasks as readily as they might give assignments to trusted direct reports. Interestingly, a significant number of the husbands of women profiled here also had high-powered jobs, and they admitted they didn't change as much as their wives, even those who took on major childrearing responsibilities. While motherhood enhanced their wives' nurturing skills, fatherhood didn't have the same impact on them.

One of these women explained this diminished impact as follows:

> My husband is a phenomenal spouse. He never imagined he would be taking on so much responsibility at home. He is a trooper and helps a lot. Even so, the workload at home is totally unbalanced. [She does far more than he does as a parent.] Men's thought processes are very different. He has made some changes due to our children, but they haven't been as dramatic as mine. He has become a little more flexible and tries to be a little less reactive.

Marla Gottschalk, the president and COO of The Pampered Chef, has a theory that it's more than just men having different thought processes, suggesting that women don't really let go of controlling the household. She said:

> Given our DNA, we take on the major roles at home and still feel the need to control. Recently, we had a party for 30. I didn't want to have the party, because my daughter had a swim meet all day. My husband said he would do it all, so I let him. But I was definitely fretting all day. I returned from the swim meet, and the party had already started. He had cleaned the house, purchased the food, and had the party well under control. It was a great party, and he totally came through. It was a big step for me. If you have a supportive husband, I recommend that working mothers try to let go of more at home.

No doubt some dads don't want or feel capable of taking on this type of parenting responsibility. If this description fits you, though, realize that not only will an increased parenting load help enhance your leadership skills, but it will also enhance your relationship with your children, wife, and friends.

YOUNG WOMEN
It's Not an Either-Or Proposition

Don't burden yourself with past thinking if you're a young woman on the cusp of becoming a business leader. Ogilvy & Mather CEO Shelly Lazarus pointed out that we are in a new era, explaining:

> The wonderful thing about today is that each woman can make her choice. There is one thing I feel strongly about. You can fit as many things as you love into your life. But if you don't love what you do at work, your life is going to be out of balance. You will resent the tediousness of work, and you will resent being away from your kids. You stay balanced if you find your work interesting and compelling and you look forward to it.

Denise Morrison, the president of global sales and chief customer officer for Campbell Soup, added:

> I would hope that younger women do not get overwhelmed by the thought of having a career and being a mother. They can do both. The world is a lot more open, and there are more enabling support systems, so they can be successful. Society needs them to continue to make progress. If we are going to have systemic change in corporate cultures, we need mothers in the workplace. I want this book to encourage young women to continue this quest. The statistics at the top for women and mothers are still really low. We still have a lot of work to do. Our journey will push it only so far. We need the next generation to take this further.

One maternal leader after the next stressed that young women should not miss out on motherhood for the sake of their careers. To a woman, they insisted that having children was the best thing that ever happened to them. To capture all their encouragement and reasons for young women to do both would take another 50 pages, so I've boiled down their arguments to a few key reasons and quotes.

Joy. According to Carol Evans of CNN Newsgroup:

> Children make your life more exciting. There is stuff to create, things to do, challenges to meet, and a lot of fun. There is joy at work, but the joy in the office is a lot different than the joy at home. There is this indescribable joy at home. And that enormous love that we feel is very much a surprise to most women. It's such a big feeling. It shifts your perspective on life.

Cindy Christy of Lucent Technologies added:

> You can look at life a lot of ways. I have a lot of jobs—mom, wife, executive, friend, volunteer, etc. I cherish my family the most. They bring me the most joy. I might not become one of the most powerful women in business, but I won't look back and have any regrets. In 15 years, I will have 4 kids and their ex-

tended families, and beyond that, I will enjoy my family for the rest of eternity. While I strive to achieve at work, I always know I will have my family.

Fulfillment. Leslie Donovan of Targetbase said, "I get great fulfillment from my job, but it will never compare to the fulfillment I get from my children." Mindy Meade agreed, saying, "I would choose to have kids again in a second . . . because it is so fulfilling." Doreen Toben, the CFO at Verizon, added, "Motherhood is a wonderful experience. There is nothing more important in life than raising your family, and there is nothing more rewarding. Making *Fortune*'s list is fine, but there's nothing that comes close to your family. Family is part of your heart. I would give up my role at Verizon in a heartbeat if need be."

Support. Nokia's Jo Anne Miller's children are now in their early 30s. She said, "My children have become my greatest cheerleaders. They have supported me through all the ups and downs of my company and brightened my life during the toughest of times. Their confidence in me flows deep into the essence of who I am."

Wisdom. Liz Clairborne's Trudy Sullivan said, "My children have helped me become a wiser person. I definitely have more gray hair, yet they keep me young. Having kids gave me a much better perspective and a more balanced life."

CHILDLESS
Seize Opportunities to Give

If you decide or have decided not to be a parent, you can still embrace maternalistic leadership skills. If you're on the corporate fast track, you should be especially alert for opportunities.

Moms don't have a monopoly on being selfless, humble, calm, confident, warm, and attentive. Some of the most giving and humble people I know are not parents. It is quite possible to hone your nurturing skills and the other traits we've discussed by helping and connecting with others. Several high-powered women I know are like Oprah. They have many giving dimensions to their life, and they are passionate about their charitable activities, their extended family, and their service-oriented roles outside of work.

Denise Morrison, for instance, believes so strongly in the benefits of learning through activities that make a difference in the community, she suggests her employees work with children:

> I encourage my coworkers to get involved with kids and take leadership roles with their soccer teams or softball teams, or scouts or community service. This typically results in developing their leadership and communication skills outside of the workplace. I see it as a win-win, producing benefits for the children and the business leader. The lessons of a coach are very relevant to work. You need to get organized, master teamwork, teach skills, inspire others to win, cope with losses, and handle the parents.

Procter & Gamble's Deb Henretta advocates finding volunteer roles that build leadership skills.

> I honed my business skills with volunteers. I had to lead through influence rather than authority. I found ways to motivate volunteers by keeping them focused on the goal. Often in community situations, you are trying to find ways to bridge different groups. I would get cooperation across these groups by keeping the common goal in the forefront of negotiations. This has had tremendous impact on my leadership style. It has made a big difference. I seek common ground rather than edict solutions.

Several of the executive moms mentioned that nursing their elderly parents or ill siblings changed their priorities and perspective on life. If you pay attention, an abundance of opportunities will surface. If you're an ultrahigh achiever (or aspire to be one), you should concentrate on doing the following:

- Break away from your addiction to work.
- Seek honest, blunt feedback.
- Find nonwork activities (preferably volunteer/philanthropic) about which you can be passionate.

In terms of the first item, you must take the addict's first step of recognizing that something has a hold on you that is not in your best interests or the best interests of other people you care about. This isn't as easy as it seems, because emotional addictions are less obvious than addictions to things like drugs and alcohol. It's also difficult to admit that the need to be the best, to constantly achieve, to be admired, to be powerful—all of which requires a great deal of work—can be harmful.

Recently, a very talented but ambitious CEO gave a speech at a conference. Numerous people in the audience had a negative reaction to her emphasis on her own ambitions. One executive said, "While she was very impressive, you can tell she doesn't just want to run a big company. She has her sights set a lot higher. She wants to run a country or perhaps the whole world." Despite this speaker's perceptive observations, people focused on what seemed to be her greed for achievement. Being addicted to work and your own ambitions is a turnoff. When you are myopically focused on your work and your business goals, you come across as self-indulgent.

Also, warn yourself that workaholics often have emotional breakdowns when they are fired or retire. It finally sinks in that making the cover of *Fortune* is no longer relevant. Their turn in the limelight is over, and the sudden loss of work from their lives takes its toll. Some workaholics experience incredible pain when they realize they have ignored the important things in life, like family. Others struggle with their identity and feel lonely, empty, and full of regrets.

One of the best ways to recognize addictive work behaviors is through the second recommendation: seeking honest feedback. As the mothers in this book point out, children brought many of their weaknesses to their attention. Though they had all been through multiple 360-degree feedback assessments at work and were receptive to feedback, they still didn't recognize the impact of all of their weaknesses.

Therefore, go beyond the standard feedback and ask your enemies or biggest critics for feedback. Have friends or family members level with you. Don't be defensive if you hear that you're obsessed with work or as tragically ambitious as a Shakespearean protagonist. In the long run, you'll be a better leader and a happier person if you accept this news now. Seeking and absorbing feedback is a catalyst to leadership growth, especially for high achievers.

In terms of the third recommendation, make an effort as early in your career as possible to engage yourself in outside activities. You'll not only benefit others, but you'll become a more nurturing, confident, and strong leader. Just realize that it will take a little experimentation to find something that lights your fire.

As I noted earlier, I took a year off from work to focus on urban education reform. I had this insatiable urge to give back to the community. I learned a lot, gained a new perspective, and returned refreshed to the corporate world. Though I'm glad I did it, it was probably the wrong choice for me. Dealing with the educational bureaucracy and the slow pace made me want to pull my hair out at times. Finding the right service opportunities is like finding the right career. You need to keep seizing opportunities until you find the one that fits who you are.

Be aware, though, that hobbies and pets do not count. I indulge myself in golf and my English garden, and I get incredibly attached to my pets, but these are indulgences and do not further my leadership development. I knew one woman entrepreneur who told me, "I don't have kids but I have a dog. He's my baby." When her dog died, she was so crushed, she bought $100,000 worth of jewelry to console herself. Clearly, the dog (not to mention the jewelry) was an indulgence; she wasn't going to be a better leader by nurturing her dog.

If you don't have children, then you have many options for service, but make sure those options involve helping other people or making the world a better place in a way that is meaningful to you.

CORPORATE LEADERS
Employ the Maternal Model

If you're a CEO or in another senior position where you can impact how your company's future leaders are trained, think of motherhood as an opportunity for your people rather than an obstacle. Support dual-centric employees, and find a way to incorporate maternal traits into leadership development regimens. Understand, too, that the more mothers you have in influential positions, the more you will attract.

Denise Morrison said:

Corporations need to do a better job with helping mothers re-enter the workforce. Most people start their business careers in their early 20s and may work until age 70. There's a point in that lengthy span of time where mothers and fathers should have choices. If they choose to spend some time outside the workplace—as stay-at-home parents or working for a nonprofit or in a volunteer capacity—that should be viewed as a positive and not a negative. In fact, companies would be wise to encourage these "giving" sabbaticals, recognizing that people will return better leaders than they were before because of these experiences. These programs might be termed "high-touch extended leaves," in that companies should remain in close contact with the employee on sabbatical, include them as much as possible in select activities with the rest of the team, and regularly recognize that their talents are appreciated.

Corporations that acknowledge the importance of their employees' lives outside of work and who provide them with a reasonable amount of work flexibility will earn the loyalty of the best and brightest people. These individuals will return from parenting and service experiences as happier and more productive employees.

MATERNAL TRENDS IN THE BUSINESS WORLD

Though organizations are increasingly receptive to women leaders in general and maternal leaders in particular, pockets of resistance remain.

Media pundits have suggested dozens of reasons why women haven't penetrated senior levels of corporations as quickly as might be expected in an age that embraces diversity and equal opportunity. Some opine that not enough women possess profit-and-loss experience; others note that more women than men drop out before getting to the top; still others declare that women remain the victims of discrimination. While all these explanations may be valid, I'm convinced that a fundamental issue is that most female trailblazers in corporate America were not mothers. As a result, they were missing a critical set of experiences needed for well-rounded, well-grounded leadership.

Parenthood is as important for success in a corporation as a college degree. Climbing the corporate ladder without such a degree is difficult, not just because you lack the toolset acquired from a formal education, but also because you're perceived to have missed a rite of passage. While some men and women make it to the top of corporations without a college degree, they are the exceptions. Likewise, if you're not a parent, besides missing the leadership lessons associated with parenting, some people will stereotype you—you're not responsible and caring, you're a workaholic, and so on. While the stereotype may not be accurate, it will skew their view of your leadership skills.

Fortunately, moms who make it to the top are providing a new leadership model in which parenting is a key component. A number of moms have penetrated the most senior levels of the largest companies and blazed fresh trails for women. The new model still mandates that they have leadership DNA, but it also embraces a kinder, gentler, more confident version of the old model; a big heart and a strong character are now as important as being a strong person.

Companies are desperate for leaders with this hybrid style and substance. They are well aware that in a global marketplace, diverse cultures, and volatile and chaotic environments, the old, male transactional model is an anachronism. Leaders who only have the hard skills (e.g., the basic leadership DNA) simply aren't suited for today's business climate. Yes, many of these types are still running companies, but the tide is turning and their days are numbered. As everyone is well aware, company populations are going to become more rather than less diverse, companies will be dealing with more rather than fewer changes, and the pace is going to quicken even further. As a result, leaders must become much more efficient at managing chaos and much more competent at dealing with the human side. Overall, they must possess the interpersonal skills and character to adapt to both new realities.

For these reasons, we're bound to see an increasing number of mothers occupying top positions in major corporations. It might not happen tomorrow, but it will happen sooner rather than later. It's instructive that some male CEOs—especially those who are parents—have already started adopting certain maternal traits. Historically, women have adopted male schemas more readily than men have adopted female schemas, because there really hasn't been sufficient motivation for men to change.

However, as mothers take hold of more corporations, and as society puts more pressure on men to be attentive fathers, those incentives will kick in rapidly. I certainly know more than one CEO who has rounded out his leadership style primarily because of his children. These men tend to be more involved in childrearing than their predecessors. Though they usually aren't equal partners, they have invested enough time and emotion in the experience to benefit as both individuals and leaders. In certain instances, these CEOs were selected for their jobs precisely because they represented a new strain of the paternal model.

As of this writing, moms run huge corporations such as Xerox, Southwest Airlines, eBay, Ogilvy & Mather, Pearson, Young & Rubicam, Lord & Taylor, Avon, and Salomon Smith Barney, and their examples will inspire more moms to try their hand at the top jobs and more executives to adopt maternal characteristics. Perhaps even more significantly, their success as CEOs will inspire more boards of directors and search committees to look for executive mom candidates.

Finally, executive moms are conditioning a new generation to accept mothers as leaders. As great mothers and great leaders, they are modeling behaviors that cannot help but have an impact on their children. Their sons are growing up as independent thinkers who are comfortable with women leaders, and their daughters are growing up knowing they can be leaders. Both are being trained in the art of managing dual-career families.

THE CASE FOR CHANGE

Though things are changing, they need to change faster. Old myths die hard, the glass ceiling still exists, and the supply of great leaders is falling short of demand. My hope is that this book can help us evolve more quickly in the direction of the maternal leadership model. If senior management recognizes the value of maternal traits and executive moms are encouraged to seek top positions, we will see changes occur that can only benefit organizations.

Motherhood has raised the consciousness of women leaders. Many of the women in this book are convinced that had they not had children, they would not have changed so dramatically. Most of them were managers before their children were born. They were already on a fast track and knew they had the basic DNA to climb the corporate ladder. With hindsight, though, most of these women recognize that their drive and talent weren't enough to get them to the top. A number of them suggested that, without becoming mothers, they would have become moderately successful—and more than moderately unfulfilled—workaholics. While a few women believe that they might have achieved their leadership positions even if they didn't have children, most look back and see motherhood as a turning point both in their lives and their careers.

I am sure that some executive dads out there have changed in similar ways, but I suspect the transformation is more difficult for men. Biologically, men's hormones work against these changes. Testosterone-filled male executives are not noted for their nurturing, calming qualities. Women executives, on the other hand, have inherent nurturing tendencies while possessing the toughness and drive that people want in a leader. Having children makes them warmer and more balanced, rounding out their leadership style. And their intense involvement in childrearing responsibilities promotes other positive behavioral changes, such as making them the most efficient people on the planet.

I have interviewed about 100 men and women who work for maternal leaders, and the far majority stated that their bosses are bringing a new culture to their executive offices and boardrooms. They not only have extraordinary leadership skills, but they lead with a clear, noble purpose; a broad perspective; and from big hearts. Their immense and intense love for their children carries over into their business lives. Their abundance of love balances their natural, results-oriented leadership style with authentic concern for people and warm-heartedness. This tough and tender combination wins the loyalty of their teams and customers and inspires incredible business results. It should come as no surprise that the men and women who work for maternal leaders love them back. They admire them and are awed, not only by their incredible business savvy but also by their genuine concern for others.

I don't think I'm overstating the case for maternal leadership. In fact, anyone who has seen an executive mom in action knows why people are positively rhapsodic in their descriptions of them. For example, I was in a Bible study group for executives in Chicago and we had just finished Apostle Paul's first letter to the Corinthians, when one participant said:

> You know, my CEO, Sally Krawcheck [of Salomon Smith
> Barney] leads just like I imagine Paul would if he were alive to-
> day. She's an amazing leader and very different from your typical
> CEO. I was present at one of her employee speeches yesterday,
> and while she exuded confidence, she was at the same time very
> down to earth and humble. She spoke freely, with great ease and
> candor, and I could tell she was leading from her heart.

Maternal leaders like Sally combine leadership DNA with a great heart. Years ago, process and quality were the key competitive differentiators. Today, maternal leadership has the potential to provide the same competitive advantage. It used to be that companies tried to stock their management teams with guys only Vince Lombardi could love—macho, intensely competitive, and obsessed with winning. While we've migrated away from that mentality, today's poised and polished leaders often do not demonstrate compassion or inspire loyalty.

The young men and women entering today's workforce expect compassion. When these children were born, their parents put signs in their cars warning other drivers: *Baby on Board*. Even after their early childhood years, they were showered with tender, loving care. Their dads, teachers, and coaches showed them a lot more compassion than previous generations experienced. As a result, they assume that parental figures at work will exhibit kindness and nurturing qualities; it's no wonder that young, fast-track employees today have grown to expect it. Companies are starting to realize that leaders with character and compassion will win the hearts and minds not only of today's workers but especially tomorrow's best and brightest people. That's why, now and in the future, the teams led by the most moms win.

A

BIOGRAPHICAL BACKGROUNDS

Colleen Arnold
Title: General Manager, Communications Sector
Company: IBM
Children: Jack and Christie
Education: BS, Nazareth College; MBA, Syracuse University

Colleen is leading IBM's global sales and marketing strategy for clients in the telecommunications, media and entertainment, and energy and utilities industries, and she has worldwide revenue, profit, and client satisfaction responsibility. Previously, she was CEO, IBM Global Services Australia, a joint venture with Telstra and IBM. She serves on the board at the School of Management, Syracuse University.

Cynthia H. Augustine
Title: Senior Vice President, Human Resources; President, Broadcast Group
Company: The New York Times Company
Children: Jen and Tommy
Education: BA, Sarah Lawrence College; JD, Rutgers Law School

Cynthia is a member of Times' executive committee, president of the company's broadcast group, and senior vice president of human resources and is responsible for all human resources functions of the Times Company, including compensation and benefits, diversity, employee relations, and organizational development. Prior to joining the Times Company, she was a partner at the law firm Sabin, Bermant, and Gould LLP, where she specialized in employment law. She serves on the boards at the Robert C. Maynard Institute for Journalism Education and the Television Bureau of Advertising as well as the NBC Affiliate Board.

Anita Beier
Title: Senior Vice President and Controller
Company: US Airways, Inc.
Children: Amy and Adam
Education: BS and MBA, University of Maryland

Anita has responsibility for the management of all accounting functions for US Airways Group, Inc. and its subsidiaries, including financial reporting, revenue accounting, accounts payable, and payroll. Previously, she was the CFO of American Commercial Lines, vice president of financial planning at CSX Corporation, and an economist for the Federal Railroad Administration.

Melinda T. Brown
Title: Vice President and Controller
Company: PepsiCo Beverages and Food, North America
Children: Rebecca and Justin
Education: BS and MBA, University of Connecticut

A Controller of PepsiCo Beverages and Foods North America, Melinda is responsible for accounting and transaction processing functions as well as customer financial services. She has held a variety of financial roles within PepsiCo. Previously, she worked for the Financial Accounting Standards Board (FASB) and in public accounting.

Elizabeth Buse
Title: Executive Vice President
Company: VISA
Children: Nicholas, Helen, and Joan
Education: BA, University of California at Los Angeles;
Graduate Fellow, Universidad Complutense, Madrid, Spain;
MBA, University of California at Berkeley

Elizabeth is responsible for the product development cycle—research, product innovation, new product development, and product deployment—and for management of VISA's consumer, small business, and commercial products. Previously, she was an executive at First Data Corporation. She also serves on the board of directors for Vital Processing Services, a leader in technology-based commerce-enabling systems.

Jocelyn Carter-Miller
Title: President
Company: TechEdVentures
Children: Alexis and Kimberly
Education: BS, University of Illinois; MBA, University of Chicago

Jocelyn manages operations for TechEdVentures, a firm that develops and manages charter schools and community-based programs. She is co-author of *Networlding: Building Relationships and Opportunities for Success*, and serves on several public and private boards. Previously, Jocelyn served as EVP and Chief Marketing Officer for Office Depot, Inc.; CMO and General Manager at Motorola; and VP of Marketing and Product Development at Mattel.

Cindy Christy
Title: President of Mobility Solutions Group
Company: Lucent Technologies
Children: Samantha, Michael, John, and Jennifer
Education: BBA, The American University in Washington, D.C.

Cindy is responsible for Lucent's business operations to bring end-to-end mobile networking solutions to service providers worldwide. She serves on the board of directors of the Cellular Telecom Industry Association (CTIA). Additionally, she is chair of the CTIA suppliers forum. Previously, she worked for AT&T Network Systems in several management positions, including chief operating officer of CDMA and TDMA networks.

Lori Craven
Title: Executive Vice President and Chief Operating Officer
Company: Tekelec
Children: Cori and Jeff
Education: BS, Oregon State University; MBA, Northwestern University; MS, Stanford University

At Tekelec, Lori leads the global sales and marketing group and is responsible for the signaling and next-generation switching business units. Lori previously worked at Lucent Technologies, where she was vice president of mobility solutions development. She also serves on the board of directors for the Alliance for Telecommunications Industry Solutions (ATIS).

Leslie Donovan
Title: Senior Vice President, Sales and Marketing
Company: Targetbase
Children: Reilly and MacKenzie
Education: BA, Ohio Wesleyan University

Leslie leads the business development team in building business strategies and solutions for clients and has been instrumental in key client acquisitions such as Procter & Gamble and Southwest Airlines. She serves on the board of the Girl Scouts of Texas Council.

Carol Evans
Title: President and Chief Executive Officer
Company: Working Mother Media
Children: Robert and Julia Rose
Education: BS, SUNY–Empire State

In 2001, Carol founded Working Mother Media by acquiring *Working Mother* magazine and the National Association for Female Executives. Prior to that, she was the COO of Chief Executive Group, publisher of *Chief Executive* magazine. She previously worked as president of Stagebill, Inc. and held a variety of positions at McCall's Publishing, the company that launched *Working Mother* in 1979. She serves as president of the Advertising Women of New York and sits on the boards for the March of Dimes, the Young Playwrights, and IMAG, the independent magazine division of the Magazine Publishers of America.

Gail Evans
Title: Executive Vice President, retired
Company: CNN Newsgroup
Children: Jason, Jeffrey, and Julianna
Education: BA, Bennington College

Gail was a member of CNN's executive committee and executive vice president of domestic networks for the CNN newsgroup. She was responsible for program and talent development, overseeing national and international talk shows, and network guest bookings. Gail is the author of two bestsellers, *She Wins, You Win: The Most Important Strategies for Making Women More Powerful* and *Play Like a Man, Win Like a Woman: What Men Know about Success That Women Need to Learn*. She is a visiting professor at Georgia Tech and on various boards, including those of the Society for Women's Health Research, the Radio Television News Directors Foundation, the Breman Jewish Heritage Museum, and the Atlanta Girls School.

Ruth Ann Gillis

Title: President of Exelon Business
Company: Exelon Corporation
Children: Edward and Alexander
Education: BS, Smith College; MBA, University of Chicago

Ruth Ann is a member of Exelon's management committee and leads Exelon's information technology services, legal and human resources services, payroll, accounts payable, and supply chain support departments. Previously, she served as Exelon's CFO. She was also a CFO for Unicom and for the University of Chicago Hospitals and Health System. She is president of the University of Chicago Cancer Research Foundations Board of Trustees and a director of Chicago State University Foundation's Board.

Marla Gottschalk

Title: President and Chief Operating Officer
Company: The Pampered Chef (Berkshire Hathaway)
Children: Amanda and Laura
Education: BS, Indiana University; MBA, Northwestern University

Marla leads The Pampered Chef's executive team, oversees long-range planning, and defines corporate strategy. Previously, she served as senior vice president of finance for Kraft Foods and executive vice president and general manager of the Post Cereal Company for Kraft. Marla serves on the board of Visteon Corporation.

Mirian Graddick-Weir

Title: Executive Vice President, Human Resources
Company: AT&T
Children: Tiffany and Danielle
Education: BA, Hampton University; MS/Ph.D., Penn State University

Mirian is a member of AT&T's executive committee and is responsible for human resources. She previously directed five AT&T customer service centers. She serves on the boards of the Harleysville Insurance Companies, the National Medical Fellowships, Inc., and the Joint Center for Political and Economic Studies. She is a trustee for Hampton University.

Joan Gulley
Title: Chief Executive Officer, PNC Advisors
Company: PNC Financial Services Group
Children: Colin
Education: BA, University of Rochester; AMP, Harvard Business School

Joan leads PNC's wealth management, institutional investment, and brokerage business units as well as PNC's specialized investment consulting services. Previously, she served as CEO of PNC business banking and as executive vice president of the Massachusetts Company. She is chairman of the board of Chatham College and sponsors the PNC Advisors Women's Financial Services Network.

Ruth Harenchar
Title: Senior Vice President and Chief Information Officer
Company: Bowne & Company
Children: Sara and Matthew, and stepchildren: Jill, Michael, and Betsy
Education: BA, University of Illinois at Chicago Circle; MPH, Northwestern University Medical School

Ruth leads the development, implementation, and operation of the global information technology platform at Bowne. Previously, she served in management positions at Ernst & Young LLP and Electronic Data Systems. Currently chairman of the Northwestern University College of Engineering Advisory Council, she also serves as the board vice chairman of New Jersey Easter Seals.

Doris Jean Head
Title: Vice President, North American Sales
Company: Marconi Communications
Children: Ashley, Rachelle, Alyssa, and Kyndrea
Education: BBA, Texas Tech University; MBA, Golden Gate University at San Francisco

Doris Jean is responsible for North American sales for Marconi's broadband Routing and Switching group. Prior to this, she held executive sales positions for Lucent and AT&T. She is also a member of the board for The Women's Museum in Dallas.

Bridgette Heller
Title: Chief Executive Officer
Company: Chung's Gourmet Foods
Children: Sara and Mariah
Education: BS and MBA, Northwestern University

Bridgette recently resigned as the CEO of Chung's Gourmet Foods. Previously, she was executive vice president of Kraft Foods North America and general manager of the Coffee Division. She is on the national board of Girls, Inc. and the board of Family Service of Westchester.

Deb Henretta
Title: President, Global Baby and Adult Care
Company: Procter & Gamble
Children: Caitlin, Connor, and Shannon
Education: BA, Bonaventure University; MA, Syracuse University

Deb is responsible for P&G's global baby and adult care division, which includes the more than $5 billion Pampers product line. She has held many different general management and marketing positions throughout her career at P&G. She serves on the board of directors at Sprint and is on the Board of Trustees at St. Bonaventure University and Cincinnati's Children's Hospital and Medical Center.

Susan C. Hogan
Title: Principal
Company: Deloitte Consulting LLP, a member of Deloitte Touche Tomatsu
Children: Thomas and Courtney
Education: BS, North Carolina State University; MBA, Harvard University

Susan leads Deloitte Consulting's Shared Services practice in the United States. She has many years of experience at developing Shared Services strategy as well as designing, implementing, and optimizing Shared Services centers.

Amal Johnson
Title: Venture Partner
Company: ComVentures
Children: Hanna
Education: BA, Montclair State College

Amal has served in the role of president for several Baan Corporation subsidiaries, including Baan Supply Chain Solutions, Baan Affiliates, and Baan Americas. Previously, she served as president of ASK Manufacturing Systems, worked in several executive positions at IBM, and was a venture partner at Lightspeed Venture Partners. Amal serves on the boards of MAE Software, Inc., Alibris, and Blue Martini.

Peggy L. Johnson
Title: President, QUALCOMM Internet Services
Company: QUALCOMM Incorporated
Children: Nicholas, Emily, and Jake
Education: BS, San Diego State University

Peggy leads the QUALCOMM Internet Services division, which is chartered with driving the development of next-generation wireless data applications and services. She is also responsible for the company's BREW® solution, which provides products and services that connect the mobile marketplace value chain: QChat™ and BREWChat™ push- to-chat products, QPoint™ location services solution, and the Eudora® e-mail client. Prior to joining QUALCOMM, Peggy worked for GE's military electronics division.

Rita Kahle
Title: Executive Vice President
Company: Ace Hardware
Children: Tim and Emma
Education: BS, University of Illinois

Rita is responsible for Ace's merchandising, finance, administration, and strategic planning initiatives. Previously at Ace, Rita served as controller and chief financial officer. Before joining Ace Hardware, she was a CPA with KPMG.

Fran Keeth
Title: President and Chief Executive Officer
Company: Shell Chemical LP (Royal Dutch)
Children: Russell
Education: BBA, MBA, and JD, University of Houston

Fran holds both global and regional positions with Shell. Globally, she is the executive vice president of customer fulfillment/product business units and deputy CEO for Shell Chemicals Limited, and regionally she is president and CEO of Shell Chemical LP. Previously, she was controller for Mobil Corporation. Fran also serves on the Dean's Executive Advisory Board at the C.T. Bauer College of Business at the University of Houston.

Ellen Kullman
Title: Group Vice President, DuPont Safety and Protection Group
Company: DuPont
Children: Maggie, Stephen, and David
Education: BS, Tufts; MBA, Northwestern University

Ellen is responsible for providing solutions in the area of safety, protection, and security and is specifically responsible for DuPont's advanced fiber systems, chemical solutions enterprise, nonwovens, safety resources, and surfaces. Previously, she held various management positions for General Electric. She serves on the boards of the Delaware Symphony and the Blood Bank of Delaware/Eastern Shore, is a trustee of Christiana Care Corporation, and is on the Board of Overseers at Tufts University School of Engineering.

Shelly Lazarus
Title: Chairman and Chief Executive Officer
Company: Ogilvy & Mather Worldwide
Children: Ted, Samantha, and Benjamin
Education: BA, Smith College; MBA, Columbia University

Shelly has been Ogilvy's CEO since 1996 and for the past 30 years has worked with blue chip clients such as American Express, Ford, IBM, and Unilever. She is a member of the board of directors for GE and Ann Taylor Stores. She is also on the board of New York Presbyterian Hospital and the World Wildlife Fund.

Donna A. Lee
Title: Chief Marketing Officer
Company: BellSouth Corporation
Children: Sean and Katie
Education: BS, Mary Washington College; MBA, Georgia State
University

Donna is responsible for market planning, business development and
alliance management, pricing, and segment marketing for BellSouth.
Prior to this position, she was president of BellSouth's Managed Network
Solutions, Inc. Previously, Donna was a senior executive with AT&T. She
serves on the board of directors of Air2Web and is also a board member
of BeVocal and of the Atlanta College of Art.

Dawn Lepore
Title: Vice Chairman
Company: Charles Schwab Corporation
Children: Andrew and Elizabeth
Education: BA, Smith College

Dawn is a member of Schwab's executive committee, a trustee of Schwab
Funds, and is responsible for technology, active trader, operations, ad-
ministration, and corporate business strategy. Previously, she served as
Schwab's CIO. Dawn is on the board of directors of eBay, Wal-Mart, and
Catalyst.

Pam Lopker
Title: Chairman and President
Company: QAD
Children: Two, ages 15 and 17
Education: BS, University of California at Santa Barbara

Pam, a manufacturing visionary, founded QAD in 1979 and has grown
its revenue to over $200 million and supports blue chip companies such
as GE, Black & Decker, and Johnson Controls.

Priscilla Lu
Title: Founder, Chief Executive Officer, and Former Chairman
Company: InterWAVE
Children: Douglas, Olivia, and Felicity
Education: BS and MS, University of Wisconsin; MBA, Northwestern University

Priscilla has recently started a new company in video networks. She was the former chairman and CEO of InterWAVE Communications for almost a decade, delivering over 140 end-to-end cellular networks worldwide. Previously, she had led product development teams at Bell Laboratories.

Kate Ludeman
Title: Founder and Chief Executive Officer
Company: Worth Ethic Corporation
Children: Catherine
Education: BS, Texas Tech; Ph.D., Saybrook Institute

Kate is an executive coach, speaker, and author who helps leaders develop and use their emotional intelligence to changing their own behaviors and transforming their organizations, making them role models for change. Previously, Kate was vice president of human resources for a high-tech Silicon Valley company.

Maria Martinez
Title: Corporate Vice President
Company: Microsoft
Children: Cecilia
Education: BS, University of Puerto Rico; MS, Ohio State University

Maria leads the Coummunications Sector Group, which is Microsoft's worldwide organization supporting sales, marketing, consulting, and support services for wireless, wireline, cable, hosting, and media and entertainment companies. She is also responsible for the transformation of Microsoft's technologies into a cohesive set of solutions. Previously, Maria was CEO of Embrace Networks, Inc., held several vice president positions at Motorola, and had a variety of management and engineering roles at Bell Laboratories.

Marion McGovern
Title: President
Company: M Squared Consulting, Inc.
Children: Morgan, Nora, and Kevin
Education: BS/BA, Boston University; MBA, University of
California at Berkeley

Marion's company, headquartered in San Francisco, is a value-added broker of senior-level independent consultants. She and her partners also created an affiliate company, Consultant Billing, Inc., which is dedicated to serving the needs of companies that payroll independent consultants. Previously, she held consulting positions with Booz Allen Hamilton, Arthur D. Little, and a subsidiary of the Boston Consulting Group. She is on the board of directors of Consulting Psychology Press, the publisher of Meyers-Briggs Type Instruments, and the American Liver Foundation. She is a member of the Young Presidents Organization (YPO) and the National Charity League.

Patricia McKay
Title: Executive Vice President and Chief Financial Officer
Company: Restoration Hardware
Children: Robert, John, and Matthew
Education: BBA, Florida Atlantic University

Patricia serves as executive vice president and chief financial officer. Previously, she was CFO at AutoNation; vice president, finance, and controller of Dole Food Company; and a CPA at Arthur Andersen & Co. She serves on the board of directors of Office Depot, Inc.

Mindy Meads
Title: Chief Executive Officer
Company: Lands' End (Sears & Roebuck)
Children: Griffin
Education: BS, University of Illinois

Mindy is responsible for Lands' End and has held numerous leadership roles in apparel merchandising at Sears. Previously, she has held senior merchandising positions at Macy's, the Limited, and Gymboree Corporation.

Jo Anne Miller

Title: Principal
Company: Nokia Innovent
Children: Christopher and Lara
Education: BS, University of Michigan; MS, University of Colorado; MBA, University of Chicago

Jo Anne now works in the venturing arm of Nokia's innovation organization and is the past president and CEO of Gluon Networks, Inc, a manufacturer of next-generation switching systems for local telephone service providers. After holding several key managerial roles at Bell Laboratories and Tellabs, Jo Anne headed down the entrepreneurial path and was involved in engineering and general management at three different wireless startups, culminating in JetCell, which was purchased by Cisco Systems. Jo Anne is a mentor for the Women's Technology Cluster.

Kathryn Kimura Mlsna

Title: Managing Counsel for Marketing and the Intellectual Property Group
Company: McDonald's Corporation
Children: Lauren, Matthew, and Michael
Education: BA and JD, Northwestern University

Kathryn supports the national and local advertising and marketing programs conducted in the United States and other markets around the world. She is a past chairman of the Promotion Marketing Association and served on Neiman-Marcus's InCircle Advisory Board. She is currently on many advisory boards, including the Japanese American Service Committee in Chicago, the DePaul University School of Law Intellectual Property Advisory Board, the Children's Advertising Review Unit (CARU), and the Girl Scouts of DuPage County Council.

Denise Morrison

Title: President, Global Sales, and Chief Customer Officer
Company: Campbell Soup
Children: Michele and Kelly
Education: BS, Boston College

Denise is a member of the executive team and has responsibility for Campbell's $6.7 billion in sales. Previously, she was executive vice president and general manager of Kraft Foods's snacks and confections divisions and held managerial roles at Nabisco, Nestle USA, PepsiCo, and Procter & Gamble. Denise serves on various boards, including the Food

Industry Crusade against Hunger, Students in Free Enterprise (SIFE), the Advisory Board for Catalyst, and Ballard Power Systems. She is also president of the New Jersey Women's Forum.

Pam Murray
Title: Executive Vice President
Company: Marriott
Children: Christopher and Stephanie
Education: BS, University of Maryland

Pam is an executive vice president of Marriott's enterprise accounting services. Her previous roles have included leadership of several transformation initiatives, including the development of Marriott's financial shared services operation. Previously, Pam held progressive positions within finance and gained operational experience as a hotel general manager. She currently serves on the board of directors for the Blount Chamber Partnership in Blount County, Tennessee.

Deanna Oppenheimer
Title: President, Consumer Group
Company: Washington Mutual, Inc.
Children: Jeni and James
Education: BA, University of Puget Sound

Deanna is responsible for the company's consumer group, which includes retail banking, financial services, customer optimization, the chief administrative office and marketing, brand management, and strategic communications. She is a board member of Catellus Development Corporation and chairs the board of trustees of the University of Puget Sound. She is also past president of the Seattle Children's Theatre board and ArtsFund.

Nayla Rizk
Title: Partner
Company: Spencer Stuart
Children: Peter and Andrew McCall
Education: BS, Cornell University; MBA, Harvard University

Nayla is a consultant in the firm's technology and communications practice and a member of the firm's board services practice. She held executive, managerial, and analyst roles respectively at Network Equipment Technologies, McKinsey, and Chevron. Nayla is a member of the Council on Foreign Relations, a member of the Pacific Council on International Policy, and a former trustee of World Affairs Council of Northern California.

Joyce Rogge
Title: Senior Vice President, Marketing
Company: Southwest Airlines Company
Children: Dan, Abbey, and Jodie
Education: BFA and MBA, Southern Methodist University

Joyce is responsible for Southwest's national advertising programs in all media and implements marketing strategies covering all sales and promotion, multicultural marketing, the frequent flyer program, and corporate sales marketing. She also has responsibility for the interactive marketing, revenue management, and customer relations departments. Previously, she was an executive for Janklow Bender Advertising in New York. She is a former participant in Leadership Texas.

Marilyn Seymann
Title: President, Chief Executive Officer, and Founder
Company: M One, Inc.
Children: Gregory, Scott, and Jeffrey
Education: BA, Brandeis University; M.A., Columbia University; Ph.D., California Western University

Marilyn is responsible for M One, a Phoenix-based consulting firm, and a founding partner for the Director's Council. She is an author and chairman of the board for NorthWestern Corporation, and she serves on the board of directors at Beverly Enterprises, Inc., MAXIMUS, Community First Bancshares, and EOS International. Formerly, she was a past vice chairman of the Federal Housing Finance Board, managing director at Arthur Andersen & Co., executive vice president of Chase Bank of Arizona, executive assistant to Arizona Governor Bruce Babbitt, associate dean of the College of Business at Arizona State University, and founder of the Arizona Association for Women.

Lorene K. Steffes
Title: Independent Business Advisor and Consultant
Children: William and Rebecca
Education: BS and MS, Northern Illinois University

Lorene is an independent business advisor and consultant. She was formerly president and chief executive officer of Transarc Corporation. She has held various executive and leadership positions at IBM, Ameritech, and AT&T. She is a director on the board of PNC Financial Services Group, Inc. and PNC Bank, National Association; a member of the Northern Illinois University Liberal Arts and Sciences Advisory Board; and formerly a trustee for Carlow College.

Trudy Sullivan
Title: Executive Vice President
Company: Liz Claiborne, Inc.
Children: Catherine and Anne
Education: BA, Manhattanville College

Trudy is responsible for the Liz Claiborne apparel brands, accessories, cosmetics, specialty retail, outlet, and licensing divisions. Previously, she was president of J. Crew Group. Trudy began her career in department stores, such as Jordan Marsh and Filenes, as well as several vertically integrated specialty stores.

Doreen A. Toben
Title: Executive Vice President and Chief Financial Officer
Company: Verizon Communications
Children: Ryan and Darby
Education: BA, Rosemont College; MBA, Farleigh Dickinson University

Doreen is responsible for Verizon's finance and strategic planning efforts. Previously, she was the controller for Bell Atlantic and held several finance and strategic planning roles at AT&T. Doreen is on the board of directors for the New York Times Company and the Lincoln Center, and on J. P. Morgan Chase's National Advisory Board.

Sophie Vandebroek
Title: Corporate Chief Engineer and Vice President of Xerox Engineering Center
Company: Xerox Corporation
Children: Elena, Arno, and Jonas
Education: BS and MS, Katholieke Universiteit in Leuven, Belgium; Ph.D., Cornell University

Sophie is responsible for platform planning, product development tools, and processes; strengthening the Xerox engineering capabilities; optimizing $1 billion annual R&D investments; and driving coherence in both the look and feel and in the interoperability of the full line of Xerox systems. Previously, she was CTO at Carrier Corporation and a researcher at the Interuniversity Microelectronic Center (IMEC) in Belgium, IBM, and Hewlett Packard. She is a senior member and has served on various committees of the Institute of Electrical and Electronics Engineers (IEEE).

Catherine West
Title: Executive Vice President and President of US Card,
Director and President of Capital One Bank
Company: Capital One Financial Corporation
Children: Will
Education: BS, Lynchburg College

Catherine is a member of Capital One's Executive Committee. As president of US Card, she is responsible for directing the company's largest line of business, and she manages enterprise operations. Previously, Catherine held executive positions at First USA Bank and Chevy Chase Federal Savings Bank. She is active in a variety of charities and civic causes that focus on children and financial literacy.

Linda Wolf
Title: Chairman and Chief Executive Officer
Company: Leo Burnett Worldwide
Children: Brinker and Michael
Education: BA, Ohio Wesleyan University

Linda is responsible for the agency's global operations spanning over 80 countries and 200 units and has expanded assignments with blue chip clients such as Kellogg's, Hallmark, Nintendo, Disney, and Procter & Gamble. Previously, Linda was CEO of Leo Burnett USA, where she played an integral part in the most aggressive growth and diversification drive in Burnett's history. Linda currently sits on the boards of Chicago's Field Museum of Natural History, Children's Memorial Hospital, the Off the Street Club, the Chicago Council on Foreign Relations, and the Economic Club of Chicago. She is a member of the University of Illinois Advisory Board, the Chicago Network, and the Committee of 200.

Ava Harth Youngblood
Title: President and Chief Executive Officer
Company: Youngblood Executive Search, Inc.
Children: Lee and Garrett
Education: BS, Northwestern University; MBA, University of
Chicago

Ava owns and operates her own executive search firm. Previously, she spent nearly 20 years at Amoco (now BP), where she had a variety of roles in research and development, operations planning, logistics, quality, sales and marketing, strategic planning, and competitive intelligence. Ava serves on the Board of Trustees of Northwestern University and holds board positions at Herzing College, Women Work!, Destiny Outreach, and Chicago Communities in Schools. She is a past director of INROADS/Chicago and past chairman of the Conference Board's Competitive Analysis Council.

B

THE EXECUTIVE PARTICIPANTS' DEMOGRAPHICS

veryone's family and career situations are unique, so there are no right answers to popular questions like when should you have children and how many should you have. I did collect demographic data from the executive mothers and saw some trends that are worth mentioning.

First, more than 90 percent of the women in this book are still married, and they are married to their first and only husband. This is pretty incredible in light of today's statistics on divorce. It's hard to determine whether having a good marriage helps one's career, or if it's the other way around and having a successful career helps a marriage. No matter how you look at it, 90 percent is such a high number, you have to believe that a good marriage is practically a requirement for success.

In fact, the married women in this book attribute a great deal of their success to their husbands. And I wish I could give all the testimonials they share about their husbands, because these men do deserve a tremendous amount of recognition. Marla Gottschalk's view somewhat typifies what they had to say. She said:

> I think a good spouse is a huge, huge factor. You need a spouse that meets you halfway. There's no way I could do it without my husband. We both travel with our work. He has made a

lot of sacrifices for my career and without a complaint. He's incredibly supportive. It would be next to impossible to do both without him. You need someone who can be there when you are not, so your kids feel that everything is totally working for them. Without his involvement with our kids, I would be living in guilt, and that would eat away at me. While some of the traditional burdens fall on me, like finding the doctor and dentist, he takes things on that I would not pay attention to. He volunteers to coach, finds the right swim team, and signs the kids up for soccer. His contributions are huge.

There was also some commonality amongst these women with respect to timing their families. Figure B.1 shows a graphical representation of the data.

Eighty-four percent had their children between the ages of 26 and 37. The three women who started their families later went to great lengths to have children. One adopted her children, one had two children via *in vitro* fertilization because she didn't have a spouse, and one used a surrogate mother to have a second child. Where there's a will to have children, there is a way. Most of the moms were happy with their timing. Most felt that having kids after establishing your work résumé and getting settled in your marriage is ideal.

Eighty percent of these mothers had two or three children, which fits within societal norms. What's somewhat surprising is that many of these women come from large, blue-collar families and had many siblings. The point of mentioning this is that executive mothers can come from any walk of life. Peggy Johnson, president of QUALCOMM Internet Services, had 14 brothers and sisters. She clearly was not afraid of leading a chaotic lifestyle. She said, "I think being from a Catholic, working-class family contributed to my success. I had to put myself through college and take responsibility at a young age. When my car broke down, I knew I had to eat macaroni and cheese until I paid off the bill. I didn't enter the workforce feeling entitled. Instead, I entered with a good work ethic."

FIGURE B.1 When Did the Executives Become Mothers and How Many Children Did They Have?

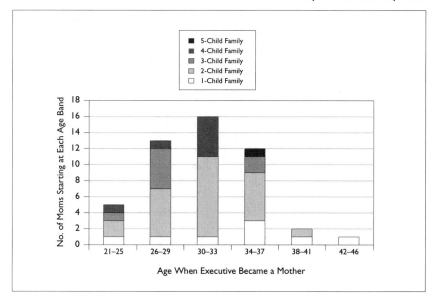

Albrecht, Karl. *Executive Tune Up*. New York: Prentice Hall, 1981.

Barletta, Martha. *Marketing to Women*. Chicago: Dearborn Trade, 2002.

Berman, Dennis and Joann Lublin. "Russo's Goal as Lucent's New Chief: Restore Luster Company Once Had." *Wall Street Journal*. 8 January 2002.

Brady, Diane and Brian Grow. "Act II: Ann Fudge's Two-Year Break from Work Changed Her Life. Will Those Lessons Help Her Fix Young & Rubicam?" *Business Week Online*. 29 March 2004.

Burrows, Peter and Rob Hof. "Meet eBay's Auctioneer-in-Chief." *Business Week*. 29 May 2003.

Editorial. *The Business Journal*. New York: World News Network, 14 June 1999.

Caliguire, Jeff. *Leadership Secrets of St. Paul*. Tulsa, OK: River Oak Publishing, 2003.

Carlin, Flora. "Women Make Better Leaders." *Psychology Today*. 17 September 2003.

Caudron, Shari. "See Jane Lead." *Controller*. June 1997.

Chira, Susan. *A Mother's Place: Choosing Work and Family without Guilt or Blame*. New York: HarperPerenial, 1999.

Conlin, Michelle, Linda Himelsteing, and Jennifer Merritt. "Mommy Is Really Home from Work." *Business Week*. 25 November 2002.

Eagly, Alice H., Mary C. Johannesen-Schmidt, and Marloes L. van Engen. "Transformational, Transactional, and Laissez-Faire Leadership Styles: A Meta-Analysis Comparing Women and Men. *Psychological Bulletin* 129, no. 4 (2003).

Erbe, Bonnie. "Trend Still Shows Women Working." Scribbs Howard News Service. 28 March 2004.

Evans, Gail. *She Wins, You Win: The Most Important Rule Every Business Woman Needs to Know.* New York: Gotham Books, 2002.

Farrell, Warren. *The Myth of Male Power.* New York: Simon and Schuster, 1993.

"The 2004 Fortune 500: Full List." *Fortune.* 5 April 2004.

Friedman, Martin B. *The Leadership Myth.* Pittsburgh, PA: Dorrance Publishing, 1992.

Galinsky, Ellen et al. "Leaders in a Global Economy." Study sponsored by Families and Work Institute, Catalyst, and the Boston College Center for Work & Family Study. 14 May 2003.

Harper, Matthew. "People." *Forbes.* 28 March 2001.

Hewlett, Sylvia Ann. *Creating a Life: Professional Women and the Quest for Children.* New York: Talk Miramax Books, 2002.

Kaplan, Robert. *Beyond Ambition.* San Francisco: Jossey-Bass, 1991.

Kawakami, Christine, Ellen J. Langer, and Judith B. White. "Mindful and Masculine: Freeing Women Leaders from the Constraints of Gender Roles." *Journal of Social Issues* 60, no. 1 (Spring 2000).

Kinsley, Craig H., et al. *Nature* 401. 11 November 1999.

Korabik, Karen and Roya Ayman. "Should Women Managers Have to Act Like Men?" *Journal of Management Development* 8, no. 6 (1998).

Kharif, Oleg. "Anne Mulcahy Has Xerox by the Horns." *Business Week Online.* 29 May 2003.

Limbacher, Carl. "Oprah: I Found My Children." *NewsMax.com.* 27 September 2003.

Ludeman, Kate, and Eddie Erlandson, "Coaching the Alpha Male." *Harvard Business Review.* May 2004.

National Parenting Association. "Groundbreaking Study Exposes a Crisis among Successful Women." *Parentunite.com.* 15 April 2002.

Pearman, Roger R. *The Leadership Advantage Training Program: Using the MBTI® Tool for Effective Leadership–Facilitator's Guide.* Palo Alto, CA: Davies-Black Publishing, 2001.

"Personal Business Diary: What Would Happen If Mom Ran the Show? *The New York Times.* 11 May 2003.

Powell, Gary. *Handbook of Gender and Work.* Thousand Oaks, CA: SAGE Publications, 29 July 1999.

Schein, Edgar, H. *Organizational Culture and Leadership.* San Francisco, Jossey-Bass, 1989.

Senge, Peter. *The Fifth Discipline.* New York: Doubleday, 1990.

Valian, Virginia. *Why So Slow? The Advancement of Women.* Cambridge, MA: The MIT Press, 1999.

Warren, Rick. *The Purpose Driven Life.* Grand Rapids, MI: Zondervan, 2002.

A

Accessibility, 128–29
Accountability, 54–58
Ace Hardware, 55
Adaptability, 99–100
Administrative assistants, 24, 94
Adventure-seeking, 55–57
Advisor mode, 144–46
Ajilon Office, 165–66
Albrecht, Karl, 92
Alliances, 5
Alpha males, 17–18
Ambition, 28–30
Amoco, 114, 152
Appropriately organized, 92–95
ARC and Associates, 40
Arnold, Colleen, 92, 97, 127–28
Aronson, Virginia, 21
AT&T, 19, 36, 50, 65, 120
Attentiveness, 126–29
Augustine, Cynthia, 150–51, 167
Avon, 196

B

Babies, and nurturing trait.
   See Nurturing
Balance, 5
   in perspective, 60–61
   transition to, 19–23
Bank One, 50
Barletta, Martha, 8–9
Barnes, Brenda, 50
Bed time, 101–2
Beier, Anita, 60, 139, 153, 160, 170
Bell Laboratories, 13, 40, 56
BellSouth, 66
Beyond Ambition (Kaplan), 20
Bias, 31

Bitterness, 48–49
Body language, 152
Boss/child-direct report response, 154
Boss/direct report response, 153–54
Boston College Center for Work and Family, 38
Boundary-setting, 5, 154–55
Bowne, 130
Brown, Melinda, 26, 83, 135
Buse, Elizabeth, 36, 169, 176–77, 179, 185
Business Week, 42, 47, 109, 121

C

Caliguire, Jeff, 172
Calmness, 102–106
Campbell Soup, 183
Caregiving, 191–92
Caring, 74
Carter-Miller, Joceylyn, 25, 63, 80, 136–37
Catalyst, 38
Caudron, Shari, 9
Change
   maternal leadership model and, 196–98
   meaningful, 184
   personal, 184
Chaos management, 87–107, 195
   adaptability and, 99–100
   calmness and, 102–106
   clear priorities and, 95–97
   creative problem solving and, 97–99
   hyperdrive, 90–92
   letting go and, 100–102
   organization and, 92–95